Racial Climates, Ecological Indifference

Studies in Feminist Philosophy is designed to showcase cutting-edge monographs and collections that display the full range of feminist approaches to philosophy, that push feminist thought in important new directions, and that display the outstanding quality of feminist philosophical thought.

STUDIES IN FEMINIST PHILOSOPHY

Linda Martín Alcoff, Hunter College and the CUNY Graduate Center

Elizabeth Barnes, University of Virginia

Lorraine Code, York University, Toronto

Penelope Deutscher, Northwestern University

Ann Garry, California State University, Los Angeles

Sally Haslanger, Massachusetts Institute of Technology

Alison Jaggar, University of Colorado, Boulder

Serene Khader, Brooklyn College and CUNY Graduate Center

Helen Longino, Stanford University

Catriona Mackenzie, Macquarie University

Mari Mikkola, Humboldt University, Berlin

Sally Scholz, Villanova University

Laurie Shrage, Florida International University

Lisa Tessman, Binghamton University

Nancy Tuana, Pennsylvania State University

Published in the Series:

Minimizing Marriage: Marriage, Morality, and the Law
Elizabeth Brake

Out from the Shadows: Analytic Feminist Contributions to Traditional Philosophy
Edited by Sharon L. Crasnow and Anita M. Superson

The Epistemology of Resistance: Gender and Racial Oppression, Epistemic Injustice, and Resistant Imaginations
José Medina

Simone de Beauvoir and the Politics of Ambiguity
Sonia Kruks

Identities and Freedom: Feminist Theory between Power and Connection
Allison Weir

Vulnerability: New Essays in Ethics and Feminist Philosophy
Edited by Catriona Mackenzie, Wendy Rogers, and Susan Dodds

Sovereign Masculinity: Gender Lessons from the War on Terror
Bonnie Mann

Autonomy, Oppression, and Gender
Edited by Andrea Veltman and Mark Piper

Our Faithfulness to the Past: Essays on the Ethics and Politics of Memory
Sue Campbell
Edited by Christine M. Koggel and Rockney Jacobsen

The Physiology of Sexist and Racist Oppression
Shannon Sullivan

Disorientation and Moral Life
Ami Harbin

The Wrong of Injustice: Dehumanization and Its Role in Feminist Philosophy
Mari Mikkola

Beyond Speech: Pornography and Analytic Feminist Philosophy
Mari Mikkola

Differences: Between Beauvoir and Irigaray
Edited by Emily Anne Parker and Anne van Leeuwen

Categories We Live By
Ásta

Equal Citizenship and Public Reason
Christie Hartley and Lori Watson

Decolonizing Universalism: A Transnational Feminist Ethic
Serene J. Khader

Women's Activism, Feminism, and Social Justice
Margaret A. McLaren

Being Born: Birth and Philosophy
Alison Stone

Theories of the Flesh: Latinx and Latin American Feminisms, Transformation, and Resistance
Edited by Andrea J. Pitts, Mariana Ortega, and José Medina

Elemental Difference and the Climate of the Body
Emily Anne Parker

Racial Climates, Ecological Indifference: An Ecointersectional Analysis
Nancy Tuana

Racial Climates, Ecological Indifference

An Ecointersectional Analysis

NANCY TUANA

OXFORD
UNIVERSITY PRESS

Oxford University Press is a department of the University of Oxford. It furthers
the University's objective of excellence in research, scholarship, and education
by publishing worldwide. Oxford is a registered trade mark of Oxford University
Press in the UK and certain other countries.

Published in the United States of America by Oxford University Press
198 Madison Avenue, New York, NY 10016, United States of America.

© Oxford University Press 2023

All rights reserved. No part of this publication may be reproduced, stored in
a retrieval system, or transmitted, in any form or by any means, without the
prior permission in writing of Oxford University Press, or as expressly permitted
by law, by license, or under terms agreed with the appropriate reproduction
rights organization. Inquiries concerning reproduction outside the scope of the
above should be sent to the Rights Department, Oxford University Press, at the
address above.

You must not circulate this work in any other form
and you must impose this same condition on any acquirer.

Library of Congress Cataloging-in-Publication Data
Names: Tuana, Nancy, author.
Title: Racial climates, ecological indifference : an ecointersectional analysis / Nancy Tuana.
Description: First Edition. | New York : Oxford University Press, 2023. |
Series: Studies in Feminist Philosophy | Includes bibliographical references and index.
Identifiers: LCCN 2022028747 (print) | LCCN 2022028748 (ebook) |
ISBN 9780197656617 (Paperback) | ISBN 9780197656600 (Hardback) |
ISBN 9780197656624 | ISBN 9780197656648 | ISBN 9780197656631 (epub)
Subjects: LCSH: Environmental justice. | Climatic changes—Social aspects. |
Race relations. | Racism. | Climate change mitigation.
Classification: LCC GE220 .T83 2022 (print) | LCC GE220 (ebook) |
DDC 304 .2/8089—dc23/eng20220917
LC record available at https://lccn.loc.gov/2022028747
LC ebook record available at https://lccn.loc.gov/2022028748

DOI: 10.1093/oso/9780197656600.001.0001

To the children I raised and love with all my being. And to the children and children's children that love brought into my life.
To Christopher and John Alexander. To Alex, Becky, Michael, Charlie, Paula, Stuart, Beth, Bonnie, Joey, Alex, Ishan, Tyson, Lucas, Lilly, Sho, and Saya.

Contents

Preface ix

1. The Interlocking Domains of Racism and Ecological Indifference 1
2. Racial Climates 34
3. Climate Apartheid: The Forgetting of Race 57
4. Through the Eye of a Hurricane 84
5. Weathering the Climate 111
Conclusion: Cultivating Anthropocenean Sensibilities 140

Acknowledgments 153
References 155
Index 185

Preface: Diving into the Wacissa with Allison Janae Hamilton

Floridawater II.[1] A doubling, a repetition. Similar, but not identical. Immersed in bluegreen waters. Ablutions.

The Wacissa River. It bubbles up from large limestone springs moving south through cypress forests, then sweetbay, maple, hickory, sweetgum. Life erupts above and below it. Aquatic birds and animals are abundant. Kingfishers, alligators, bald eagles, water moccasins, crayfish. Enter its waters and one enters a domain of fish and river plants.

> *I was in a swamp and I did the photographs with me in the water. And so there's a strength in the posture, but there's also a vulnerability. You're very aware of the environment, and you're not sure if the character is in danger, or if they are the villain. So there's a little bit of everything.* (Allison Janae Hamilton, quoted in Ellis 2021)

The Wacissa is also infused with human history. The intersection of river and sea offers a land rich in resources. The original inhabitants settled in the region fourteen thousand years ago, carving tools from the chert easily found along the route of the Wacissa. Their ceremonial and shell mounds dot the river. From at least 1000 CE a group of Indigenous people lived in the region who farmed and prospered from the riches of the land and waters. Called Apalachee by the Spanish, they were a large community of about fifty thousand at the time of Ponce de León's arrival in 1513 in what came to be called Florida. Spain sent missionaries into the region, and by the end of the seventeenth century missions dotted the route of the Wacissa and beyond: San Antonio de Bacuqua, San Luis de Apalachee, San Lorenzo de Ivitachuco, Santa María de Ayubale, San Martin de Tomole, San Miguel

---

[1] Allison Janae Hamilton gifted *Floridawater II* as the cover image of this book. Born in Kentucky, raised in Florida, and deeply connected to the Tennessee farm that was part of her mother's lineage, Hamilton's focus in her work is immersed in landscapes and vulnerabilities of particular places and "the histories and narratives of displacement, land loss, bodies, ownership of space, and migration" (Goodalle 2019) that infuse those places.

de Asile, La Concepcion de Ayubale, San Francisco de Oconi, San Juan de Aspalaga, San Joseph de Ocuya. The missionaries brought with them new lifeways along with new infectious diseases that resulted in large losses of Indigenous communities both within the land they called *La Florida* and beyond. Apalachee and the Spanish missionaries had complex relationships but nonetheless lived together until the early eighteenth century, when Colonel James Moore along with eighty British and fifteen hundred Creek soldiers attacked the area, killing or enslaving many Apalachee and forcing the relocation of others. The Adams-Onis Treaty signed in 1819, not long after the raids, granted the land then referred to as Spanish Florida to the United States.

> *In order to justify something horrific, there has to be a story. That's the effect of the narrative; you're creating a storyline that excuses or makes it okay. Exploring that was interesting to me. That's something you see all over the world. What are the stories and what are the myths that become entrenched and ingrained that were originally meant to justify something? How are those myths operating now? What does that mean for the future?* (Allison Janae Hamilton, quoted in Donoghue 2021)

The Spanish had slaves, both captured Indigenous and African people. But theirs was not a system of chattel slavery. Their slaves' choices were limited, but they had the right to marry, to own property, even to buy their own freedom. Under US rule a new system of slavery emerged, a system of chattel slavery in which kidnapped individuals were permanently owned and their children automatically enslaved. When Florida became a state in 1845 almost half of its population were enslaved people.

> *The folks that have been people who have been the most vulnerable on this landscape—and who continued to be—also find this place home. They have used the landscape for their own ritual, their own healing practices, modalities, their own medicine, and their own spiritual rituals. So, it's the land. The Southern land is not just this thing to be afraid of; it doesn't only present the obvious.* (Allison Janae Hamilton, quoted in Alipour 2021)

Even before Florida became a state there were plans to create a navigable water passage from the Wacissa River to the Gulf of Mexico. Plantation owners needed a route to ship goods, and the overland routes available were difficult for markets to access. Appeals for land were made to Congress, but the labor that created dams, cleared banks, dug up limestone boulders, built levees, and dug channels in the swampy land was the labor of slaves. Still known as the Wacissa Slave Canal, only a few cotton barges navigated its waters before it was largely abandoned at the end of the Civil War and with the arrival of railroads in the area.

> *My work resists the idea of climate change being this future thing. It also resists climate change being universal because it's not going to affect everybody the same, and it's not affecting everybody the same. The Wacissa River is part of this river system that was cut through by the slave canal. And as the name suggests, the slave canal was dug out by the labor of enslaved Black folks here in Florida. The purpose was to bring cotton from Georgia to the Gulf of Mexico. But as soon as it finished, the railroad came to town, so it never really got used for its intended purpose. I was riding through that particular river system that has this history of violent labor, and I'm showing the aftermath of this hurricane. These two things are coming together in Wacissa. There's a current reality of people living here, but how it's affecting and will always have the affectation of historical impetus.* (Allison Janae Hamilton, quoted in Alipour 2021)

As the labor-intensive plantation economies began to wane, other industries arrived in their place. One of these, the logging industry, transformed the Wacissa River area well beyond anything that had come before. In the 1930s the Wacissa watershed was clear-cut for its old growth longleaf pine and bald cypress trees. With the destruction of the forest the ecology of Wacissa changed, resulting in losses of land and water life.

> *If you look at landscape, there's really a lot there: access to different types of space, land loss, migration (forced and otherwise), property, materials of labor, and what's been mined for economic, cultural and spiritual uses by communities at the margins, like medicine and hoodoo. It's a very complex terrain, in a physical and metaphorical sense.* (Allison Janae Hamilton, quoted in Radley 2020)

Although logging continues in the area, the area around the river has been protected and has become a region renowned for its beauty and abundant birdlife and used by many for recreation.

> *I'm exploring these myths that allowed the South to be cultivated, for this violent exploitation of people forced to labor on it, and the people for whom, in the aftermath of that, this land is now home. My work is an exploration of what all that means, and what it means today. A lot of people categorize the South as this place stuck in history, but for me, all these myths, all these metaphors, all these historical actions have a bearing on today's lived experience. I'm really thinking about that original idea of paradise but propelling it forward. Dragging the examination of that myth into today so that we can see what the through lines are, particularly in the face of climate change and environmental injustices.* (Allison Janae Hamilton, quoted in Alipour 2021)

My goal in writing this book is to weave a complex narrative that touches on some of the lineages that entangle environmental indifference and systemic racisms. My work is designed to disrupt the more traditional narratives that justify and enforce oppression as well as treat environments as sources of consumption by emphasizing the intimate yet complex interrelations of these narratives.

> *The effects of climate change are happening now. You look at the way cities were designed, and you look at the aftermath of American slavery during the reconstruction era, how certain communities were placed in certain areas—all of that was deliberately thought of. There were conversations about this, like where are we going to put these formerly enslaved people? And when you think about something like a hurricane, well, who tends to be on the wrong side of the levee or which community tends to be in the most vulnerable parts of the city or community? What's going to happen to those folks as climate change makes the storms more intense, more frequent? That means that climate change is not really an equal thing.* (Allison Janae Hamilton, quoted in Donoghue 2021)

I cannot tell all the stories, but my desire is that this collection of examples will serve to help us look differently, to see how these intersections shift and shape in different locations and in different time periods. And in seeing differently, we are inspired to push back against the limits of traditional accounts of environmentalism. I look to the past and to the entanglements of environmental indifference and systemic racisms in order to reshape futures.

I don't want to be representative. I have this one experience and I'm literally drawing from what I know. I'm staying in my lane. I don't want to speak for the South; I don't want to speak for any one particular Black American experience. I flesh things out from my own experience. I don't want to translate because I'm not going to translate it the same way my mom or my brother or my grandmother would. I'm not even going to try. I'm threading the historical narratives I've studied, the experiences that I've had, the family histories that I've heard passed down from my elders, the visceral experience, the sonic experiences. I'm threading it through a narrative that is partially tangible, partially archetypal and mythic. (Allison Janae Hamilton, quoted in Alipour 2021)

My goal in *Racial Climates, Ecological Indifference* is not to detail every instance in which systemic racisms and ecological indifference are infused, but to identify a range of diverse examples from specific locations as a way to amplify attunements to this interaction, to provide a strategy for seeing anew that builds on and with the work of others, like Allison Janae Hamilton, who are dedicated to exposing how environmental degradation and oppression are interlaced. To provide a practice in which we cultivate how to listen across histories of harm and learn how to take responsibility for them. I believe that cultivating such attunements can provide thresholds to new ways of living and enable us to appreciate alternative ways of world-making.

A lot of [my work] is bound up with the land and the ways that landscape operates in the context of healing, and of ritual. That is one way that the concept of land in my work connects to other parts of the Black diaspora—through the ritual practice of land, and through intimate connections to nature. The ways that the land operates as a mechanism of agency, not only as a burden. In the US context, Hoodoo is a big part of that. And I draw from those rituals, patterns, and habits I witnessed from my elders growing up. . . . I'm curious about the multiple, complex, and sometimes conflicting meanings that landscape and nature has in the context of my own culture, as well as throughout the world. (Allison Janae Hamilton, quoted in Alipour 2021)

1
The Interlocking Domains of Racism and Ecological Indifference

Working on *Racial Climates, Ecological Indifference* in the midst of a global pandemic and widespread Black Lives Matter protests shines a bright light on the complex interconnections of social issues and environmental issues.

As COVID-19 and protests against racism spread across countries and continents,[1] we begin to appreciate how globally interconnected we are and how interconnected are the problems that face us. We see as well how seemingly small individual choices can have important impacts, whether those choices are wearing a mask, signing a petition for sustainable transformation in our communities,[2] providing support to food banks, or developing a curriculum to discuss privilege and oppression. While the COVID-19 pandemic has rendered transparent how oppression and health are interconnected, we see only part of the complexity of this interconnection if we do not also recognize the ways such social issues are intertwined with environmental issues.

Consider the problem of air pollution. The Environmental Protection Agency's (EPA; 2021b) study of particulate matter pollution documents the many negative effects of this type of pollution on environments: it damages forests, affects the diversity of ecosystems, and changes the nutrient balance in coastal waters and large river basins. Remember that most particles form in the atmosphere as a result of complex reactions of chemicals that are pollutants emitted from power plants, industries, and automobiles—some of the main causes of climate change.

---

[1] The World Health Organization (n.d.) noted that as of January 2022 incidents of COVID-19 have been officially reported in all but four countries: Nauru, Turkmenistan, Tuvalu, and the Democratic People's Republic of Korea. During the first year of the pandemic, tens of millions of people protested against racism in many countries, including South Africa, Japan, Canada, Zimbabwe, Belgium, Australia, France, United States, Syria, Britain, New Zealand, Italy, Mexico, Spain, Sweden, and Kenya.

[2] The Black Lives Matter movement's #DefundThePolice is designed to support "radical, sustainable solutions that affirm the prosperity of Black lives"; see https://blacklivesmatter.com/defundthepolice/.

Racial Climates, Ecological Indifference. Nancy Tuana, Oxford University Press. © Oxford University Press 2023.
DOI: 10.1093/oso/9780197656600.003.0001

Air pollution affects humans as well. Exposure can result in lung disease, heart disease, and premature death. The World Health Organization (n.d.) estimates that over 4.2 million deaths a year are due to exposure to ambient air pollution. But the effects of air pollution on humans are not equally distributed. Consider the situation in the United States. The American Lung Association's 2020 report, "State of the Air," as well as a study by researchers at the EPA on the health effects of particle pollution (Mikati et al. 2018) have documented that non-White people in the United States face higher exposure to and risk from particle pollution.[3] According to "State of the Air," "approximately 74 million people of color live in counties that received at least one failing grade for ozone and/or [either short-term or year-round] particle pollution. Over 14 million people of color live in counties that received failing grades on all three measures" (American Lung Association 2020, 11).

To connect the disproportionate impact of air pollution on Blacks to the pandemic and to the Black Lives Matter movement, we can begin with the fact that Blacks in the United States are disproportionately impacted by COVID-19. This fact is the result of many issues, but one of them is the disproportionate exposure of Blacks to air pollution—an issue that intertwines the social and the environmental. Blacks have 1.54 times higher burden from small particulate air pollution than the overall population in the United States (Mikati et al. 2018, 480). A Harvard public health study conducted at the height of the coronavirus pandemic documented that "many of the preexisting conditions that increase the risk of death in those with COVID-19 are the same diseases that are affected by long-term exposure to air pollution" (Wu et al. 2020, 2). The study identified correlations between long-term exposure to fine particulate matter air pollution and increased mortality risks from COVID-19 due to air pollution's impact on the respiratory and cardiovascular systems of those exposed to it over long periods. Air pollution impacts both human and environmental health, hence the importance of addressing the complex intersections between social and environmental issues when we address racial injustices.

Another example of the complex interconnections between environmental issues and social issues is the impact of the pandemic on Indigenous

---

[3] I capitalize racial designations to signal that they are social categories with histories, not biological kinds. That said, these histories are often both geographically and historically complex, do not always have a shared history, and are not fixed. Hence what a particular race term means in different locations or even within the same location at different times is often not the same. For a discussion of this practice, see Appiah (2020).

populations. The United Nations Department of Economic and Social Affairs (2020) report, "COVID-19 and Indigenous Peoples," warned that the pandemic "poses a grave health threat to Indigenous peoples around the world." Indigenous populations often experience limited access to healthcare services and significantly higher rates of underlying health conditions that result in far higher risk from COVID-19. Indigenous conceptions of well-being and health can impact how or whether Indigenous people seek medical attention, particularly if health systems are oriented around typical European and North American norms and values and are not provided in Indigenous languages.

To take just one example, consider Indigenous populations in Brazil. In March 2021, Brazil reported more new COVID-19 cases and deaths per day than any other country in the world: over 12.5 million cases and over 314,000 deaths and rising. In that same month, Articulação dos Povos Indígenas do Brasil (APIB; Articulation of the Indigenous People of Brazil), a large coalition of Brazil's Indigenous organizations, identified over one thousand COVID-19 deaths and over fifty-one thousand cases across 110 Indigenous communities (see website of Emergência Indígena, updated regularly).[4] Given the nature of the disease, Indigenous communities often lose leaders, elders, and traditional healers. The losses, then, are not only of lives and relationships but of history, culture, and knowledge. "Our elders are guardians of traditions, custodians of wisdom, advisors and holders of unique spiritual knowledge," said Nara Baré, coordinator of Coordenaçãções das Organizações Indígenas da Amazónia Brasileria (Coordination of the Indigenous Organizations of the Brazilian Amazon), a large regional Indigenous organization composed of several indigenous rights organizations of the Brazilian Amazon Bason and a member of APIB. "To see them go is, in a way, to witness another aspect of the destruction of our people" (quoted in Teixeira 2021). Trajectories of infection are complex. Some blame government interventions. Katia Silene Akrãtikatêjê, a chief from the Gavião community in the state of Pará, for example, attributes the spread of COVID-19 to a government health team who visited her village to give flu vaccines. "Everyone got sick from there on," she asserted (quoted in Phillips 2020). Others blame the government for taking too long to send emergency food kits to people isolated in their villages, which required that they travel to nearby towns for resources. Others, such as

---

[4] https://emergenciaindigena.apiboficial.org/dados_covid19/

the Yanomami, blame *garimperios*, illegal miners seeking gold, for spreading the coronavirus.

Let me dwell on the example of illegal mining on Yanomami land in order to trace just a few of the relevant interconnections between human well-being and environmental well-being. The Brazilian NGO Instituto Socioambiental (Socioenvironmental Institute) estimated that in 2020 up to twenty thousand *garimperios* invaded Yanomami land in northern Brazil. The *garimperios* bring with them not only COVID-19 but environmental degradation[5] that, in turn, impacts human well-being. The pits they dig destroy ecosystems and fill rivers with mud that upsets the cycles of fish breeding. The mercury *garimperios* use to separate out the gold pollutes the rivers and contaminates the food chain (Soares et al. 2018). Mercury negatively impacts vertebrates' development as well as their neurological and hormonal systems, harming fish and then harming the predators that eat them—humans, otters, river dolphins, and Yacaré caimans alike (Tan, Meiller, and Mahaffey 2009). Mercury exposure in humans can result in numerous systematic toxicological effects, including irreversible damage to children's development, as well as kidney damage, heart disease, blindness, and digestive problems in adults. A study of mercury exposure that was requested by Davi Kopenawa Yanomami, chairman of the Hutukara Yanomami Association, documented clear correlations between proximity to gold mining and high mercury concentrations in the hair of Yanomami community members (Vega et al. 2018). The *garimperios* not only are a disease vector for coronavirus, but their mining activities over the years have often resulted in underlying conditions that make Yanomami individuals more susceptible to the virus.[6]

President Jair Bolsonaro of Brazil, rather than trying to stop illegal mining, is instead working to legalize mining in Indigenous reserves in the Amazon. Bolsonaro, who is infamous for his racism toward Brazil's Indigenous populations, has argued that the Yanomami territory in Brazil, which constitutes over 9.6 million hectares, including many acres of rainforest, is more extensive than they require or deserve.[7] He is working to remove

---

[5] The term "environmental degradation" refers to a complex set of phenomena that result in the deterioration of environments, including deterioration of air, water, and soil quality, destruction of ecosystems or habitats, and the extinction of flora or fauna.

[6] According to the NGO Survival International (2019), the illegal invasion of gold miners in the 1980s, when the number of *garimperios* swelled to about forty thousand, resulted in the loss of 20% of the Yanomami population due to violence by the miners and the illnesses they brought with them.

[7] Yanomami territory crosses the border into Venezuela, where the Yanomami live in the 8.2-million-hectare Alto Orinoco-Casiquiare Biosphere Reserve. The combined land forms the largest forested Indigenous territory in the world.

protections and open some Indigenous territories to agriculture and mining. To bring about this shift, he removed responsibility for the creation and limitation of reserves from FUNAI, Brazil's National Indian Foundation, the Brazilian government body that established and carried out policies relating to Indigenous peoples and was responsible for mapping out and protecting lands traditionally inhabited and used by these communities. He transferred this responsibility to the Agriculture Ministry, which has little, if any, commitment to Indigenous communities.

Bolsonaro, as did former president Donald Trump in the United States, downplayed the urgency of the pandemic. He did not support a national lockdown or a national testing campaign. But it is not only the coronavirus or Bolsonaro's efforts to seize ancestral lands that is placing the health of Indigenous communities at high levels of risk. Climate change is threatening the sustainability of Indigenous lifeways. Many Indigenous peoples live in ways that are interdependent with their environments and its resources. As climate change impacts animal and plant species, it often negatively impacts traditional food sources and lifeways. Environmental and political shifts due to climate change can also result in restricted access to traditional gathering areas for food and medicine. Loss of water due to glacier melt or precipitation changes often has highly negative impacts on environments and the living beings who depend on them. Climate impacts can lead to loss of land or forced displacement, as well as to negative social impacts such as intensified discrimination and marginalization (Alvarez 2017). The challenges being faced by the Yanomami are a complex entwining of social and environmental issues.

Resources for Transformation—Genealogical Sensibilities

These brief examples illustrate one of the key claims of *Racial Climates, Environmental Indifference,* namely, that any effort to focus on the many facets of environmental injustice requires a broad and complex approach, one that reveals the many visible as well as hidden strategies, economies, causes, vectors of power, and the like that contribute to current situations and future risks. This means we must consider each instance of environmental injustice with attention to the multiple processes that constitute it. If we search for simplifying generalizations or overarching principles, we risk obscuring the complex histories and multiple vectors of power that constitute the injustices.

In particular, we risk occluding structural injustices emerging out of complex lineages such as racism, sexism, and colonialism. Michel Foucault's conception of a polyhedron of intelligibility is a helpful lens for addressing the complexities of environmental injustices. Foucault (1991, 77) refers to the complex factors relevant to a particular event as a polyhedron, "the number of whose faces is not given in advance and can never properly be taken as finite. One has to proceed by progressive, necessarily incomplete saturation. And one has to bear in mind that the further one breaks down the processes under analysis, the more one is enabled and indeed obliged to construct their external relations of intelligibility.... This process thus leads to an increasing polymorphism as the analysis progresses. Each instance I documented above reveals only a few of the facets of the problem. As we begin to address any one dimension of environmental injustice, whether it be air pollution or the impacts of illegal mining, we begin to see that it is linked complexly and inexorably to other dimensions, each of which has multiple histories, indeed histories that often shift not only over time but also spatially as we examine the issue's relevance to different geographical regions. Hence the need for historical and contextual specificity both in terms of the particular nature of injustices as well as the complex processes that contribute to environmental degradation. Efforts to understand the complexity of environmental injustice will thus require carefully situated efforts to examine the particular phenomena under question from their many and often intersecting facets, recognizing that the phenomena in question are neither singular nor simple but are informed by multiple and, at times, conflicting processes, beliefs, histories, institutions, laws, scientific views, moral stances, and much more.

While this study is situated in the broad field of environmental injustice, my particular focus is climate injustice. Working on issues of climate injustice requires facing the fact that so many people are oblivious to or, worse, deny the complex injustices linked to climate change. It also means confronting the harsh reality that some see the injustices but remain indifferent. As Jean Drèze and Amartya Sen (1989, 275–276) explain in the context of hunger: "The persistence of widespread hunger is one of the most appalling features of the modern world. The fact that so many people continue to die each year from famines, and that many millions more go on perishing from persistent deprivation on a regular basis, is a calamity to which the world has, somewhat incredibly, got coolly accustomed. It does not seem to engender the kind of shock and disquiet that might be reasonable to expect given the enormity of the tragedy. Indeed, the subject often generates either cynicism ('not a lot can be done about it') or complacent irresponsibility ('don't blame me—it is not a problem for which I am answerable')." Tracking such indifferences, whether to human injustices or to harms to environments, and understanding the causes of such indifferences is key to addressing climate injustice.

Even those who accept the reality of climate injustice and advocate action too often see only one facet of the problem. Indeed, such actions are frequently focused on technological or policy responses such as limiting greenhouse gases by transitioning to renewables or implementing carbon taxes. But such perspectives risk obscuring the ways systems of oppression and indifference to many lives and lifeways are so intertwined in the problem that solutions that touch only on one facet of the problem risk failure or, worse, exacerbating the underlying issues. To attune us to the complexities of issues in the field of climate injustice, I advocate developing what I refer to as *genealogical sensibilities*. I use the term to name habits of alertness to the complex histories of the movements of power, with particular alertness to systems of oppressive practices, beliefs, and institutions.[8] Genealogical sensibilities are attuned to those lineages of injustice that are often silenced or suppressed, but also to those that have been so normalized that they are simply accepted as "the way things happen." Genealogical sensibilities serve to thwart the habit of looking for simple solutions or quick fixes to climate injustice; instead they endeavor to understand the complex lineages of oppressive histories, practices, and structures and their continuing impacts in order to disrupt them, and to do so with the aim of transformation.

My account of genealogical sensibilities is informed by Foucault's sense of genealogy and his attention to heterogeneous infusions of beliefs, practices, events, and institutions. These complex infusions give rise to subjectivities, to multifaceted formations of historically formed identities that are assumed to be innate and universal for human beings, who in turn shape regimes of truth with claims to universality. In some instances, genealogies give accounts of the formations of such capacities as reason and conscience. In others they explore the emergence of identities—gender, or sexual or racial types— and how they are differentiated. As Ladelle McWhorter (1994, 49) phrases

---

[8] In addition to developing this concept in my work on climate change, this conception has been informed and influenced by my work with Charles Scott and developed in our book *Beyond Philosophy: Nietzsche, Foucault, Anzaldúa* (Tuana and Scott 2020).

it, "Genealogies begin with the birth of the being to be accounted for. They note the supporting conditions at the time—those that brought forth the new creature and nurtured it—and then move back in history through the ever-increasing confluences of contingencies that engendered those supporting conditions. These "births" are not simple, according to Foucault (1977). His genealogies find "not the inviolable identity of . . . origins . . . [but] the dissensions of other things" 142). They find conflict, friction, strife, discord, contention, and, in Foucault's words, the "disparity" of multiply interrelated things that give rise to many beginnings. Genealogies trace the complex and at times inconsistent relations of power that stabilize or destabilize institutions, identities, values, habits, senses of commonality, and social boundaries.

While those with genealogical sensibilities might not carry out complex, archival genealogical studies when they turn to issues of climate injustice, they are nonetheless attuned to movements and histories of power, to the often ignored or obscured ways relations of power function in social structures, systems of justice, and standards of normalcy. They are attuned to what Foucault (1977, 150) refers to as "the endlessly repeated play of dominations" from which such phenomena as concepts, desires, knowledge-practices, institutions, and lifeways emerge. This attunement carries with it a desire to question unquestioned values, beliefs, stabilities. It involves a willingness to dwell in the domain of the unthought and to risk movements beyond the limits of reason in order to understand how and why we hold some things to be rational and others irrational, deem some things knowledge and others superstition, view some things worthy of protection and others as fungible, accept some things to be natural and others abnormal. It involves, as well, attention to how even the very conception of justice that seems to guide our paths when we work in the field of climate justice might itself be permeated with injustice.

Genealogical sensibilities thus attune us to the complexity and multiple lineages of climate injustices, whether these be lineages of oppressive practices and institutions or those of indifference to the flourishing of some lives and lifeways. Genealogical sensibilities include habits of considering the histories that shaped and informed beliefs, institutions, patterns of behavior. They involve attunements to patterns and consistencies, as well as inconsistencies embedded and reproduced in practices, discourses, institutions. Genealogical sensibilities provide a way of rotating the polyhedron, to see climate injustices from their many and situated domains so as to reorient thought, to disrupt habituated patterns of action and belief, to open up new desires, new ways of thinking about the problems at hand.

The genealogical sensibilities I advocate arise from strong passions, such as anger in the presence of perceived entrenched injustices or what is identified as corruption, corruption not only of individuals but of institutions, societies, or cultures. They arise from experiences of suppression, ostracism, and harmful prejudgments concerning such things as gender, race, species, unquestioned axioms of meanings and values, or other economies of inequality. Genealogical sensibilities are attuned to complex movements of power not only in order to disclose them but also to disrupt them and provide openings for different ways of living. They might reanimate suppressed lineages that offer different ways of valuing and recast the ways people engage the world around them. Genealogical sensibilities can incite change in how people think and feel. They can contribute to a shift in subjecting values of domination, habitual forms of recognition and identification, and institutional practices that attach to genders, sexual preferences, skin colors, species type, etc. Such passions, encounters, and experiences, when they create new ways of seeing and knowing and behaving, impact the sensibilities and systems of the practices in which they arise. Genealogical sensibilities aim to loosen the soil of fixed beliefs and practices, to expose relations of power that silence and marginalize certain kinds of people and relations, and to open new prospects of exposure to what we cannot now perceive or think. The force of genealogical sensibilities has less to do with providing the true account than with inciting transformations. *Racial Climates, Ecological Indifference* is informed by a genealogical sensibility.

Resources for Transformation—
Ecointersectional Analyses

I opened this chapter with a discussion of instances in which Blacks in the United States and Indigenous communities in Brazil are impacted by the infusions of social and environmental issues. I did so in part to call attention to the ways issues of environmental injustice demand an intersectional approach. Foucault's polyhedron of intelligibility is, I contend, incomplete without it. Emerging from the insights of US Black feminist thinkers such as Francis Beal (1969), Patricia Hill Collins (1990, 2019), members of the Combahee River Collective (1979), Anna Julia Cooper (1892), Kimberlé

Crenshaw (1989, 1991), and many others who made evident the double jeopardy of being Black and being a woman, intersectionality offers an "analytic sensibility" through which to examine "sameness and difference and its relation to power" (Cho, Crenshaw, and McCall 2013, 795). Collins (2019, 27) explains that Crenshaw's metaphor of intersectionality "arrived in the midst of ongoing struggles to resist social inequalities brought about by racism, sexism, colonialism, capitalism, and similar systems of power. The metaphor of intersectionality could move among and through these forms of domination, providing a snapshot view of their sameness and difference as a way to see their interconnections." In a recent book on intersectionality, Collins and Sirma Bilge (2016, 2) offer the following general description: "Intersectionality is a way of understanding and analyzing the complexity in the world, in people, and in human experiences. The events and conditions of social and political life and the self can seldom be understood as shaped by one factor. They are generally shaped by many factors in diverse and mutually influencing ways. When it comes to social inequality, people's lives and the organization of power in a given society are better understood as being shaped not by a single axis of social division, be it race or gender or class, but by many axes that work together and influence each other. Intersectionality as an analytic tool gives people better access to the complexity of the world and of themselves."

The central goals of intersectional analyses are (1) to examine the interrelations of systems of oppression in order to understand how they overlap and infuse[9] and, in these infusions, alter the experience of the oppression and (2) to shine a light on the all too frequent omission of attention to race, especially to the complex situations of women of color, particularly those from disadvantaged communities (Carbado et al. 2013). Crenshaw (2020) describes intersectionality as "a lens, a prism, for seeing the way in which various forms of inequality often operate together and exacerbate each other." "We tend," she explains, "to talk about race inequality as separate from

---

[9] I use the term "infuse" and its variants to signal that systems of oppression are not additive, nor are they separate nor separable. The prefix "inter-" with its connotation of being between or among, risks separation of vectors of power and oppression. Great efforts have been made to undermine this connotation of the term "intersectionality" and to make clear that systemic racisms infuse and are infused by other forms of systemic oppression such as those involving class, gender, ethnicity, ability, or sexuality. My contribution to this effort is to argue that systemic racisms are also not separate or separable from systemic practices of environmental degradation. While remaining cautious about terms that employ the preface "inter-," I use the terms commonly associated with intersectionality, namely, intersecting, interlocking, and intermeshing with the understanding that I do not intend to signal separation.

inequality based on gender, class, sexuality or immigrant status. What's often missing is how some people are subject to all of these, and the experience is not just the sum of its parts." As Collins (1990, 18) reminds us, "oppression cannot be reduced to one fundamental type"; rather "oppressions work together in producing injustice." Intersectional analyses thus are without specified limits as dimensions of power and oppression and their interactions often shift and change. Nor are the impacts of the interactions predictable. In some cases, the intersection of facets might diminish the force of the oppression; in another they might exacerbate the oppression. Intersectional analyses are prisms that call attention to different facets of systems of power, the components of Foucault's polyhedron of intelligibility, that contribute to social inequality and provide an important optic for examining the complexities of climate injustices. And like Foucault's (1991, 77) polyhedron, the nature and number of intersections of axes of power "is not given in advance and can never properly be taken as finite." As Devon Carbado (2013, 304) explains, an intersectional analysis "is never done, nor exhausted by its prior articulations and movement; it's always already an analysis-in-progress."

What this means is that it is crucial to cultivate our commitment to seeing complexities, to situating our intersectional analyses both spatially and temporally, as well as working to understand the many interactions among beliefs, values, institutions, comportments. It means accepting that our analyses will always be limited, that there are always more facets of the problem than any one analysis is able to comprehend. I focused my analysis of the greater impact of COVID-19 on Blacks in the United States around the facet of exposure to air pollution. While this is clearly one important facet, it is hardly the only one. The startling facts collected by the Centers for Disease Control (2022)—among them, that as of January 2022, 21.5% of reported COVID-19 deaths in the United States are of non-Hispanic Blacks, even though this group makes up only 12.8% of the total population—cannot be explained by exposure to air pollution alone.[10] Tracing the myriad facets in this situation would require us to consider a number of issues, including how and why incidents of noncommunicable diseases such as diabetes and high blood pressure that cause an individual to be more susceptible to the coronavirus are higher in Blacks than Whites in the United States. Why and how

---

[10] Rates for groups considered Latino are similarly troubling as they account for 29.9% of all reported COVID deaths yet are only 19.6% of the population.

access to health insurance or even healthcare is more limited for Blacks than for Whites. The impact of the greater numbers of Blacks, particularly Black women, who are involved in both paid and unpaid caregiving and the multifaceted reasons why they are so situated. The complex histories of housing and job discrimination that result in greater numbers of Blacks living in more crowded spaces, either smaller homes and/or with more people, making social distancing difficult and at times impossible. The reasons behind greater numbers of Blacks using public transportation and working in jobs that do not provide options for social distancing. The myriad reasons doctors are less likely to refer Black individuals for COVID testing when they come in with fever, coughing, and trouble breathing (Farmer, 2020). The reasons why in some predominantly Black low-income neighborhoods in the United States it can take longer to get a COVID-19 test than it does in other neighborhoods or why testing centers in these areas are more likely to be closed because they are unable to acquire equipment and protective gear. And the reasons why the COVID vaccination rate among White people is nearly twice as high as the rate for Black people (19% vs. 11%), as well as over twice as high as the rate for Latino people (19% vs. 9%) (Ndugga et al. 2021). An intersectional approach that foregrounds structural inequalities in income, housing, jobs, and healthcare provides a prism for understanding the complex ways multiple facets of social inequalities contribute to the racial disparities in COVID-19 rates that we are seeing in the United States.

The relevance of an intersectional approach to climate injustice is obvious, yet surprisingly understudied. The Intergovernmental Panel on Climate Change in their Fifth Assessment Report in 2014 (Olsson et al. 2014) provided a figure that highlighted what they labeled "the intersecting dimensions of inequality," listing gender, class, ethnicity, age, race, and (dis)ability as relevant and intersecting factors contributing to what they referred to as multidimensional vulnerability (Figure 1.1).

The report, a summary of the best available peer-reviewed scientific evidence, documented with very high confidence based on robust evidence that "climate change and climate variability worsen existing poverty, exacerbate inequalities, and trigger both new vulnerabilities and some opportunities for individuals and communities" and concluded that "climate change interacts with non-climatic stressors and entrenched structural inequalities to shape vulnerabilities" (Olsson et al. 2014, 796).

The report correlated multiple lines of support to conclude that "socially and geographically disadvantaged people exposed to persistent inequalities

RACISM AND ECOLOGICAL INDIFFERENCE 13

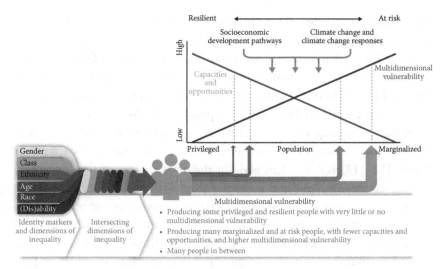

Figure 1.1 Multidimensional vulnerability driven by intersecting dimensions of inequality, socioeconomic development pathways, and climate change and climate change responses. Authors of the report argued that vulnerability depends on the structures in society that trigger or perpetuate inequality and marginalization, not just income poverty, location, or one dimension of inequality in itself, such as gender.

Source: Figure 13-5 from Olsson, L., M. Opondo, P. Tschakert, A. Agrawal, S.H. Eriksen, S. Ma, L.N. Perch, and S.A. Zakieldeen, 2014: *Livelihoods and poverty. In: Climate Change 2014: Impacts, Adaptation, and Vulnerability*. Part A: Global and Sectoral Aspects. Contribution of Working Group II to the Fifth Assessment Report of the Intergovernmental Panel on Climate Change [Field, C.B., V.R. Barros, D.J. Dokken, K.J. Mach, M.D. Mastrandrea, T.E. Bilir, M. Chatterjee, K.L. Ebi, Y.O. Estrada, R.C. Genova, B. Girma, E.S. Kissel, A.N. Levy, S. MacCracken, P.R. Mastrandrea, and L.L. White (eds.)]. Cambridge University Press, Cambridge, United Kingdom and New York, NY, USA, pp. 793-832.

at the intersection of various dimensions of discrimination based on gender, age, race, class, caste, indigeneity, and (dis)ability are particularly negatively affected by climate change and climate-related hazards. Context-specific conditions of marginalization shape multidimensional vulnerability and differential impacts" (Olsson et al. 2014, 796). The report cited only two papers that provided intersectional analyses: Andrea Nightingale's (2011) "Bounding Difference: Intersectionality and the Material Production of Gender, Caste, Class and Environment in Nepal" and Anna Kaijser and Annica Kronsell's (2014) "Climate Change through the Lens of Intersectionality." While there have been subsequent efforts to bring an intersectional analysis to bear on issues of climate change, given the significance of the approach, the numbers are surprisingly small.[11]

While the relevance of intersectional analyses to issues of climate injustice seems obvious, even within those handful of studies that bring an intersectional lens to issues of climate change, there is, perhaps unsurprisingly but nonetheless regrettably, too often a practice that Bilge (2013, 412) refers to as the "whitening of intersectionality," caused by "decentring the constitutive role of race in intersectional thought and praxis." As Crenshaw (1993, 112–113) reminded us early in the development of the conception of intersectionality, "political strategies that challenge only certain subordinating practices while maintaining existing hierarchies not only marginalize those who are subject to multiple systems of subordination but also often result in oppositionalizing race and gender discourses." In comparison to the large number of studies of the differential impacts of gender and climate change or the intersection of gender and class as it is relevant to climate change, few studies foreground race as one of the key elements of intersecting social inequalities that comprise climate injustice.[12] My aim in this book is to focus attention on this crucial component.

The subtitle of this book, *An Ecointersectional Analysis*, is designed to call attention to an additional lens of the prism that is often overlooked in intersectional analyses.[13] An analytic sensibility that attends to the ways social

---

[11] In addition to the special issue of *Race, Gender & Class* devoted to intersectional approaches to climate change edited by Phoebe Godfrey (2012) and the two anthologies she coedited with Denise Torres (2016a, 2016b), there is a small but growing number of publications, many quite recently published, that explicitly apply an intersectional lens to the topic of climate change including: Djoudi et al. (2016); Garutsa (2021); Hathaway (2020); Lykke (2009); McNamara and Clissold (2019); Nesmith et al. (2021); Nicoson (2021); O'Brien (2020); Osborne (2015); Quandt (2018); Ravera, Martín-López et al. (2016); Ryder (2018); Sultana (2013); Thompson-Hall, Carr, and Pascual (2016); Tuana (2019); Vinyeta, Whyte, and Lynn (2015); Walker et al. (2019); Wood et al. (2021).

[12] There is a growing literature on race and environmental injustice; see, e.g., Hage (2017); Merchant (2003); Mills (2001); Pellow (2007, 2016); Pellow and Brulle (2005); Pulido (2015, 2017a, 2017b); Whyte (2018). However, work on race and climate change is more limited, despite the fact that there have been four special journal issues devoted to the topic: Baldwin and Erickson (2020); Godfrey (2012); Lewis (2016); Tuana and Bernasconi (2019). Authors whose work has directly focused on race and climate change include Wynter and McKittrick (2015); Vinyeta, Whyte, and Lynn (2015); Whyte (2017); Yusoff (2018); Vergès (2017); Pulido (2018); Mirzoeff (2018).

[13] Rachel Hallum-Montes (2012) was the first to coin the term "eco-intersectional." Hallum-Montes's account was designed to build "on the more materialist branches of ecofeminism as well as the ecogender perspective" and to provide "an examination of how histories and systems of power, privilege, and exclusion based on gender, race, class, and other social markers work together to shape human-human and human-environment relations" as well as allowing "for an understanding of how people are mobilizing across borders of race, gender, class, and nationality in shared struggles for environmental justice" and adopting "the feminist commitment to positive social change by linking academic scholarship with activist and advocacy work" (108). Although my use of the term differs from Hallum-Montes's, it is synergistic with it.

injustices and environmental degradation are not only infused but are often co-constitutive is key to fully understanding the complexity of climate injustice. Too often accounts of harms to environments are viewed as separate from the impacts and effects of social inequalities. While it is often acknowledged that environmental degradation frequently causes greater harms to groups of people and communities who also suffer from social oppressions, the two phenomena are treated as separate and, at best, additive. Racism, for example, even when it is conceived as systemic, is typically seen as separate from environmental degradation or the two are seen as additive—e.g., racism results in Blacks living in more toxic environments. Here a component of environmental racism is acknowledged: Blacks are more likely to be exposed to environmental harms. However, this approach can obscure the fact that systemic injustices and environmental degradation are at times and in complex ways infused. One of my aims in this book is to provide case studies that shine a light on these complex intersections through the lens of ecointersectional analyses.

Systemic Racisms—A Short Excursus

Throughout the book, my focus will be on systemic rather than individual racisms. I acknowledge the impact of the racist beliefs, habits, prejudices, affects, and behaviors of individuals and the ways they impact their and others' sense of self-worth in both positive and negative ways as well as inform their interactions with others. However, my emphasis throughout the book will be on systemic racisms, namely, the structures, beliefs, images, and collective practices that permeate social and political systems such as healthcare, education, law, politics, media, employment, and religious organizations and that serve to maintain racial domination.

The distinction between individual racism and institutional or systemic racism was introduced in 1967 by Stokely Carmichael (Kwame Ture) and Charles V. Hamilton in *Black Power: The Politics of Liberation*. Their work made clear the importance of the distinction: "Racism is both overt and covert. It takes two, closely related forms: individual whites acting against individual blacks, and acts by the total white community against the black community. We call these individual racism and institutional racism. The first consists of overt acts by individuals, which cause death, injury or the violent destruction of property. This type can be recorded by television cameras; it can frequently be observed in the process of commission. The second type is less overt, far more subtle, less identifiable in terms of specific individuals committing the acts. But it is no less destructive of human life. The second type originates in the operation of established and respected forces in the society, and thus receives far less public condemnation than the first type. When white terrorists bomb a black church and kill five black children, that is an act of individual racism, widely deplored by most segments of the society. But when in that same city—Birmingham, Alabama—five hundred black babies die each year because of the lack of proper food, shelter and medical facilities, and thousands more are destroyed and maimed physically, emotionally and intellectually because of conditions of poverty and discrimination in the black community, that is a function of institutional racism. When a black family moves into a home in a white neighborhood and is stoned, burned or routed out, they are victims of an overt act of individual racism which many people will condemn—at least in words. But it is institutional racism that keeps black people locked in dilapidated slum tenements, subject to the daily prey of exploitative slumlords, merchants, loan sharks and discriminatory real estate agents. The society either pretends it does not know of this latter situation, or is in fact incapable of doing anything meaningful about it" (4).

The distinction between individual racist beliefs or behaviors and the ways racist regimes permeate social and institutional structures is an important lens for understanding the complexity of oppressions. The distinction has been the subject of many studies where scholars have worked to identify features of different types of systemic racism—institutional, structural, economic, ontological. My use of the concept turns less on making such distinctions and more on working to reveal the systemic components relevant to specific instances of the intersections between systemic racisms and environmental exploitations. However, to underscore that there is not a "unified" or universal system or structure of racial exploitation, but rather a complexly situated and changing process of racialization, I modify Carmichael and Hamilton's original term to *systemic racisms*. To speak of systematic racism in the singular risks reducing its complexity. I use the plural to signal that there is neither an unchanging and unified structure to racism nor a particular form of racialization that is the dominant model through which other types of racism are formulated. The plural is designed to serve as a reminder that the structures of racial domination or exploitation differ both historically and geographically. The term as I use it is designed to include the complex lineages and histories that are part of the fabric of current racial formations. It is also important to remember that systemic racisms are never separate or separable from other forms of systemic oppressions based on formations such as gender, sexuality, class, ethnicity, or ability. Nor are they, as I will argue, separate or separable from systemic practices of environmental degradation.

Racist Climates, Ecological Indifference

Ecointersectional analyses are a powerful resource that reveal that environmental degradation and systemic oppressions not only co-occur but are often mutually constitutive. As described by Ghassan Hage (2017, 40) in *Is Racism an Environmental Threat?*, racism is "a mode of relating to the world that, in the process of relating, creates the very world it is relating to." He argues that "racism reproduces the attitudes and dispositions that are behind the ecological crisis" (61). To understand how, for example, racism gives rise to and is in turn shaped by environmental degradation entails careful, genealogically informed analyses of the many and often shifting ways systemic racisms and ecological degradation are infused. It also means that we cannot address one problem without also addressing the other. Indeed, one of my aims in this book is to provide an account of why the fight to protect the environment must also be a fight against systemic racisms and other forms of systemic inequity. Ecointersectional analyses engage the complex exchanges between forms of systemic injustice, including the ways the vectors of power and oppression informing them are saturated with beliefs, values, and practices concerning animals, plants, minerals, mountains, rivers, oceans, and the like.[14] Doing so, as I demonstrate in the examples I develop throughout this book, will require going well beyond the current focus on unequal distribution of risks and harms in environmental justice and climate justice discourses.

---

[14] My aim is to develop a usage of the term "ecointersectional" that does not reiterate or reinforce problematic ontological divides so common in Western sensibilities, such as those between humans and nature or between life and nonlife, and the various permutations thereof which are often at the ontological heart of the links between environmental exploitation and the exploitation of groups of animals, including humans. An ecointersectional lens is particularly helpful here in that just as race is not separate or separable from gender—does not constitute an ontological divide—so too we begin to appreciate that *geos* is not separate or separable from *bios*; they infuse in complex ways.

Part of what blocks an appreciation of the deep interconnections between systemic oppressions and environmental degradation is the habit of separating social factors from environmental factors and seeing the play of power primarily affecting the former domain. While acknowledging that social factors impact environmental factors and vice versa, what is seldom seen are the ways systemic injustices *emerge out of and give rise to* harms to the environment. Even the term "environmental justice" in much of the scholarship refers not to impacts on environments per se but on how those impacts disproportionately harm or benefit certain groups of people. Environmental justice approaches typically focus on the ways people of color and people who live with poverty are disproportionately exposed to environmental harms and lack access to environmental benefits. Even those who develop an environmental racism lens, while they often use an intersectional lens to consider how race, gender, class, and other vectors interact, typically focus on two dimensions: (1) equality and fairness in the distribution of environmental harms and benefits (distributive justice) and (2) the rights of affected communities to participate in decision-making regarding these distributions (procedural or participatory justice). Too often studies of environmental justice or even environmental racism focus only on co-occurrence—Black populations in the United States are more likely to be exposed to toxins; waste disposal facilities in the United States have a greater likelihood of being sited close to Native American lands.[15] This lens, while important, occludes the often complex and long history of the *co-constitution* of systemic racisms and environmental degradation.

Environmental justice and environmental racism approaches too often emerge from frameworks in which humans are the central actors, with environments playing a key role in their health and well-being. The focus is typically on ensuring that humans have the environmental resources they need to flourish and are not disproportionately disadvantaged or unjustly advantaged. What such approaches overlook is that the conception of the environment as separate from humans and in its service is complicit with the sensibility that also sees some life forms and lifeways as more important than, indeed superior to others, including some human life forms and lifeways.

---

[15] Luke W. Cole and Sheila R. Foster (2001) provide a history of the environmental justice movement tracing its origins in numerous movements such as the United Church of Christ (1987) Commission for Racial Justice's study "Toxic Wastes and Race in the United States," Native American activist movements to protect land, and labor movements to protect farm workers from dangerous pesticides.

My conception of *ecological indifference* is designed to signal an often muted component of environmental injustice, particularly in research on climate injustice, namely, the disposition of seeing animals, plants, and/or the ecosystems of which they are a part as resources for human consumption and enjoyment—usable, fungible, disposable, without intrinsic worth or standing. The phrase "ecological indifference" signals a sensibility that both separates the "human" from the "nonhuman" and views the latter as essentially lacking in worth apart from what it might offer the former domain.[16] To refer to ecological indifference is not to indicate that people experience no feeling for "nature," that is, that they are indifferent to many aspects of "nature." Indeed, many people enjoy a refreshing walk through a park or forest, laugh at the antics of the birds and squirrels at their feeders, or marvel at the wildness of the animals they see on safari. Ecological indifference instead signals a disposition to view the nonhuman world as, well, nonhuman and thus to view it as having only instrumental value, that is, that the nonhuman world's value is measured primarily by its usefulness for humans. As David Abram, Tema Milstein, and José Castro-Sotomayor (2020, 7) phrase it, "The term 'environment' locates us humans at the center, as the only thing that's not 'environment,' since all these other beings are 'our' environment. They are what surrounds us." In addition to the ways this conception of "nature" habituates attitudes of indifference, another of the many problems of this conception is that the separation of humans from nature is often not clean cut. Indeed, systemic racisms and sexisms serve to both trouble the divide—humans who are seen as less than fully human—and to provide a basis for seeing and treating some humans in the same way as nature is viewed and treated, namely, as valuable only based on their use value.[17]

Let me be clear that while ecological indifference signals a general disposition, indeed one that is dominant in the global economy,[18] it is not one shared

---

[16] In a similar fashion, Val Plumwood argued that in dominant worldviews nature is "backgrounded," her term for nature being relegated to a role that allowed usefulness without entailing moral considerability. As Plumwood (1993, 21) explained in *Feminism and the Mastery of Nature*, "What is involved in the backgrounding of nature is the denial of dependence on biospheric processes, and a view of humans as apart, outside of nature, which is treated as a limitless provider without needs of its own. Dominant western culture has systematically inferiorised, backgounded, and denied dependency on the whole sphere of reproduction and subsistence. This denial of dependency is a major factor in the perpetuation of the non-sustainable modes of using nature which loom as such a threat to the future of western society."

[17] This theme is developed around the concept of fungibility in the work of Saidiya Hartman (1997) and Tiffany Lethabo King (2016). For a discussion of the racialization of the human/nature divide, see Joshua Bennett (2020) and Zakiyyah Iman Jackson (2020).

[18] This theme has been developed by Jason W. Moore (2015, 2016).

by all. There are many cultures and communities in which the various life forms and environments that make up more-than-human[19] worlds are animate and valued parts of the co-relational world of which we are a part.[20] The First National People of Color Environmental Leadership Summit, to take just one example, drafted a statement in 1991 designed to reframe the environmental justice movement. The first of its seventeen principles "affirms the sacredness of Mother Earth, ecological unity and the interdependence of all species, and the right to be free from ecological destruction" (Delegates to the First National People of Color Environmental Leadership Summit 1991).

When environmental justice and climate justice approaches focus on systemic injustices in the ways environmental or climate harms and benefits are distributed to different groups of people, they risk overlooking a more fundamental linkage between seeing and treating environments as exploitable, disposable, fungible, and ways of seeing and treating certain groups of people as exploitable, disposable, fungible.[21] My aim in positioning climate injustice alongside ecological indifference is to demonstrate that these two seemingly disparate phenomena are in fact infused. *That is, ecological indifference and*

---

[19] David Abram (1996) introduced the term "more-than-human" in his book *The Spell of the Sensuous*. In my earlier work (Tuana 2001), I built on Abram's conception to avoid the realist/constructivist divide and developed a conception of the happening of things where no sharp divide is posited between so-called nature/culture. The term "more-than-human" is also designed to affect a shift from seeing humans as separate and separable from "environments" to seeing more-than-human worlds as both encompassing and exceeding human worlds. That said, the habit of juxtaposing the human and the more-than-human world threatens to keep the division circulating. Even placing the term "human" within the locution risks retaining an emphasis on the uniqueness of *Homo sapiens*, while at the same time occluding the ways in which some people have been excluded from full membership in the category "human." While not minimizing these risks, I believe the locution "more-than-human" has the potential to disrupt ontological habits of separation and keep in question efforts to collapse dichotomies as well as to find ways to make distinctions. My aspiration is that the term can become, as Penny Harvey, Christian Krohn-Hansen, and Knut G. Nustad (2019, 4) phrase it, a "way of keeping open an unsettled space that allows us to remain attentive to a multiplicity that does not settle, and to uncertainties that are never simply resolved." Stephanie D. Clare (2019) addresses issues such as this in *Earthly Encounters*. I do, however, continue to make a distinction between systemic racisms and harms to environments. While I realize that in doing so I risk reanimating a human/nature split, I do so with care and caution in order to talk about the ways systemic racisms are implicated in harms in the more-than-human world.

[20] This conception of the relationality of things is often found in Indigenous cosmovisions. For example, Glenn Coulthard's (2014) conception of "grounded normativity" and its development by Leanne Betasamosake Simpson (2017) encompasses such a conception, as does Brian Burkhart's (2019) conception of "locality" in *Indigenizing Philosophy through the Land*. Melanie L. Harris (2017) points to a similar conception of relationality in African American earth-honoring faiths. My conception of animacy here is kin to that of Mel Chen (2012) and is not designed to separate life from nonlife, bios from geos.

[21] This is what Hage (2017, 43) refers to as "generalized domestication": "[G]eneralized domestication as I want to develop the concept is a way of inhabiting the world through dominating it for the purpose of making it yield value: material or symbolic forms of sustenance, comfort, aesthetic pleasure and so on."

environmental or climate injustice are two sides of the same coin. The examples offered in each of the chapters provide illustrations of this infusing in various locations and times. They are designed to provide resources for appreciating the intersections not only among social identities but also intersections within the wider, more-than-human context, and, given my focus on climate change, to offer resources for recognizing intersections among the biological and the geophysical, and to do so with attention to the specificities of particular historical and geographical locations. This attunement arises from ecointersectional approaches.

In positing ecological indifference as a key component of environmental injustice, my account may sound similar to accounts by proponents of ecological justice (e.g., Baxter 2005; Garner 2013; Nussbaum 2006; Schlosberg 2014). Ecological justice perspectives view nature as having intrinsic value and acknowledge the mutual interdependence of all species. Proponents often seek to expand the domain of moral considerability so that it includes animals, plants, and ecosystems. I support one core concern of proponents of ecological justice, namely, that how we live with and think about the environments we are of and in[22] is a key element in efforts to address climate or environmental injustice. However, while I am in full agreement with many ecological justice theorists that the human-nonhuman, social-natural dichotomies of dominant sensibilities are key drivers of ecological indifference, what is often missing from such accounts is recognition of the ways systemic oppressions and attitudes about the environment are entangled. My goal is not to take a stand on whether the biocentric or ecocentric[23] positions offered by such accounts can be refined to correct these omissions. My focus is rather to investigate the ways climate injustice and ecological indifference

---

[22] This admittedly awkward locution—"of and in"—is an effort to speak in ways that do not draw a divide between environments and humans. We, you and I, are as much a part of the ecosystems of prairie, forest, and ocean as are the birds, trees, and fish. What constitutes an environment is not fixed for all organisms. Indeed, a human body is the environment for a multitude of organisms: viruses, bacteria, fungi. There is no fixed "environment" but rather the places in which we live together where what counts as the environment for one is not the same for all. Nonetheless, in talking about ecological indifference and climate justice, I will refer to environments. The tendency to separate and background environments—humans here, environment as the nonhuman remainder—is what I'm trying to undo. Hence, environments that we are of. But I keep the "in" to recognize, nonetheless, that there are differences and distinctions between parts of ecosystems.

[23] Biocentrism views all living things as having intrinsic moral worth and believes that the human species is not inherently superior to other species (see, e.g., Taylor 1986). Ecocentrism extends intrinsic value and moral worth to ecosystems, not just to the organisms, including humans, that are part of it (see, e.g., Leopold 1949; Callicott 1989). Theorists in these schools push back against the view that "nature" is without moral worth. However, they often do not see the ways the fungibility of "nature" and the fungibility of certain groups of humans are infused.

inform one another and to argue that efforts to address systemic oppressions will not succeed without also contesting dispositions, beliefs, and institutions that incline us to ecological indifference. Coming to understand that the systemic injustices that give rise to intersecting oppressions and the ingrained habits of ecological indifference that result in environmental degradation are interlocked is crucial.

New Materialisms?

Many theorists have questioned the separation and hierarchizing of "nature" and "culture" and their many linked conceptions.[24] My own work has been richly informed by Donna Haraway's process philosophy–influenced account regarding material-semiotic processes (where the hyphen is a signal of interconnection, not separation) and the ways in which her work offers an account of how the social and the physical in all of their manifestations co-emerge (see especially Haraway 1997, 2016). Her account of the material embeddedness of things—economies, ecosystems, institutions, weather events—is a model I've followed as I've worked to remove the slash between nature/culture with its attendant power dynamics.

Advocating a form of materialism, whether it be "old-school" Marxist-inspired or the so-called new feminist materialisms, is, of course, one way to begin to disrupt such hierarchizing dichotomies. Haraway's (1991, 150) brand of socialist feminism is a good example of attention to multiple axes of power and the ways they carve the world at joints that sediment oppressions: "In the traditions of 'Western' science and politics—the tradition of racist, male-dominant capitalism; the tradition of progress; the tradition of the appropriation of nature as resource for the productions of culture; the tradition of reproduction of the self from the reflections of the other—the relation between organism and machine has been a border war." One of the central goals of Haraway's work is to draw attention to the situatedness of the

---

[24] While the list would go on for more than a page, two notable examples relevant to environmental injustice are Sylvia Wynter's (2001, 2003) engagement of Frantz Fanon's conception of a "Manichean divide" between categories such as White/Black, culture/nature as divides that ground relations of domination through a logic of mutual exclusion that renders one side superfluous and fungible and Plumwood's (1993) conception of "hyperseparation," the structure of dominance that undergirds binaries in Western thought such as nature/culture, human/nonhuman, male/female, mind/matter, and does so by seeing one side of the binary as the superior form toward which the other side is an inferior subordinate.

interrelations of production, reproduction, and imagination—historically, culturally, and ecologically. But centering the more-than-human in Marxist-inspired materialisms is not as common as one might hope.[25]

Feminist "new" materialism attempts to foreground the agency of more-than-human worlds and manifests in many guises centered on various resources, from phenomenology to Western science.[26] Jane Bennett (2001), for example, in *The Enchantment of Modern Life: Attachments, Crossings, and Ethics* deploys the term "enchanted materialism" to call attention to the agency of organic as well as inorganic phenomena. Others, like Karen Barad (2007), turn to the natural sciences to identify resources for disrupting such dichotomies as mind/body, human/nonhuman, or nature/culture. Troubled, for example, by the divide between language and matter, Barad develops a theory of agential realism in which discursive practices and materiality co-emerge (44–45). Matter is on this account a continuous becoming; both matter and meaning materialize together.

While the "new" materialisms keep the facet of the more-then-human in clear sight, their efforts to grasp power "in the fullness of its materiality" (Barad 2007, 66) often overlook, or at least downplay, the relatively durable structures that support hegemonic positions and the ways that they function to oppress differently positioned individuals and groups. Bonnie Washick and Elizabeth Wingrove (2015, 71) object that in theories developed under the label of "new materialisms," "systemically (re)produced relations of inequality and domination by and among (agentially nonsovereign) humans recede in the face of a new materialist metaphysical (and rhetorical) aesthetic." Indeed, as Chelsea M. Frazier (2016) clearly demonstrates, the human/nonhuman divide cannot be effectively troubled without recognizing the racialized nature of Western notions of the human. Frazier's goal is to show that "'the West' itself—its divisions of space and its rigid notions of the human subject—are insufficient frameworks through which 'global warming, severe climate change, and the sharply unequal distribution of the earth's resources' can be effectively addressed" (44).[27] These

---

[25] Myra Hird (2009, 329), to take just one example, offers an intersectional lens, but one that focuses only on the domain of the human when she argues that materialist feminism must be "concerned with women's material living conditions—labor, reproduction, political access, health, education, and intimacy—structured through class, race, ethnicity, age, nation, ableism, heteronormativity, and so on."

[26] I leave the term "new" in scare quote to recognize concerns such as those of Sara Ahmed (2008) concerning the alleged newness of such approaches to materiality.

[27] As Alfred López (2018, 374) states, the new materialism as reflected in the work of theorists such as Jane Bennett "preclude[s] or occlude[s] the presence of the raced enfleshed subject."

concerns are further complicated by many who argue that "new" materialists' claims to newness are made at the expense of such traditions as those of "First Nations and Indigenous peoples; to those humans who have never been quite human enough as explored, for instance, in postcolonial and revolutionary black thought . . . and to other non-Western medical and spiritual modalities" for whom dichotomies such as human/nature were never part of their ways of being (Wazana Thompkins 2016; see also Todd 2015a, 2016).

The Interlocking of Injustice and Indifference

Climate injustice, indeed environmental injustice as a whole, and ecological indifference are not separate or separable phenomena; they are one and the same. My focus in many of the chapters concerns the complex interrelationality between environmental degradation and systemic racisms. Here I follow the lineage of intersectionality in working to avoid the whitening of ecointersectionality, while recognizing that far more work has been done on the intersections of climate injustice and the axes of oppression due to gender or to class.[28] As with any intersectional analysis, my focus on the infusing of systemic racisms and environmental degradation is not designed to erase other dimensions but rather to attend to what can be seen when the focus is on this particular facet of the prism and its intersections with other facets. In the words of Kara Thompson (2017, 93), we need to see that "racism and climate change are genealogical and scalar. They belong to the procession of anthropogenic histories premised on white supremacy over black and brown bodies and nonhuman worlds, and on making these two at times indistinguishable."

There are three distinctive but interrelated domains in which the intersections between systemic racisms and ecological indifference are manifest.

---

[28] In addition to books devoted to issues of gender and climate change by Buckingham and Masson (2019), Dankelman (2010), Nagel (2016), Roy (2019), and Sen Roy (2018), there are a number of special issues of journals devoted to the topic including, *Ambio* (Ravera, Iniesta-Arandia et al. 2016), *Climatic Change* (Huyer and Partey 2020), *Gender, Technology and Development* (Huyer 2016), *Hypatia: A Journal of Feminist Philosophy* (Cuomo and Tuana 2014), and *International Journal of Environmental Research and Public Health* (Balbus and Sorensen forthcoming). The number of journal articles on the topic is far too large to list them all. An overview of this literature is provided in Pearse (2017). I will discuss this issue in more detail in Chapter 5.

1. Differential distribution of harms/benefits due to systemic racisms.
2. Racist institutions and practices fueling or causing environmental degradation.
3. The social structures that generate environmental degradation are the same ones that generate systemic oppression of certain groups of people.

The various case studies offered in this book are designed to illustrate instances of these domains and of the interrelations among them.

Differential Distribution of Harms/Benefits Due to Systemic Racisms

Attention to differential distribution of ecological harms and benefits is the best-known dimension of environmental racism. Efforts to identify and rectify the ways racism results in certain groups being more protected from environmental harms and other groups being subject to higher levels of risk from environmental harms are key components of environmental justice scholarship and activism.[29] In addition to concerns over inequitable distributions of environmental burdens and benefits, environmental justice proponents have advocated for equitable representation in the decision-making processes concerning environmental risks. Work on environmental justice has had such a significant impact that even governmental agencies such as the US EPA include these two dimensions in their definitions of environmental justice. The EPA offers the following definition:

> Environmental justice is the fair treatment and meaningful involvement of all people regardless of race, color, national origin, or income, with respect to the development, implementation, and enforcement of environmental laws, regulations, and policies. This goal will be achieved when everyone enjoys:
> - the same degree of protection from environmental and health hazards, and

---

[29] See, e.g., Bullard (1994); Bullard et al. (2007); Cole and Foster (2001); Pulido (2015, 2017a, 2017b).

- equal access to the decision-making process to have a healthy environment in which to live, learn, and work.

Fair treatment means no group of people should bear a disproportionate share of the negative environmental consequences resulting from industrial, governmental and commercial operations or policies. (Environmental Protection Agency 2021a)

Recognition of differential distribution of environmental harms and benefits is coupled with attention to the causes of such injustices and the most effective means to remedy them. From the placement of hazardous-waste landfill sites (Mohai and Saha 2007, 2015), to the location of heavy industry (Taylor 2014; Mele 2016), to protection or the lack thereof from lead exposure (Pulido 2016), to the exposure of workers to toxic chemicals (Guthman and Brown 2016; Sánchez Barba 2020; Saxton 2015), the question of *how* some social groups come to be disproportionately exposed to environmental risks and how best to remedy such harms falls within this first domain. Investigating what either directly caused or at least contributed to the unequal burdens or benefits is often controversial and contentious. Debates frequently center around the question of whether class or race or the intersection of class and race is the most salient causal factor in environmental racism. Another point of controversy surrounds questions of culpability, that is, whether the unequal burdens are the result of intent or accident.

The first domain of the intersection of systemic racisms and environmental degradation is widely recognized, and many theorists are working to expand the original focus on heavy industries that pollute the air or the water and the siting of waste facilities.[30] But surprisingly, this domain has had comparatively little application to the field of climate justice. As previously noted, far more work has been done on inequities in climate impacts due to gender, to class, and to geographical location than in examining how race and racism intersect with risks due to anthropogenic climate change. One of my goals in this book is to foreground the complex interrelations of systemic racisms and differential climate impacts. However, as important as it is to include this theme in climate justice scholarship and activism, I do so through its intersections with the other two domains. Indeed, it is essential that the other two domains in which the intersections between systemic racisms and

---

[30] See, e.g., studies of environmental racism and the prison industrial system (Gilmore 2006; Pellow 2018).

ecological indifference are manifest become components of climate justice scholarship and activism. This book, then, serves as a call to transform climate justice scholarship and activism so that it becomes attentive to all three components of racial climates.

Racist Institutions and Practices Fueling or Causing Environmental Degradation

The second domain, how racist practices themselves fuel or cause environmental degradation, shifts the focus from the question of how systemic racisms affect the risk burden of oppressed groups to the question of how systemic racisms and racist practices result in harms to environments—to nonhuman animals and life forms, to plants, to ecosystems. The first domain of the intersection of racism and ecological indifference—differential impacts on humans—has received robust attention in the past three decades in the wider domain of environmental justice, although remaining largely absent from the climate justice literature. The second domain—how systemic racisms lead to or contribute to harms to the environment—has not been a common theme in either the environmental justice literature or the climate justice literature. While the second domain is perhaps more difficult to document, it is, nonetheless, an important gap in the environmental justice literature as a whole, as well as in the climate justice literature.

As the second domain is far less prevalent in the literature, I will provide an illustrative example, namely the nineteenth-century extermination of buffalo in the United States.[31] As with any analysis of the links between systemic racisms and environmental degradation, accounts must be historically and geographically situated. While additional research in this second domain of the intersection of racism and ecological indifference might unearth helpful generalizations about the ways such links occur, attending to the specifics of such instances is an important first step. As I argue throughout this book, the move to generalization often occludes the complexities of the interfusions of racial climates and ecological indifference.

Consider the near extermination of the buffalo in the United States in the nineteenth century. An appreciation of the dramatic change that

---

[31] Here I refer to the American bison by the commonly used term "buffalo."

happened at this time helps us understand the extent of the impact. While there were huge herds of approximately 30 million buffalo in the sixteenth century, by the late nineteenth century they had been hunted to near extinction. At the end of the nineteenth century, only a few hundred buffalo remained across the United States, and fewer than one hundred remained in the wild in the Great Plains states (Taylor 2011; Isenberg 2000). William Hornaday, the superintendent of the National Zoological Park, writing in 1889 of what he referred to as the extermination of the American bison, referred to the writings of Daniel Boone, Lewis and Clark, and others who spent time in the Great Plains to document the abundance of bison in the Great Plains prior to that time. Included in his illustrative quotes is one from Lieutenant Colonel Richard Irving Dodge, who was the commander of Fort Dodge, Kansas, in the 1870s. Dodge's (1877) book *The Plains of the Great West and Their Inhabitants* provided a sense of the abundance of the buffalo:

> The great herd on the Arkansas through which I passed could not have averaged, *at rest*, over fifteen or twenty individuals to the acre, but was, from my own observation, not less than 25 miles wide, and from reports of hunters and others it was about five days in passing a given point, or not less than 50 miles deep. From the top of Pawnee Rock I could see from 6 to 10 miles in almost every direction. This whole vast space was covered with buffalo, looking at a distance like one compact mass, the visual angle not permitting the ground to be seen. I have seen such a sight a great number of times, but never on so large a scale. (quoted in Hornaday 1889, 390)

There were, of course, various economic reasons for the destruction of the herds, given the value of buffalo products, particularly hides. But to limit the explanation to profit overlooks an important facet, one that illustrates how racism, in this case the view of Plains Indians as savages in need of eradication or at least control, was a central factor in the extermination of the buffalo (Hubbard 2014).[32]

After the end of the Civil War, President Ulysses S. Grant appointed William Tecumseh Sherman to serve as the commanding general of the

---

[32] Even before advances in tanning made buffalo hides a more valuable commodity, there were efforts to eradicate the buffalo in order to destroy the resources Indigenous communities relied upon.

army, a post he held from 1869 until 1883. Sherman considered it to be a central aim of his administration to ensure that the Western and Plains states were "safe for settlement," an aim that was linked to his belief that the land must be cleared of its original inhabitants. To clear the central plains for settlement and clear the path for the Union Pacific and Kansas Pacific railroads, Sherman advocated exterminating the buffalo in the region. In a letter to General Philip H. Sheridan in May 1868, Sherman wrote, "[A]s long as Buffalo are up on the Republican [River] the Indians will go there. I think it would be wise to invite all the sportsmen of England and America there this fall for a Grand Buffalo hunt, and make one grand sweep of them all. Until the Buffalo and consequent Indians are out from between the road we will have collisions and trouble."

Sherman and Sheridan supported this aim by providing civilian hunting expeditions with supplies, military escorts, and scouts. Sherman and other military commanders also endorsed the killing of buffalo by troops in order to address the so-called Indian Problem. Pony soldiers, for example, were required to shoot buffalo from horseback, a skill that would then be turned directly against the Indigenous populations. The intention was explicit: control the Indigenous population by destroying the buffalo. In a letter to Sherman dated October 15, 1868, Sheridan set forth his plans for dealing with the Indigenous populations: "The best way for the government is to now make them poor by the destruction of their stock, and then settle them on the lands allotted to them." In 1881, Sheridan expressed his views in the following way: "If I could learn that every Buffalo in the northern herd were killed I would be glad. The destruction of this herd would do more to keep Indians quiet than anything else that could happen, except the death of all the Indians. Since the destruction of the southern herd . . . the Indians in that section have given us no trouble" (quoted in Smits 1994, 337). Racism against Indigenous people, which manifested in systematic efforts to control and in many instances eradicate them, is a key reason for the extermination of the large buffalo herds on which Indigenous communities relied.[33]

---

[33] Simon Lewis and Mark Maslin's (2015) proposal of the Orbis spike as the anthropogenic signature marking the start of the Anthropocene Epoch at 1610 reflects the devastating impact of colonialism on populations in the Americas. They argue that the decrease in atmospheric carbon dioxide resulting from to the large and rapid decline in human population in the Americas due to genocide and disease exposure by Europeans that resulted in the deaths of more than 50 million people alongside the "geologically unprecedented homogenization of Earth's biota" and the "annexing of the Americas" for resources that provided the material causes of the Industrial Revolution are sufficient to demarcate this period as the start of a new geologic era (175, 177). As Lewis puts it, "[P]lacing the Anthropocene at this time highlights the idea that colonialism, global trade and the desire for wealth

This is just one brief account of an instance when systemic racisms fueled or caused environmental degradation. But as is often the case, the intentional environmental harm, in this case the extermination of the buffalo, had other, unintended environmental impacts. Buffalo are a keystone species, that is, a species that plays an essential role in maintaining the ecosystem of which it is a part (Knapp et al. 1999; Freese et al. 2007).[34] Their grazing practices and wallowing behavior resulted in increases in biodiversity in the prairie ecosystem (Fuhlendorf and Engle 2001), and the intentional efforts to eradicate buffalo led to near "simultaneous reduction in herbivore abundance and grassland extent" (Knapp et al. 1999, 39).

The particular manner in which systemic racisms contribute to environmental degradation will differ in different locations and different time periods. Nonetheless, understanding how past and current racist practices, institutions, and beliefs fuel environmental degradation or impact the practices leading to current levels of greenhouse gases is an important and generally overlooked element in the intersections of systemic racisms and environmental degradation. While I do not believe that the nature of the linkages will all be the same, my contention is that attention to this domain will reveal linkages that go beyond mere correlation. Hence, ecointersectional analyses are an important but often overlooked component of analyses of environmental injustices and, in particular, climate injustices. This study endeavors to begin to rectify that omission.

The Social Structures That Generate Environmental Degradation Are the Same Ones That Generate Systemic Oppression of Certain Groups

The third domain of the intersection of systemic racisms and environmental degradation has only recently become the subject of study.[35] Hage (2017), as

and profits began driving Earth towards a new state" (quoted in Biello 2015). While I do not engage classification debates concerning the Anthropocene, my position is akin to that of Michael Simpson (2020, 55), who explains that "rather than seeking to definitively resolve the question of the status of the Anthropocene and its relationship to coloniality . . . my call is for scholars to destabilize the stories of the Anthropocene that remain framed in colonial narratives of progress, advancement, and civilization."

[34] The analogy is to the keystone in an arch, which if removed will result in the collapse of the arch. The concept of a keystone species was introduced by Robert T. Paine (1969).
[35] In addition to Hage, the work of Claire Jean Kim (2015), Wynter (2001, 2003), and Kathryn Yusoff (2018) would be included in this domain.

one example, offers an affirmative answer to the title of his book *Is Racism an Environmental Threat?* His view is that racism intensifies the environmental crisis not through the "direct causal effects of racist practices on the environment," the second domain above, but because "it reinforces and reproduces the dominance of the basic social structures that are behind the generation of the environmental crisis—which are the structures behind its own generation" (14–15), the third domain. Focusing on Islamophobia, Hage argues that "the racial crisis manifested by Islamophobia and the ecological crisis not only happen to have an effect on each other, they are in effect one and the same crisis, a crisis in the dominant mode of inhabiting the world that both racial and ecological domination reproduces" (14). Hage focuses on the dominance of what he calls "structures of generalized domestication," arguing that they constitute a way of relating to the world: "Generalized domestication is a mode of inhabiting the world through dominating it for the purpose of making it yield value: material or symbolic forms of sustenance, comfort, aesthetic pleasure, and so on" (87). The dominance of this sensibility "initiates a mode of being where otherness is always an otherness that is instrumentalized and perceived to exist 'for me'" (120). Generalized domestication, on Hage's account, includes a process of polarization that "works through the valorization of a certain definition of 'humanity' that the domesticator aims to 'evacuate' from the domesticated, be it 'nature,' a particular animal, blacks, or Muslims" (100–101). His argument is that the practices that constitute systemic racisms and the practices that have led to ecologically destructive modes of domination emerge from the same dominant sensibility.

While I disagree with Hage's decision not to attend to the causal effects of systemic racisms on the environment, the second domain, in arguing that ecological indifference and racial climates are two sides of the same coin, I am in agreement with Hage's (2018, 274) insight that "the classifications and the practices that constitute colonial racism and the practices that have generated the destruction of the natural environment are mutually self-reinforcing because they share a common root in a common mode of existence, the dominant manner in which we humans are inserted, and deploy ourselves, in the world, and which works as their generative principle." My position is that climate justice theory and activism must become more attuned to the ways in which ecological indifference and systemic racisms are interlocked through a dominant sensibility that accepts the fungibility and thus the disposability of certain types of things *and* certain types of beings. In other words, dominant sensibilities have led to modes of inhabiting the world where the disposability of certain life forms, including groups of people, and the disposability of environments are intertwined.

The Interrelations of the Domains

Ecological indifference goes hand in hand with resource-extractive practices of colonization and capitalism. A focus on consumption and conquest in a sensibility that rejects a conception like the more-than-human world and instead conceptualizes the human world as separate and separable from the rest of the world and views "nature" as having, at best, only use-value has led to *sacrifice zones*. Sacrifice zones include areas of the environment that have been stripped of the resources viewed as valuable—logged-over forests, spent or abandoned uranium mines, the remains of mountaintop removal mining for coal—or have been designated as repositories for the unusable byproducts of consumption—landfills, waste dumps, injection wells, and Superfund sites. These sacrifice zones contain all the inhabitants, including the human inhabitants, who are relegated to living in what have often become toxic environs and who have thus been sacrificed along with the forests, mountains, and waterways. Steve Lerner (2010) in *Sacrifice Zone: The Front Lines of Toxic Chemical Exposure in the United States* provides a detailed description of sacrifice zones that go beyond the phrase's original meaning of sites that have been contaminated by radioactivity due to uranium mining and processing. Lerner uses the phrase more broadly to refer to areas of chemical pollution because it "dramatizes the fact that low-income and minority populations, living adjacent to heavy industry and military bases, are required to make disproportionate health and economic sacrifices that more affluent people can avoid"; he argues that "this pattern of unequal exposure constitutes a form of environmental racism that is being played out on a large scale across the nation" (3).

While such an account makes clear the injustice of differential impacts (the first domain), a more comprehensive understanding of environmental and climate injustice must also consider the ways in which the creation and acceptance of environmental sacrifice zones and the creation and acceptance of people and other life forms that are sacrificable are interdependent and mutually reinforcing (the third domain). But to be complete, such an account also requires that we remain alert to those instances where systemic racisms cause or contribute to environmental degradation (the second domain). Understanding the various beliefs, habits, practices, dispositions through which systemic racisms reinforce and are reinforced by environmental degradation is an important and often missing component of the climate justice literature. As Hop Hopkins (2020), with the Sierra Club, wrote, "You can't have climate change without sacrifice zones, and you can't have sacrifice zones without disposable people, and you can't have disposable people without racism." Each of the chapters that follow includes efforts to illustrate and elucidate the complexity of such interconnections between systemic oppressions and ecological indifference.

2
Racial Climates

> Here is a lesson: what happens to people and what happens to the land is the same thing.
> —Linda Hogan (1995)

In *A Billion Black Anthropocenes or None,* Kathryn Yusoff (2018, 51) argues that "the Anthropocene is configured in a future tense rather than in recognition of the extinctions already undergone by black and indigenous peoples." Indeed, she contends that "black and brown death is the precondition of every Anthropocene origin story" (66). Yusoff's is a reminder, one that echoes many others, that the *anthropos* of the Anthropocene is not the universal category it appears to be.[1] It is, on the contrary, framed by virtue of the very same divisions between the human, the less than human, and the nonhuman from which our current environmental issues arise.

Yusoff urges us to see that racism and environmental exploitation are not separate and separable phenomena but are inextricably linked. As Romy Opperman (2019, 58) phrases it, we need to "reframe the problem of environmental racism in terms of racist environments" in which we "see racism as an atmospheric force that shapes the relations of individual and milieu." This insight necessitates a transformation of the very framing of theories of climate justice. Appreciating that racism is an atmospheric force requires attention to *racial climates*.

Climate justice efforts have typically focused on the disproportionate impacts of anthropogenic climate change on so-called less developed countries or in-country disparities due to gender roles or income status, as well as the impacts on future generations. The United Nations (2019), for example,

---

[1] A small sample includes Baldwin and Erickson (2020); Mirzoeff (2018); Pearse (2017); Sealey-Huggins (2018); Todd (2015b); Vergès (2017); Weizman and Sheikh (2015); Whyte (2017); Wynter (2003).

defines climate justice as follows: "The impacts of climate change will not be borne equally or fairly, between rich and poor, women and men, and older and younger generations. Consequently, there has been a growing focus on climate justice, which looks at the climate crisis through a human rights lens and on the belief that by working together we can create a better future for present and future generations." As I argued in the previous chapter, a focus on injustices concerning distribution of the negative impacts of climate change and other environmental harms, while important, can serve to inadvertently obscure underlying sources of oppression that are woven into our shared climate. Iris Marion Young (1990, 8, 15) long ago emphasized that a focus on distributive justice, on the question of disproportionate impacts, "obscures other issues of institutional organization"; in particular, "this focus tends to ignore the social structure and institutional context that often help to determine distributive patterns." In other words, while attention to differential impacts is important and a guide for debates on climate reparations,[2] it is crucial that we do not ignore the structural dimensions that permeate the maldistribution of environmental and climate impacts.

Understanding the institutional structures, habituated actions, and sensibilities, as well as the histories and their afterlives that are infused in the happenings of differential impacts is a crucial and often overlooked component of climate justice.[3] Missing from conceptions of climate justice such as that of the United Nations is a recognition of *racial climates*: the complex exchanges of oppressions that gave rise to anthropogenic climate change. Targeting the lineages of the values, concepts, and practices that give rise to current climate regimes, in this case those values, concepts, and practices animated by (though never exclusively by) systemic racisms, provides a richer understanding of the ways *lineages of oppression and climate injustice are interwoven*.

In the previous chapter I introduced three interlocking domains in which the lineages of systemic racisms and ecological indifference are interwoven.

1. Differential distribution of harms/benefits due to systemic racisms.
2. Racist institutions and practices fueling or causing environmental degradation.

---

[2] See, for example, Klinsky and Brankovic (2018).
[3] I use the term "infuse" with the goal of signaling a break from an additive model, namely, sex + class + sexuality + race + environment. I see this term as in deep resonance with the intention of the term "intersection" in the work of Crenshaw.

3. The social structures that generate environmental degradation are the same ones that generate systemic oppression of certain groups of people.

To flesh out the infusing of these domains in the context of climate justice I turn to research on racial climates in education. We who work in the field of climate justice would benefit by learning from and augmenting insights from this literature. Sylvia Hurtado and colleagues (1998), for example, argue that when addressing diversity, most educational institutions focus on increasing the number of minority students. While not denying the importance of this effort, the authors address other dimensions of the climate that have an important impact. They offer a five-dimensional conception of racial climates, dimensions that often entwine and co-emerge.[4]

1. The impacts of governmental and institutional policies, programs, initiatives—financial aid policies and programs, affirmative action policy, state and federal policy on affirmative action, etc.
2. An institution's historical legacy of inclusion or exclusion of various racial/ethnic groups—the vestiges of past discrimination and of state-imposed segregation including policies, behaviors, beliefs, and attitudes of teachers, administrators, and students.
3. An institution's structural diversity—the balance or lack thereof in the representation of diverse racial/ethnic groups in the composition of the student population as well as in the faculty and their roles within the institution.
4. The psychological dimension of the institution's racial climate—individual and community perceptions of group relations, perceptions of discrimination or racial conflict, and attitudes toward those from racial/ethnic backgrounds other than one's own.
5. The institution's behavioral dimension—the nature and extent of social interactions between and among individuals from different racial/ethnic groups, as well as pedagogical practices, e.g., integration of diversity issues in the course content, promoting interaction across racial/ethnic groups in classes. (282)

---

[4] Hurtado et al. (1998) make a distinction between external and internal forces. Here I have combined them.

We can adapt and modify this framework to develop a multidimensional understanding of racial climates which includes but is not limited to differential impacts.

1. The impacts of the framing of governmental and institutional policies, programs, and initiatives relevant to climate change and to the impacts of climate change, including attention to adaptation and mitigation policies and other policies that impact anthropogenic climate change.
2. The historical legacies and inherited sensibilities informing the treatment of various racial/ethnic groups, with emphasis on those legacies and sensibilities that entwine environmental exploitation and the exploitation of certain groups of people.
3. Structural dimensions of diversity, such as the governmental and institutional policies, practices, and norms that privilege some lifeways over others, including more human-focused policies such as current and past labor policies, housing policies, aid policies, and health policies, as well as more environment-focused policies such as waste and water management and regulations concerning biodiversity and ecosystem protection.
4. Psychological dimensions of individual and group perceptions and attitudes and the related affective responses regarding which lives and lifeways are considered valuable and which are seen as less worthy of protection.[5]
5. Differential impacts of unavoidable and unavoided climate change.[6]

Such a multidimensional lens will enable us to understand why and how the fifth dimension, differential impacts, is grounded in and often reanimates multiple legacies of oppression. It is an approach that reveals that environmental harms such as the impacts of anthropogenic climate change and racist practices are not, as is often assumed, separate and separable phenomena but are *entwined historically, structurally, and psychologically.* These are the

---

[5] While I will weave this dimension throughout various chapters, Chapter 5 brings this dimension to the foreground most explicitly.

[6] The distinction between unavoidable and unavoided impacts is drawn to acknowledge that there are some climate-related impacts that we cannot avoid no matter what choices we now make. However, there are also impacts that could have been avoided but where a choice was made—either intentionally or not—not to take the action needed to avoid them. Failure to take effective action to reduce emissions as well as choices not to invest in adaptation options once we have knowledge of anthropogenic climate change are situations in which the impacts related to such choices are labeled "unavoided" to signal that we had the knowledge and ability to make a difference, but chose not to.

intersecting dimensions to which I refer when I speak of racial climates in the context of climate justice. In this chapter I use these five dimensions to refine our understanding of the different ways in which lineages of systemic racisms and ecological indifference are entangled and often co-emerge.

To address environmental racism in terms of racist environments with the complexity it demands requires new tools for analysis. As I previously argued, a key tool, and one that I both adopt and adapt from the work of US Black feminist thinkers, is ecointersectional analyses. Intersectional analyses have not only sensitized us to marginalizations due to the entwinings of different types of oppression and discrimination but also to the ways efforts to correct such injustices can unwittingly reproduce or legitimize the very marginalizations they attempt to address. As Saidiya Hartman warns, "What then does this language—the given language of freedom—enable? And once you realize its limits and begin to see its inexorable investment in certain notions of the subject and subjection, then that language of freedom no longer becomes that which rescues the slave from his or her former condition, but the site of the re-elaboration of that condition, rather than its transformation" (Hartman and Wilderson 2003, 185).

To augment the insights of Black feminist figurations of intersectionality I include as a crucial dimension the infusions of ecosystems with and in human systems, the coupling I refer to as the more-than-human, which, of course includes humans and their various lifeways.[7] Ecointersectional analyses are essential to understanding how the disposability of certain types of ecosystems are often entwined with the disposability of certain groups of people. Let me underscore, however, that it is important to recognize that "all intersectional moves are necessarily particularized and therefore provisional and incomplete" as each such analysis "must necessarily limit itself to specific structures of power" (Carbado et al. 2013, 304). In other words, *what is needed are carefully situated, historically informed, contextually sophisticated studies of the intricacies of the linkages of the disposability of some groups of humans and the disposability of other life forms and ecosystems.* I refer to the latter as "ecological indifference." The ways systemic racisms and ecological indifference are entwined are not the same in every location, for every group,

---

[7] This locution is designed to catalyze a shift from seeing humans as separate from other life forms and environments to recognizing the complex interrelations between things. Hence the importance of not referring to humans and the more-than-human world. It is an easy slip and one that I've made in my own work. I urge readers to be attentive to such slips within this book. They are not intended, but habits of thought are difficult to transform.

or in every historical period. Mapping the contours of those shape-shifting processes and tracing their afterlives is important for any effort to understand and respond to racial climates. Hence my contention that genealogical sensibilities that focus attention on the various histories, differences, and permutations of systemic racisms and ecological indifference are another essential tool for understanding racist environments, or what I'm referring to as "racial climates."

The preface "eco-" is an inclusive, gathering word that refers to the ways things happen together. Ecointersectional analyses include attention to ecosystems, those complex interactions between life forms, which of course include human life forms, and between life forms and life places, the physical, abiotic conditions in which life forms exist. My aim is to use the term "ecointersectional" in ways that do not reinforce but will perhaps trouble the ways in which a divide between humans and nature is made, and the many manifestations of this divide in dominant Western sensibilities. Attention to the many ways worldings happen is another important component of ecointersectional analyses, one I focus on in my final chapter.

Ecointersectional analyses enable us to see that the pathways to protecting environments from degradation and biodiversity loss often infuse with efforts to address oppression in its myriad and often interlocking forms. It is my aspiration that ecointersectional analyses will contribute to more robust understandings of climate justice, as well as environmental justice in general, that hold the promise of avoiding, as Hartman phrased it, the re-elaboration of the condition. My focus in this chapter is on how ecointersectional analyses augment current understandings of environmental racism by demonstrating that a focus on differential impacts is too narrow a lens to understand the complexities of racial climates. What is needed is an appreciation of the ways the five dimensions entwine and inform racial climates. My aim in identifying these dimensions is to enhance ecointersectional analyses of climate injustices by providing a resource for more comprehensive analyses of the various dimensions of racial climates.

The Infusing of the Dimensions—Mitigation Policies and Heatwaves

While we can begin with the framing of climate-related policies, *dimension 1*, in order to understand racial climates, we soon find ourselves in the midst of the interrelations of all of the dimensions. Attending to racial climates can help us see how climate adaptation and mitigation strategies often interact with structural dimensions of diversity in ways that privilege some ways of living and some life forms over others, *dimension 3*. Attention to that dimension enables us to understand how historical legacies of systemic racisms, *dimension 2*, can contribute to forms of climate adaptation apartheid where, in the words of Bishop Desmond Tutu (2007, 166), "the citizens of the rich world are protected from harm, [and] the poor, the vulnerable and the hungry are exposed to the harsh reality of climate change in their everyday lives." Climate adaptation apartheid certainly results in differential impacts, *dimension 5*. But to respond to such differential impacts it is essential to understand that climate apartheid, like South Africa's apartheid, involves deeply held systemic beliefs, values, and dispositions regarding racial superiority and inferiority. Such beliefs, values, and dispositions not only impact individual understandings and practices, *dimension 4*, but are infused into and supported by the interactions of various social institutions, such as education, waste management, labor, and policing and the practices and dispositions they authorize, *dimension 3*, as well as informing the values underlying policies governing mitigation and adaptation policies, *dimension 1*. Careful examination of histories and current practices of environmental exploitation often reveal that the labor used to mine resources as well as the ecosystems that those engaged in such exploitation saw as expendable are linked to systemic beliefs regarding racial superiority and inferiority and to ecological indifference. Systemic racisms and environmental exploitation are often infused throughout all the five dimensions of racial climate.

To provide an illustration of the entwining of the five dimensions, I begin with mitigation targets, *dimension 1*, and focus on one of the many infusions of racial climates, namely, the interactions of mitigation targets and the urban heat island effect.

Mitigation Targets

Attention to racial climates in the framing of mitigation and adaptation policies leads to careful analysis of who and what is targeted for protection and who and what is not. Consider the target of 2 °C that has been treated as an acceptable and manageable target threshold for mitigation. Many nations have committed to international agreements such as the Copenhagen Accord designed to limit increases in the global average surface temperatures from rising more than 2 °C (3.6 °F) above pre-industrial levels. The oft repeated claim is that doing so will limit dangerously disruptive climate impacts for future generations.

But as Joni Seager (2009, 16) made clear over a decade ago, the 2 °C target is safe only "for temperate-latitude, rich countries. For the millions of people in poor countries, low-latitude countries, low-lying states, and small island states, 2° is not acceptable. For the dozens of states already pushed to adaptive limits, a 2° cap, even if achievable, is too little, too late. For fragile ecosystems, perhaps especially coral reef and other marine communities, 2° of warming is not a safe target."

The recent report by the Intergovernmental Panel on Climate Change (2018), *Global Warming of 1.5 °C*, echoes Seager's warning by showing that 2 °C of warming would expose many life forms—from humans to corals—to life-threatening heatwaves, coastal and river flooding, and water shortages. Extreme heat, for example, will be much more common if the global average surface temperature increase is close to 2 °C. While the report does address differential impacts (*dimension 5*), little attention is paid to the intersections between systemic racism and mitigation targets (*dimensions 2, 3,* and *4*). To appreciate this intersection, consider extreme heat events.

Heatwaves and Histories of Structural Racism

Decisions on mitigation targets will have an impact on the prevalence and severity of extreme weather events such as heatwaves. Rising global temperatures have already impacted the intensity, frequency, and duration of heatwaves. It is estimated that extreme heat events have caused more human deaths than hurricanes, floods, and tornadoes combined (Wong, Paddon, and Jimenez 2013), as well as degrading many land and marine ecosystems (Stillman 2019). The June 2020 heatwave in the Pacific Northwest, for example, when temperatures were higher than ever recorded in the region from Oregon to Vancouver, killed humans, birds, and many marine plants and animals (Rosen 2021). Hence the significance of mitigation targets on the prevalence of heatwaves.

The "urban heat island effect" refers to the phenomenon of cities being significantly hotter than surrounding rural areas due to the greater concentrations of roads and buildings and the relative lack of vegetation. Buildings and roads absorb and re-emit heat from the sun more than farmlands or forests do, resulting in a temperature differential between cities and rural areas. But heat island effects can also happen *within* a city, causing some neighborhoods to be hotter than others due to the density of the buildings or lack of green spaces or tree canopies. Mitigation policies affect global temperature increases, which in turn affect the frequency and intensity of heatwaves, which affect those who live in neighborhoods that lack green spaces.

Consider the intermeshing of histories of structural racism and heat waves in the US. The urban heat island effect intersects with past histories of racial segregation in US cities (*dimension 2*). The racial isolation of Blacks in northern cities, for instance, began in the early decades of the nineteenth century, as neighborhoods that had been integrated shifted over a period of thirty years into segregated Black neighborhoods, segregation that has persisted to this day in many cities.[8] This ghettoization of Blacks was initially fueled by acts of violence by Whites desiring to remove Black residents from the integrated neighborhoods. There was a significant increase in race riots during and after World War I in which Whites violently attacked Black residents. In 1919 alone, in what has been called "Red Summer," race riots took place in almost forty cities across the United States when Whites, buoyed by White supremacist propaganda, attacked Blacks and their property (*dimension 4*). In Chicago, as just one example, hundreds of Blacks lost their homes when Whites set fires and then blocked roads to prevent fire trucks from reaching the burning houses. Following the riots, many Blacks were unwilling to move back to their home neighborhoods, justifiably fearing additional violence, and instead moved to outlying regions. The resulting "Black neighborhoods" were often "policed" by Whites with threats of violence or actual violence should residents attempt to expand into White neighborhoods. In *American Apartheid: Segregation and the Making of the Underclass*, Douglas Massey and Nancy Denton (1993, 35) note that "during and after World War I, a wave of bombings followed the expansion of black residential areas in cities throughout the north. In Chicago, fifty-eight black homes were bombed between 1917 and 1921.... [I]n Cleveland, a wealthy black doctor who constructed a new home in an exclusive white suburb had his house surrounded by a violent mob, and when this attack failed to dislodge him, the home was dynamited twice." After the 1920s,

---

[8] A detailed study of this history can be found in Massey and Denton (1993).

while violent tactics did not disappear altogether, the rise of neighborhood "improvement" associations worked to secure and maintain the "color line" by lobbying for zoning and covenant restrictions in which Blacks would be barred from owning or leasing properties. Real estate boards supported such covenants. The National Association of Real Estate Boards (1924, 7, article 34), in their 1924 code of ethics, included an article supporting such efforts, stating that "a Realtor should never be instrumental in introducing into a neighborhood a character of property or occupancy, members of any race or nationality, or any individuals whose presence will clearly be detrimental to property values." In these examples we see infusions of *dimensions 3* and *4* as individual and group beliefs and prejudices concerning racialized groups informed corporate as well as governmental policies.

Racial segregation was solidified in the 1930s through the practice of "redlining." The Home Owners' Loan Act of 1933 was passed as part of a federal program to address the impacts of the Depression by refinancing mortgages at low interest rates to prevent foreclosures. The resulting Home Owners' Loan Corporation (HOLC) was charged with identifying neighborhoods considered desirable for such refinancing. The HOLC "graded" and color-coded neighborhoods into four categories based on whether the *neighborhood* was judged to be a good risk for a mortgage loan rather than on the qualifications of the individual applicants. The underlying concern was that the home value not be negatively impacted by the condition of the neighborhood. These decisions were largely based on the racial makeup of the neighborhoods. Those that were judged undesirable for mortgage support, and were literally outlined in red on maps, tended to be Black or Latino neighborhoods.[9] This assessment led to increases in loan denials and greater refusal by insurance companies to issue policies to businesses or individuals in these areas. The color-coded maps created by HOLC were used by the Federal Housing Administration (FHA) as well as the Veterans Administration to determine areas where it would be safe to insure mortgages. A 1935 FHA manual for mortgage underwriters stated that acceptable ratings would depend on neighborhoods not being at risk for "the occurrence or development of unfavorable influences" such as the "infiltration of inharmonious racial or nationality groups" (quoted in Calmore 1993, 1511).

---

[9] Working-class neighborhoods, particularly those with "less desirable Whites," namely Jewish, Irish, or Italian communities were classified as in the third category, resulting in few mortgages being approved in such neighborhoods. Those neighborhoods that were predominantly Black or Latino were redlined regardless of the wealth of the residents (Massey and Denton 1993).

Despite being banned under the Fair Housing Act of 1968, redlining practices continue to impact today's urban landscapes.[10] Neighborhoods historically redlined are still dominantly low- to moderate-income (74%), and most remain minority neighborhoods (64%), with cities in the South showing the least change in both dimensions (Mitchell and Franco 2018, 4–5). Through violence, the threat of violence, and legal brokering, many of the once integrated cities of the North became strictly segregated, while many cities and suburbs in the South cemented their segregation practices. The lineages of those practices continue to impact these cities and their residents to this day.[11]

Current climate targets (*dimension 1*) intersect with historical legacies of violence and housing policy gerrymandering (*dimension 2*) and current policies, practices, and norms concerning housing (*dimension 3*), often reinforced by individual and group prejudices concerning racialized groups (*dimension 4*), which in turn intersect with urban heat island effects (*dimension 5*). According to a recent study, formerly redlined districts across the United States are, on average, 2.6 °C/4.68 °F warmer than non-redlined districts; in some cities the difference is as much as 7 °C/12.6 °F (Hoffman, Shandas, and Pendleton 2020). Combine the dramatic increase in extreme heat events likely under a 2 °C-warming scenario with the impacts of systemic racisms in the United States, and we begin to understand the inextricable interconnections between histories of systemic racisms and climate apartheid, in this case, climate mitigation apartheid. Differential impacts (*dimension 5*), in this instance the disproportionate risk for Blacks of heat-related health impacts and mortality in US cities, are interwoven with histories and current instantiations of systemic racisms (*dimensions 2, 3,* and *4*) and current mitigation policies (*dimension 1*). While my focus is on systemic

---

[10] Despite its intent to prohibit discrimination concerning the sale, rental, or financing of housing based on race, religion, national origin, or sex, the impact of the Fair Housing Act was to further segregate Blacks in cities by financing Whites to move into basically segregated suburbs and financing Blacks to purchase inner-city homes (Massey and Denton 1993; Rothstein 2017; Taylor 2019).

[11] Lineages are both complex and shifting. Formerly redlined areas remain on the whole typically denser neighborhoods and have less greenspace or green canopy and thus are subject to the urban heat island effect. However, while such neighborhoods remain majority-minority, their geographical location is a significant factor in their racial makeup. For example, a Brookings study found that formerly redlined areas in the city of Los Angeles, California, which is currently the third-most populous formerly redlined area, has a population comprised of 70% Latino or Hispanic and 6% Black, while formerly redlined neighborhoods in Birmingham, Alabama, remain majority Black (Perry and Harshbarger 2019). In other regions the majority-minority in formerly redlined neighborhoods is often a mix of Latino and Black, with a smaller percentage of Asian American. The afterlives of the lineages of systemic racisms are complex.

racisms, it is crucial remain attentive to the infusions of other dimensions such as age, gender, and class that contribute to each of these dimensions. Consider, for example, their role in differential impacts (*dimension 1*) through the example of the Chicago heatwave. Most of the 739 people who died over the course of three days of record high temperatures in the 1995 Chicago heatwave were elderly and poor, and a disproportionate percentage were Black.[12] Gender also played a role, as a significantly higher percentage of men died compared to women. A study of the heatwave attributed this gender disparity to women having stronger social ties, which meant their friends and neighbors were more likely to check on them and offer assistance (Klinenberg 2015).[13]

As Leon Sealey-Huggins (2018, 100) forcefully phrases it, "we can only properly understand the harm being wrought by weather events and climate change by directly connecting it to broader social and political processes of which structural racism is a central part." Doing so requires "consideration of the relationships between the colonial and imperialist histories either underpinning climate change's causes, or structuring societies' capacities to respond" (100). An ecointersectional approach attentive to the ways global climate change exacerbates historically codified inequities will help to ensure that policies designed to alleviate disparities in climate impacts identify all the dimensions of racial climates in order to avoid reanimating them.

In the previous chapter, I identified three interlocking domains in which the lineages of systemic racisms and ecological indifference are interwoven. In one of those domains are instances where racist institutions and practices fueled or caused environmental degradation. My example was the near extinction of buffalo herds in the United States resulting from efforts to remove Indigenous peoples from the land. I contend that racial segregation

---

[12] A sense of the devastation of those three days can be experienced through the *Chicago Magazine*'s oral history of the event (Thomas 2015).

[13] Though my focus is on the urban island heat effect, this is not the only example in which rising temperatures and systemic racisms infuse. Consider, for example, the impact of rising temperatures on farmworkers in the United States. Rising temperatures have serious implications for farmworkers who are typically paid per piece rather than an hourly rate. One study of farmworkers in Florida, for example, found what they labeled "a strikingly high prevalence" of dehydration and acute kidney injury (Mix et al. 2018). There are currently no federal regulations concerning protection from heat exposure for farmworkers. Only three states, California, Minnesota, and Washington, have instituted heat-related protections for farmworkers. While often very basic—providing water, shade, and breaks—the absence of even such rudimentary regulations in other states has resulted in many heat-related incidents. Current efforts to establish federal regulations have focused on passage of the Asunción Valdivia Heat Illness and Fatality Prevention Act. The Act is named in honor of Asunción Valdivia, who died in 2004 of heat stroke at the age of fifty-three after picking grapes in Washington for ten hours straight in 105-degree temperatures.

in US cities is another instance of this domain, where racist policies and practices result in environmental harms. Neighborhoods were destroyed and slums created in order to remove Blacks and Latinos from some neighborhoods and contain them in others. While very different from the buffalo hunts in form, there are clear resonances in intent: to control and contain people viewed as inferior. And the impacts of the measures used included harm to aspects of the environment—in the case of racial housing segregation these include the environmental impacts of failing to provide adequate waste and water services and of deteriorating and substandard housing. Granted there are differences. In the case of the buffalo hunts, the harm was to a nonhuman species in order to control a group of humans; in the case of redlining and segregation, the harm is to city neighborhoods, environments that have been largely shaped by humans, to control a group of humans. Thus when we are examining the ways racist institutions and practices fueled or caused environmental degradation, it would be a mistake to limit our attention to "naturally" occurring environments, such as oceans, grasslands, rivers, and forests and the inhabitants thereof. Urban ecosystems, with their complex assemblages of buildings, birds, parks, mammals (including human mammals), rivers, bridges, gardens, fish, tunnels, reptiles, and insects, are as much a part of the environment to which environmental justice movements need to attend as the so-called wilderness areas and everything in between. Ecological indifference is as rife in urban environments as it is in rural environments.

Intermeshing of Systemic Racisms and Environmental Degradation

While it is certainly essential to unveil the many ways climate apartheid is supported by climate adaptation or mitigation choices and policies, *dimension 1*, understanding the circulations of racism in the context of climate change will require examining historical lineages of systemic racisms entwined in the causes and impacts of anthropogenic climate change, *dimension 2*. It will also require that we identify the many ways systemic racisms are infused in the very institutions and practices that contribute to the acceleration of greenhouse gases, *dimension 3*. It is only by tracing the sometimes subtle, often normalized, habituated beliefs and attitudes regarding racial, gender, or ethnic superiority or inferiority, *dimension 4*, that we can begin to appreciate that climate injustice is about far more than differential impacts, *dimension 5*.

While many approaches to climate justice focus on current vulnerabilities and impacts, to fully address climate injustices, indeed to advocate for environmental justice as a whole, we also need to understand how the legacies of racial, gender, and ethnic oppressions informed and continue to impact social institutions such as education, waste management, housing, forest management, labor, nature reserves, and policing. Further, we need to know how these legacies were, and continue to be, imbricated in the mining of resources, shifts in land use, and the eradication of some species and the safeguarding of others. This requires that we understand the histories of injustices buried beneath the differential impacts of anthropogenic climate change as well as understand the legacies that inform the unspoken ground of the choices made or ignored regarding how to adapt to climate impacts.

As I argued in the first chapter, to fully develop our ecointersectional analyses requires genealogical sensibilities which provide an important lens for understanding the historical legacies that entwine current practices of environmental exploitation and the exploitation of certain groups of people. Genealogical sensibilities involve cultivating a disposition to be attuned to the interlocking, interpenetrating, and infused processes from which normative practices and hierarchies of authority and values emerge in order to understand their complex histories and trace the vestiges of those histories in contemporary institutions, beliefs, and practices. Let me illustrate these claims with another example of the entwinings of exploitation: the practices that have led to deforestation in Brazil. An ecointersectional lens reveals that the disposability of the forest in Brazil is intermeshed with the disposability of certain groups of people. This is an instance in which systemic racisms infuses ecological indifference, resulting in multidimensional exploitation.

Brazil's Charcoal Industry

Brazil has the largest charcoal industry in the world, producing up to 13 million tons of vegetal charcoal per year, 80% of which is used by steel and iron makers. Production of Brazilian charcoal requires logging and burning, often of native forests, compounding the problem of deforestation with the destruction of the rainforest. The Brazilian Forest Code, *Código Florestal Brasileiro*, first introduced in 1934, with amendments in 1965, 1989, 2001, and 2012, was designed to protect native forests and savannas by requiring landowners in the Amazon to maintain a percentage of their property under native vegetation and put an end to illegal deforestation. Although the Forest Code has had a significant impact on deforestation rates in Brazil, illegal deforestation continues at an often devastating pace.

The production of charcoal and its history are reminders of the complexity of responding to anthropogenic climate change. Using biomass fuels, like charcoal, can have environmental benefits. One major benefit is the reduction in the use of fossil fuels and the consequent lowering of sulphur and nitrogen contents, resulting in less environmental pollution and fewer health risks (Rousset et al. 2011). However, since burning biofuels releases carbon dioxide, to strike a balance, many advocate planting fast-growing crops to recapture carbon dioxide. But such an approach to biosequestration in the Amazon is as much of a threat to Indigenous lifeways and highly biodiverse ecosystems as is the original deforestation. There are several hundred Indigenous groups living in the Brazilian Amazon. The traditional lifeways of most of these groups involve complex interactions with the ecosystems of which they are a part in ways that, while providing them with ample resources for a healthy life, vitalize and rejuvenate the forest, "adding to its diversity and the size of its faunal and floral populations" (Taylor 1988, 138). Reforestation and other forms of biosequestration often do little to address degradation of Indigenous lifeways or the Amazon's biodiverse ecosystems.

During the past fifty years, the Amazon has lost approximately 17% of its forest cover, with deforestation rates in Brazil higher than in any other country.[14] Scientific projections indicate that the rainforest's tipping point before it stops producing enough rain to sustain itself and begins to degrade into a savannah is about 20% to 25% loss of forest cover (Lovejoy and Nobre 2018). And the loss of forest cover is significant beyond the Amazon itself. The Amazon system plays a significant role in the world's climate. It produces about 20% of the world's oxygen supply and acts as a carbon sink, absorbing large amounts of carbon dioxide from the atmosphere. Nutrients delivered by the Amazon River to the Atlantic Ocean help to foster oceanic life that sequesters globally relevant amounts of carbon (Subramaniam 2008). In the terrestrial realm the Amazon rainforest is responsible for 10% of the carbon

---

[14] The *Time* online story about the loss of the Amazon rainforest, "The Amazon Rainforest Is Nearly Gone" (Sandy 2019), provides a number of images that depict the extent of the loss. An immersive experience narrated by Jane Goodall (2019), "Inside the Amazon: The Dying Forest," provides additional insights.

stores in ecosystems. But when trees are logged and the forest is burned, that carbon is released into the atmosphere at alarming rates.

While charcoal production is not the only cause of deforestation in Brazil, it is one of the arenas in which there is a complex intermeshing of racism and environmental degradation. It is therefore essential to develop methods that expose such intermeshings. Françoise Vergès (2017, 74) queries, "What methodology is needed to write a history of the environment that includes slavery, colonialism, imperialism and racial capitalism, from the standpoint of those who were made into 'cheap' objects of commerce, their bodies as objects renewable through wars, capture, and enslavement, fabricated as disposable people, whose lives do not matter?" In response, I advocate developing *genealogical sensibilities* as a key component of ecointersectional analyses. Genealogical sensibilities attune us to the legacies of oppression that infuse both the phenomenon of climate change and the actions and reactions to it. The goal of genealogical sensibilities is to become attuned to the often silent workings of power in its manifold deployments and to do so in order to identify legacies of oppressive practices, particularly the silenced or suppressed lineages that continue to animate oppression. Genealogical sensibilities dispose us to be alert to the often ignored or suppressed ways relations of power function in policies, social arrangements, accounts of justice, desires for purity, and demands for certainty. This alertness—this attunement—is designed not only to understand but also to animate the instabilities of such deployments of power by disrupting the fantasies of stability that sustain them and the illusions of unchanging truths and values that help to bolster those fantasies. Unsettling unquestioned assumptions and axioms by ecointersectional and genealogically informed methods of investigation is an essential path to effectively addressing the devastation of the Brazilian rainforest.

Unfree Labor and Environmental Degradation

Genealogical sensibilities help us understand how attitudes in Brazil toward Indigenous peoples and Afro-Brasileiros (*preto,* Black, and *pardo,* mixed-race) are informed by the legacies of Portuguese invasions and histories of enslavement of Indigenous people, as well as by the legacies of the transatlantic slave trade in Brazil. Understanding their enduring vestiges and their circulations in unfree labor is key to an ecointersectional analysis of current systems of racist oppression and its links to environmental degradation. A genealogical tracing of the lineages of unfree labor practices in modern Brazil would require a study of the afterlives of the transatlantic slave trade[15] and also of the complex histories of sugar and coffee plantations in Brazil, the so-called Amazon rubber boom, and the impact of the privatization of public land to corporations that opened the region to the international market and to essentially unrestrained development.[16] My focus in this section offers only one facet of such an analysis: the impact of livestock farming and the charcoal industry on deforestation in Brazil. While certainly incomplete, this study nonetheless reveals some of the ways systemic racisms and environmental degradation are infused in Brazil.

The Portuguese trafficked slaves to Brazil starting in the early years of the transatlantic slave trade. Brazil established slavery in the mid-fifteenth century, earning the ignoble distinction of becoming the first slave society in the Americas (Bergad and Schwartz 2007). The Portuguese developed a large-scale sugar industry in northeastern Brazil, eventually becoming the principal supplier of sugar to European markets. This effort, however, required laborers. When enslaving Indigenous peoples provided insufficient labor, the Portuguese instead enslaved peoples from Africa resulting in Brazil becoming the leading African slave trafficker in the Americas by the end of the sixteenth century. Approximately 40% of the people trafficked in the transatlantic slave trade came through Brazil (Issa 2017). As the demand for more slave labor intensified, the indifference toward African and Indigenous people and ecological indifference toward the land they were forced to transform infused. Brazil was slow to abolish slavery due in part to the centrality of slave labor for both sugar and coffee plantations as well as for diamond and gold mining. Indeed, while the Brazilian slave trade ended in the early 1850s, full emancipation was not granted until 1888, when Brazil became the last country in the Americas to abolish legal slavery (Klein and Luna 2010). However, slavery by other names continued to be practiced in Brazil. We can find its most recent manifestation in the rainforest.

Slavery within Brazil was grounded in deep-seated beliefs regarding racial superiority and inferiority. The legacy of systemic racism continues to

---

[15] Hartman (2008) introduced this phrase to signal the enduring impacts of slavery's racialized violence.

[16] One facet of this genealogy is offered by Joshua Eichen (2020) in his study of sugar plantations in Northeast Brazil in the sixteenth and seventeenth centuries. Histories of slavery in Brazil can be found in Bergad and Schwartz (2007) and Klein and Luna (2010).

circulate in contemporary Brazil and remains linked to environmental degradation. According to the research of Kevin Bales (2012, 106), the charcoal that fires the modern industries of Brazil "comes from denuded forests and the hands of slaves." The Global Slavery Index (2018) estimates that 369,000 people a day are being exploited by unfree labor practices in Brazil. The racial climate of Brazil's unfree labor involves both class and race. It is the press of poverty that leads men and women into contemporary slave labor or, as it is labeled in Brazil, *trabalho escravo contemporâneo*.[17] Poverty in Brazil is entwined with systemic racisms—one of the pervasive afterlives of the transatlantic slave trade. Most who are tricked or coerced into *trabalho escravo contemporâneo* are Afro-Brasileiros from the northern regions, where over 51% live in poverty, in part due to the disparity between educational opportunities for Afro-Brasileiros and Whites.[18] Many who are subject to slave labor in Brazil are Afro-Brasileiro men, and almost all leave their homes to seek out work to provide basic needs for themselves and their families.

Systemic racisms in Brazil are interwoven with environmental degradation. Research carried out by the NGO Repórter Brasil found that the region with the highest incidence of slave labor is the "deforestation arch" in northern Brazil, where trees are cut down to create charcoal-burning camps and to clear land for pasture and farming (Melo 2007).[19] The nonprofit Amazon Watch (2019) interviewed a Brazilian environmental protection employee who claimed the men working in illegal deforestation and mining in the forest are badly paid and exploited by rich bosses. "Deforestation," he explained, "is not exactly slave work but it is not far off."

Trabalho escravo contemporâneo in modern-day Brazil, like unfree labor in the United States and many other countries, does not involve the ownership dimension of chattel slavery. While it is no longer legal to own another person, fear and intimidation are used to force individuals to work long hours under inhumane living conditions for barely subsistence wages.[20]

---

[17] In 2003 labor laws were amended to define and prohibit slave labor. Yet according to a study of forced labor in Brazil, "the number of legal actions brought for slave labour crimes is very small when compared to the number of victims freed in the country" (Maranhão Costa 2009, 26).

[18] The Borgen Project (2018). In 2014 the weekly earnings of Black and mixed-race Brazilians averaged only 58% that of White Brazilians (*The Economist* 2016).

[19] *Trabalho escravo contemporâneo* is not limited to charcoal and land clearing in Brazil. It can also be found in sugar and coffee industries and has recently been found in the textile and construction industries (Osava 2020).

[20] According to the NGO Repórter Brasil, in 2007 inspections of charcoal camps found that "working conditions and the supply of food were precarious, and the average working day was ten hours, including Sundays and bank holidays" (quoted in Maranhão Costa 2009, 46).

Recruiters lure the poor of Brazil, particularly those from the impoverished northeastern region, with the promise of good wages for hard work, but the workers find themselves conscripted hundreds of miles from their homes in logging camps, and are then informed that they will be responsible for the costs of their transportation, food, and housing, all furnished by the "employer" at highly inflated rates.[21] As described by Bales (2012, 137, italics in original), "They are trapped, believing that trust *might* pay off and knowing that running away is of no avail. A charcoal worker explained the situation to me: *The charcoal always goes to the smelter but the money never comes back. So we have to wait and see. Maybe we decide to wait for two more months. From time to time we ask the gato [the recruiter]; he always says that he is not paying us because we all owe him so much money, but in fact no one owes him anything.*"

These workers are not property, but they are viewed as *disposable*. They are readily replaceable, so there is little interest in providing safe working conditions or adequate food, housing, or healthcare. Those engaged in deforestation or charcoal production are expected to work ten-hour days with few, if any, days off. Violence, including brutal murders, are used to control workers and curb resistance. The landowners accept the profits and deny accountability. Government inspectors have little impact; the police seldom enforce the law as they are often bribed by the businesses who profit from the exploitation. "Although they own the land and keep most of the profits from making charcoal, these companies insulate themselves from any charge of slavery by arranging the work in a series of subcontracts. . . . [I]f central government inspectors or human rights activists find and publicize the use of slaves, the company can express horror, dump (temporarily) the guilty gatos, tighten up security to prevent further inspections, and go on as before" (Bales 2012, 143).[22]

---

[21] In recognition of the problem of unfree labor practices, Brazilian law (Article 149 of Law 10.803) renders illegal "reducing someone to a condition analogous to that of a slave, either by subjecting him/her to forced labor or exhausting workdays, by subjecting him/her to degrading work conditions, or by restricting, by any means, his/her mobility because of a debt contracted with an employer or his/her agent" (translated in Issa 2017, 101).

[22] In his recent study *Blood and Earth*, Bales (2016, 242) makes a clear link between modern slavery and environmental degradation. He concludes by listing a series of facts his work has revealed: "*We know* that the hidden crimes of slavery and environmental destruction are not just inextricably linked but mutually reinforcing and reach around the planet. *We know* that slaves are used to destroy the environment, and that when an ecosystem is devastated the people who live within it are pushed closer to slavery." While his is an important study of modern slave labor, the solutions he poses fall short in that they are not informed by the many complex lineages to which I gesture in this section.

Ecological indifference and systemic racisms are infused in the rainforests of Brazil. The International Labour Organization's (ILO) study of forced labor in Brazil found that "the crime of reducing workers to a condition analogous to that of a slave is often accompanied by environmental offences (a large number of the workers are contracted to clear native forests)" (Maranhão Costa 2009, 18). According to the ILO report, the links between environmental exploitation and slave labor intensified in the 1970s and 1980s with the movement of cattle farmers into the region. Currently 62% of the slave labor in Brazil occurs in activities related to livestock farming: "[I]n the bovine meat production sector (for which Brazil is the world export leader), farmers use slave labour to clear land and plant pasture, to build fences, and to increase the area of usable farmland by clearing native forest" (45).

While deforestation in the Brazilian Amazon significantly declined in the mid-2000s[23] due to government interventions, efforts by civil society, and macroeconomic factors such as international soy and beef importation moratoria, our genealogy would include the election of Jair Bolsonaro. In 2019, the year Bolsonaro became president, Brazil had a 34.4% *increase* in deforestation. According to the Instituto Nacional de Pesquisas Espaciais (INPE; National Institute for Space Research), over 10,000 square kilometers of the Amazon were cleared in 2019 (cited in Butler 2020). This increase has continued to accelerate. The Brazilian Amazon Deforestation Monitoring Program found that deforestation rates in 2020 increased by 9.5% over rates in 2019, at the time the highest rate of deforestation in the decade (Silva Junior et al. 2021). The German branch of the World Wildlife Fund published a study in 2020 arguing that the higher rates of deforestation were due to the coronavirus pandemic, which has restricted state and watchdog control as well as causing increases in poverty, resulting in more people using the forest as a resource for income (Winter 2020). An INPE study published in November 2021 reported that deforestation in Brazil's portion of the Amazon reached a fifteen-year high, with an estimated 13,235 square kilometers of forest lost between August 2020 and July 2021, an increase of 22% from the previous year (cited in Taylor 2021). There is every reason to believe that such increases will continue given Bolsonaro's policies.

Since his election in 2019 Bolsonaro has advocated the expansion of mining and industrial farming into protected areas of the Amazon. He has

---

[23] Deforestation rates in the Amazonia in 2012 were 84% lower than the 2004 peak; 27,772 km^2 of forests were clear cut in 2004 compared to 4,571 km^2 in 2012 (Silva Junior et al. 2021).

reduced the budget of the country's environmental protection agency by 24% and canceled a range of environmental fines. Those shifts have in part contributed to over 100,000 fires in the Brazilian Amazon in 2020 and over 80,000 fires in 2019 documented by the INPE. These fires were primarily set by illegal miners and loggers, as well as by farmers as part of slash-and-burn agriculture designed to clear the land for crops and livestock and create a nutrient-rich layer of ash to fertilize crops and grasslands. The impact on the rainforest is compounded by the impact on those in Brazil with COVID-19 from the increased air pollution caused by the fires that can exacerbate COVID impacts.

Bolsonaro's ecological indifference is laced through with racism. In his campaign for the presidency, he promised to end the demarcation of Indigenous land. After being elected he insisted that pro-environment and pro-Indigenous policies were blocking the northern state of Roraima from becoming the richest in the nation. Bolsonaro, who has compared Indigenous communities living in protected lands to animals in zoos, has been trying to amend the Constitution to open Indigenous lands to farming and logging as well as resource extraction, efforts Indigenous activists have been working to block. Bolsonaro says his aim is to "integrate" Indigenous communities. What he means by "integration" can be gleaned from his statement that it was "a shame that the 'Brazilian chivalry' hadn't been as efficient as the North American ones that have effectively exterminated the 'Indians'" (quoted in Salamanca 2019).

Bolsonaro's racist statements are playing out in his efforts to pass laws such as Bill 490/2007 which would reduce the amount of ancestral land of Indigenous groups subject to government protection.[24] His position echoes decades of treating Brazil's Indigenous people as "obstacles to progress."[25] These policy revisions combined with years of illegal logging on Indigenous land and clear-cutting by cattle ranchers are having devastating impacts on Indigenous communities. Once again, we see the complex infusions of ecological indifference and racial climates. An interview in 2012 with Pire'i Ma'a, a member of the Awá people, offers a glimpse of the extent of the interlocking harms: "They are chopping down wood and they are going to destroy

---

[24] Bill 490/2007 was approved under the Constitution and Justice Committee in June 2021 and as of April 2022 it was pending before the House of Deputies.

[25] The 1967 Figueiredo Report, submitted by public prosecutor Jader de Figueiredo Correia, documented wide-scale abuse and human rights violations of Indigenous peoples by the Indian Protection Service.

everything. Monkeys, peccaries, tapir, they are all running away. I don't know how we are going to eat—everything is being destroyed, the whole area. This land is mine, it is ours. They can go away to the city, but we Indians live in the forest. They are going to kill everything. Everything is dying. We are all going to go hungry" (quoted in Chamberlain 2012).

Despite the brevity of my genealogical account, what I hope shines through is the importance of seeing the linkages between the disposability, fungibility, and consumability of natural resources and the disposability, fungibility, and consumability of certain groups of people. All five dimensions of racial climates are woven together: Bolsonaro's policies to weaken environmental protections and the concurrent impacts on deforestation and climate change, *dimension 1*; the legacies of slavery of Indigenous and African peoples, *dimension 2*; Bolsonaro's policies on Indigenous land and the lack of educational resources in the northern arch, which contribute to the extreme poverty of the Afro-Brasileiros who live in that region, *dimension 3*; attitudes of governmental officials, cattle ranchers, and mine owners concerning which lives and lifeways are valuable, *dimension 4*; differential impacts of environmental degradation, *dimension 5*.

The complexities of racial climates are best understood through a multi-dimensional lens, one that will foreground the ways *dimension 5*, differential impacts, emerges from and often reanimates multiple legacies of oppression. To appreciate the complexities of racial climates we need to understand these dimensions, understand their multifarious lineages of values and their attendant habits of thought and action, and see the ways ecological indifference and indifference toward the lives and lifeways of some people are woven together in practices that result in environmental degradation.

Kairos: The Time of the Break

I opened this chapter with a reflection on the *anthropos* of the Anthropocene to frame this study with the reminder that this anthropos does not in fact encompass all humans. If we do not understand the myriad ways that the anthropos of the Anthropocene is *not* the universal category often reinscribed in its repetition, we reinforce the very divisions—human/less than fully human/nonhuman—that are woven tightly into environmental exploitation and entwined inexorably with exploitation of certain groups of people.

I end with a reflection on the *cene* of the Anthropocene. *Cene,* from the Greek *kainos* is a word-forming element used in geology to mean "new," as in "a new epoch." Like the implicit but dangerously inaccurate universality of anthropos, genealogical sensibilities reveal that this epoch, this *cene,* is far from new.[26] The circulations of the past continue not only in the atmosphere but in our institutions, dispositions, and desires. Perhaps, following McKenzie Wark (2016, 222), we might desire a *kainos* that "ought to be, not what it is." Wark asks whether, given such a desire, this *cene* might instead invoke *kairos* in its sense of an opportune time for action or, as Wark sees it, the critical moment, the time of the break, a nonhuman time. Remembering as well that *kairos* also means "weather" in modern Greek, we might take this alternate meaning of *cene* as a reminder that while systemic racisms are a central lens of this study, to fully appreciate the deep formations that led to our current climate crises and to formulate responses that are not simply a re-elaboration of the condition, we must recognize the circulations of the *inhuman*—not only those that have been used to enslave or control groups of humans through the trope of fungibility but also those that drove a sharp divide between humans and the world we are of and in. Such genealogies expose the entwining of disposable people and disposable environments. Perhaps they provide a path to a time of the break from such divides. A propitious time for action for the sake of the more-than-human.

One last caution. To understand the nature of the entwining of disposable environments and disposable people we cannot desire simple answers. What I quoted earlier is worth repeating: "[A]ll intersectional moves are necessarily particularized and therefore provisional and incomplete." Each such analysis "must necessarily limit itself to specific structures of power" (Carbado et al. 2013, 304). Our ecointersectional analyses must be detailed historically and geographically situated genealogies of the incorporations of systemic racisms and environmental exploitation. They must be nimble, able to track fluctuations in the often quickly shifting power formations. In other words, as we reflect on and respond to racial climates, no simple answer will suffice.

---

[26] Kyle Whyte (2016, 89) reminds us, "For many Indigenous peoples today, the concept of societies having to adapt constantly to environmental change is not new." He goes on to explain that "settler colonialism seeks to erase Indigenous peoples' adaptive capacity and self-determination by repeatedly containing them in different ways, destroying the ecological conditions that are tightly coupled with Indigenous cultural and political systems" (92).

3
Climate Apartheid
The Forgetting of Race

Not Without Us

"Not without us" is a slogan of several gender and climate change movements. It was, for example, adopted by gendercc-Women for Climate Justice to emphasize their motto "No climate justice without gender justice." Thanks to the work of various activist organizations and feminist scholars, the past two decades have been witness to a growing recognition of the gender dimensions of climate change. Scholars and activists have called attention to such issues as the paucity of women in the climate policy domain, the effect of gender roles on climate change impacts, as well as the importance of considering gender in the context of adaptation policies (e.g., Alaimo 2012; Alston and Whittenbury 2013; Dankelman 2010; Nagel 2016). More recently scholars have begun to examine gender-specific causes of climate change, the role of gender in mitigation strategies, and even the gendered dimensions of the discourses of climate change (e.g., Arora-Jonsson, 2011; Djoudi et al 2016; Ravera, Martín-López et al. 2016).

While not denying the importance of this work, it often proceeds as though through a narrow lens in which gender is the central dynamic. To be sure, authors often bring in issues of culture to direct attention to the specific gender roles that can result in differential impacts or examine the effects of poverty on women in the context of climate impacts. However, there is seldom a richly intersectional perspective.[1] In particular, there is rarely attention to the role of race or racism in discussions of climate justice.[2] We are

---

[1] Despite a number of calls for more research on climate change from an intersectional perspective (Kaijser and Kronsell 2014; Djoudi et al 2016) and a recent book devoted to intersectional approaches (Godfrey and Torres 2016b), there are, as I discussed in Chapter 1, still relatively few instances of such approaches and even fewer that bring the lens of race to the foreground of the analysis.

[2] The writings of those working in the field David Naguib Pellow has labeled "critical environmental justice" have argued for the importance of examining the ways racism and environmental justice issues are linked beyond issues of differential harms. Many in this field do so by developing an intersectional lens. This work, according to Pellow (2016, 223), "extend[s] beyond [the] question of

here witnessing analogous silences, absences, and forgettings that scholars such as Kimberlé Crenshaw and Patricia Hill Collins called to our attention in their accounts of the illegibility of Black women. Crenshaw (1991, 1282), for example, working in the domain of legal studies, focused on the ideological role of law in constructing particular types of legible and illegible juridical subjects and identities:[3] "With respect to the rape of Black women, race and gender converge so that the concerns of minority women fall into the void between concerns about women's issues and concerns about racism. But when one discourse fails to acknowledge the significance of the other, the power relations that each attempts to challenge are strengthened." My position is that similar types of illegible lives are being constructed in the domain of climate practices and policies, and these illegibilities have not been made decipherable in climate justice literature.

To situate my analysis, I rely on the approach to intersectionality offered by Anna Carastathis (2016 3-4), who urges us to see intersectionality as "an analytic sensibility, a disposition, or a way of thinking . . . into which most of us have not yet become habituated" and to see it as "a profound challenge, as opposed to a determinate resolution, of cognitive essentialism, binary categorization, and conceptual exclusion." While my attention turns here on the forgetting of race, I underscore my firm conviction that we can unmute the circulations of systemic racisms in the context of climate change only through a disposition that is inclined to question and trouble all one-dimensional understandings of the silences and mutings of our current understandings of climate injustice. While informed by a careful and determined attention to silences and illegibilities formed by oppressive beliefs, practices, and institutions, an ecointersectional approach is designed to add to the prism of intersectionality by attending to the ways the harms to environments are impacted by and implicated in systemic oppressions. Carastathis's admonition to develop a disposition, a habit of attention to silences and illegibilities, is an important resource for ecointersectional analyses. We need to develop attunements to how the lineages of oppressions between differences such as

---

distribution to incorporate a deeper consideration of theory and the ways that gender, sexuality and other categories of difference shape EJ struggles." See also Pellow (2018), Pellow and Brulle (2005), and Pulido (2015, 2016, 2017a, 2017b). The topic of climate justice has yet to become a dominant theme of this literature. As I noted in Chapter 1, the theme of racial climates is still muted in the climate justice literature.

[3] While the literature on intersectionality is huge, I find Devon Carbado's (2013) radicalizations of intersectionality a rich resource for avoiding misreadings of intersectionality.

sex, class, sexuality, and race can be intermeshed, but we must also develop dispositions that animate attention to the infusing of such lineages with environmental exploitation. The profound challenges of climate change are coupled with an urgent need for cultivating sensibilities that attend to the complexities of the sites of injustices,[4] sensibilities that recognize the inextricable entanglements of humans and environments.

Inspired by ecointersectionality, my goal in this chapter is to further illuminate the forgetting of race in the context of climate justice. My examples aim to begin to untangle the weave of racism as it circulates in the causes of and responses to anthropogenic climate change. The mainstream approach in literature on gender and climate change, or even what literature there is on race and climate change, has been to focus on the *differential impacts* of climate change on certain groups of people. As I previously argued, such an approach will be insufficient to understanding the complex circulations of racism in the context of climate change. We need in addition to understand how racism is deeply incorporated into various institutions and social practices relevant to the current climate regime. Ecointersectional analyses must, thus, arise in genealogical sensibilities that attune us to the lineages of oppressive practices, past and present, that infuse action and inaction in the context of climate change. A genealogical sensibility not only discloses the workings of power, it loosens the soil of fixed beliefs and practices and reminds us to attend to its stirrings. As Foucault (1966, xxiv) says in *The Order of Things*, "I am restoring to our silent and apparently immobile soil its rifts, its instability, its flaws; and it is the same ground that is once more stirring under our feet." And through such animations, such movements, we may become open to subversions that can materialize in the insecuring ground. Genealogical sensibilities thus do not involve abstract study of historical movements. They involve attunements to formations of power, both past and present, attunements that are dedicated to insubordination and refusal. Bringing genealogical sensibilities to our ecointersectional analyses

---

[4] Sensibilities encompass not just ways of knowing but also affective responses, habitual dispositions, bodily comportments, and forms of desire that are constitutive of social and cultural meanings and values. While they certainly influence individual comportments, they do so through systems of meaning and values that we internalize in being part of a culture, which often include many communities with common and deep dispositions that compose networks of circulating, interfused oppressions. Sensibilities in this sense are what allow people to make sense of and be especially alert to some values, practices, and things while ignoring, rejecting or finding senseless other values, practices, and things.

animates the desire for new values, for new ways of feeling, thinking, and living.

This chapter, indeed this book, is designed to be provocative. My desire is to catalyze a different approach to climate justice and to call for a far deeper understanding of the phrase "environmental racisms" than is currently embraced.[5] To do so I analyze three instances of the infusions of racism and environmental exploitation: climate adaptation practices in Lagos, Nigeria; the enmeshment of race and coal mining in the post–Civil War United States, and the infusing of poverty and urban ecosystems in Brazil.

My investigations are precipitated by a series of questions: What do we see when we work within the institutions, discourses, and practices devoted to climate justice? What remains inaudible, silenced by a failure of attunement, by forms of muting at times so profound that forms of habituated amnesia emerge that, while not always unintended, have profound impacts on those already affected by complex systems of injustice and oppression? When we engage in the work of climate justice, to whom are we speaking, and for what purposes? Who remains silent or silenced? What lives have been rendered illegible? What is it we wish to affect, and what are we affected by? How will our efforts, our actions, and our new conceptualizations be used or used against us? How do our liberatory theories travel or fail to do so? How can we learn to experience what is silenced by them? These are the types of questions that have the potential to transform our understanding of what is required for a climate justice that is truly and thoroughly "not without us."

---

[5] The concept of environmental racism was introduced by the Reverend Benjamin Chavis in the 1987 United Church of Christ Commission for Racial Justice report "Toxic Wastes and Race in the United States." The study documented the disproportionate targeting of Black and Latino communities in the United States for the siting of hazardous waste facilities. The original definition of environmental justice has been expanded to encompass a wide variety of environmental harms that disproportionately impact individuals and groups, both in the United States and internationally, on the basis of race or color, and the history in the United States of excluding Blacks and Latinos from policymaking processes relevant to environmental issues. Romy Opperman's (2019) essay "A Permanent Struggle against an Omnipresent Death: Revisiting Environmental Racism with Frantz Fanon" provides a helpful discussion of the recent move from a focus on environmental racism to a broadened focus on critical environmental justice. This shift and Opperman's conception of racist environments are designed to offer a more radical approach to environmental racism. My aim in this book is to further this more radical approach by demonstrating the inextricable links between systemic racisms and environmental exploitation.

Climate Change Apartheid

"We do not need climate change apartheid in adaptation."[6]

Climate change apartheid. A concept born of his experience of South Africa's violently enforced racial segregation and coined by Archbishop Desmond Tutu in the *Human Development Report 2007–2008*. This concept is a vivid reminder of the imperative to attend to the practices, habits, legal institutions, discourses, and impacts of anthropogenic climate change from an ecointersectional lens. Tutu's (2007, 166) admonition that climate "adaptation is becoming a euphemism for social injustice on a global scale" serves as a guidepost for the genealogical sensibilities essential to ecointersectional analyses. Tutu has issued a call for attunements to inequalities at times of environmental and social transformation. Inequalities that, in this case, are being caused by anthropogenic climate change.

It is important to recognize that, like apartheid, we do not appreciate the complex nature of climate change apartheid if we understand it simply as differential impacts or differential treatment. Apartheid in South Africa involved deeply held systemic beliefs and dispositions regarding racial superiority that not only impacted individual beliefs and practices but were infused into and supported by the interactions of various social institutions, such as education, labor, and policing, and the practices and dispositions they authorized.[7] This infusion of beliefs and dispositions with institutions and legal policies played a major role in maintaining the systemic subordination of those who were, by these very dispositions and policies, deemed inferior. Such institutional practices became normalized. They became commonplace; they were, and arguably still are, taken for granted, habituated in the ways of the privileged. To appreciate the nature and import of climate change apartheid, then, requires attention to the more subtle, normalized, and often muted ways in which systemic, institutional racism circulates in societies, as well as attention to the ways in which it is impacted by other forms of systemic oppression, such as those due to gender, sexuality, or class.[8] And in

---

[6] This is the title of Tutu's (2007) report.

[7] For a rich discussion of the beliefs and institutions that grounded apartheid in South Africa, see Saul Dubow (1989, 2014).

[8] Charles Mills's (1997) *Racial Contract* provides an extraordinarily fertile resource for understanding these mutings. See in particular his analysis of the active production and preservation of ignorance, what he calls "an epistemology of ignorance," which is designed to occlude the effects of prejudice, privilege, and oppression. An exciting literature has blossomed thanks to his insights (see, e.g., Medina 2012; Sullivan and Tuana 2007; Kidd, Medina, and Pohlhaus 2017).

addition to these circulations, an ecointersectional analysis brings to bear the infusions of ecological indifference.

The climate apartheid which Tutu called to our attention emerges not out of differential impacts of anthropogenic climate change due to a group's geographical location. Rather, climate apartheid emerges from complex exchanges between systemic racisms and environmental exploitation. The sensibility I urge us to develop is one that is attuned to the injustices infused throughout the differential impacts of anthropogenic climate change as well as to those injustices that permeate climate action and inaction. Only in this way can we become attuned to the mutings and forgettings of racism in the context of climate change and work to achieve genuine climate justice.

Tutu (2007) turns our attention to climate mechanisms, such as mitigation and adaptation, and to the impacts of choices of climate mechanisms whether or not those choices are intended. The focus of Tutu's concern is threefold: (1) the emphasis on adaptation over mitigation, (2) the meaning of the term "adaptation," and (3) adaptation practices. Climate justice ultimately depends on responsible mitigation strategies that will address the causes of anthropogenic climate change by reducing levels of greenhouse gases and, in this way, reduce the rate and severity of climate-related impacts. However, until responsible mitigation policies are put in place and we have adapted to the climate impacts unavoided to that point, adaptation to unavoidable and unavoided climate impacts is our only recourse for the near to long-term future.[9] But here, Tutu maintains, we come up against the inadequacy of language and practice. What, he asks, does adaptation mean? He argues that in practice it has resulted in a form of adaptation apartheid in which "the citizens of the rich world are protected from harm, [and] the poor, the vulnerable and the hungry are exposed to the harsh reality of climate change in their everyday lives" (166). Embedded in his conception of climate apartheid is a series of questions: To what are we willing to adapt? What do we see as being in need of adaptation, and what remains unseen or, if seen, not valued? Who and what gets protected? Who and what is rendered

---

[9] Some loss and damage from anthropogenic climate change is unavoidable, despite current mitigation and adaptation measures. For example, sea level rise will result in some land loss no matter how aggressive our adaptation measures. Avoidable impacts are both foreseeable, that is, predictable, and of a scale subject to feasible mitigation or adaptation measures. The category of unavoided impacts, though shifting, identifies those impacts that could have been but were not avoided due to insufficient mitigation policies or insufficient commitment to and/or funding for effective adaptation measures. The latter category of impacts is growing exponentially as nations and regions fail to effectively address the root causes of anthropogenic climate change. For further discussion, see Van der Geest and Warner (2015).

more precarious? Do we see or even care about these types of, perhaps unintended, harms of adaptation practices?

Let us begin with the insights of Bishop Tutu and, attuned to his sense of injustice, travel to the city of Lagos on the Nigerian coast. As with many coastal cities, sea level rise is threatening Nigeria's largest city. With a population of well over 14 million, Lagos is one of the busiest ports on the African continent and has become a major financial center. As in many coastal cities, sea level rise and warming oceans are placing Lagos at risk of serious impacts from storm surges and flooding that result not only in loss of lives and infrastructure but also intrusion of sea water into freshwater sources and ecosystems (Fashae and Onafeso 2011). Scientific projections show that sea levels could rise by one meter over the next fifty years or so. Such a rise would have devastating effects on Lagos. As Stefan Cramer, Nigeria's director of Germany's Heinrich Boll Foundation and an adviser to the Nigerian government on climate change, explained, "In 50 years with a one-meter sea level rise, two million, three million people would be homeless. . . . By the end of the century we would have two meters and by that stage Lagos is gone as we know it" (quoted in Tattersall 2008).

As have New Orleans, Venice, Rotterdam, and many other cities, Lagos is responding to rising seas and intensification of storms by building a sea defense barrier, in this case one that will span 8.5 kilometers upon completion. The barrier is being built to protect Victoria Island, one of the most affluent neighborhoods in Lagos.[10] The difference is that atop this barrier, called "the Great Wall of Lagos," the city of Eko Atlantic is being erected.[11] Eko Atlantic is championed as a sustainable city designed to become the financial and commercial center that will "pav[e] the way for Nigeria to become a top 20 global economic power within the next decade" (South Energyx Nigeria Limited n.d., 1). The goal is to provide homes to a quarter-million residents.

---

[10] Land erosion rates for Lagos Bar Beach have been very significant (30 meters per year). While the erosion has many causes, there is general agreement that the primary cause was the dredging of the Lagos harbor and construction of large stone breakwaters by the British between 1908 and 1912 to ease the movement of ships into the harbor (Okude and Ademiluyi 2006).

[11] The area now known as Lagos, colonized by the Portuguese and British, is known to its Indigenous inhabitants as Èkó, which, according to Kristin Mann (2007), author of *Slavery and the Birth of an African City: Lagos, 1760–1900*, most likely derives from the Edo word for "war camp." There are multiple ironies in choosing the name Eko Atlantic for a city that will be closed to the vast majority of Nigeria's Indigenous peoples: a city that is being built as a walled fortress; a city that provides its own services, from water and electricity to security, and maintains its separation from the poor by the not so invisible wall of housing prices that will keep out all but the most affluent.

Who will live in Eko Atlantic's gleaming towers? It certainly will not be the over 60% of Nigeria's population, almost 100 million people, who live in extreme poverty. The World Bank's 2017 Atlas of Sustainable Development documents that 5 million more Nigerians were living in extreme poverty in 2013 than in 1990. The high poverty rate is clearly visible in Lagos, where 70% of the city's residents live in slum settlements subject to extreme flooding that regularly sweeps raw sewage and refuse into living spaces (Ajibade and McBean 2014). Approximately sixteen thousand millionaires live in Nigeria, almost ten thousand of whom also live in Lagos. This economic discrepancy exists alongside Nigeria's oil wealth, with annual revenues of over US$41 million from petroleum exports alone.[12] Eko Atlantic's shiny towers of luxury apartments are targeted to the wealthy, a majority of whom will likely be wealthy foreign business representatives, along with a minority of the wealthiest Nigerians. Two- to three-bedroom flats in Eko Atlantic are selling for US$710,000 to US$3 million. Even the income of Nigeria's middle class, estimated as constituting only 11% of the nation's population, will not open the shiny doors of Eko Atlantic. According to a recent Pew Research Center (2015) study, the monthly income of Nigeria's middle class averages between US$1,000 and US$2,000, which translates to an annual average income of US$14,600 to US$29,200 for a family of four.[13]

This is a vision of Tutu's climate apartheid writ large. Given these income demographics, the majority of the residents of Eko Atlantic are not likely to be Nigerians. And those who are Nigerians will be the wealthy, living in the equivalent of a walled and fortified community, with its own energy and water resources. And they will live upstream, so to speak, of the poor of Lagos, who have limited access to electricity and clean water. Echoing Tutu, we must interrogate for what and to whom is this adaptation? Here the axis of climate apartheid is distributed by class, but it is also seldom separate from race.

Race and class circulate in complex ways in Lagos. Tracing these lineages to their contemporary resonances is part of understanding the impact of systemic racisms in the context of climate change. Doing so requires genealogical sensibilities attuned to lineages that are entangled and often altered by

---

[12] Organization of the Petroleum Exporting Countries 2022.
[13] In response to criticism concerning the high cost of properties, the marketing group shifted the narrative on the Eko Atlantic webpage. Rather than the earlier discourse about its various luxuries, the opening statement on the webpage (accessed 2022) is "One common misconception about Eko Atlantic is that all properties are priced above the market. While the city will naturally feature a range of high end luxury apartments, it also houses many opportunities for more competitively-priced accommodation."

their entwinements. The complexities of a history of slaveholding in the territory that has come to be known as Lagos is one such lineage. The lineage of enslaving individuals and groups within Nigeria was transmuted by the rise of the external slave trade in the eighteenth century, which was fueled by the rise of sugar plantations in the Caribbean, gold mining in Brazil, and tobacco, rice, and cotton plantations in the Americas (Klein 1999; Mann 2007). The growth of the external slave trade and Lagos's role as a central shipping port for the trade led to the accumulation of wealth for certain groups, including ruling groups who leveed mandatory taxes or required substantial gifts from those, typically foreigners, involved in the slave trade (Mann 2007). Complex circulations of warfare and the disruption of the Oyo Empire, often compounded by the slave trade, contributed both to political instability in Lagos and to shifting attitudes toward various ethnic groups. British annexation of the territory that included Lagos and colonial rule of all of what subsequently became Nigeria rethreaded lineages as British economic interests, in this instance the growing demand for palm oil, intersected with their mid-nineteenth-century campaign to end slave trading. The latter lineage tightly knit a growing abolitionist sentiment with the economic concern that the slave trade would undermine the stability needed for commerce in other types of goods (Mann 2007).

The treaties signed with the British that served to suppress the external slave trade, however, made no mention of the internal slave trade. The internal slave trade, yet another thread in this complex weave of lineages that contribute to racism in Lagos, continued without impediment. Its continuation was supported by missionaries promoting the view of West African slavery as a benevolent practice as well as claiming that the palm oil trade, which was dependent upon such slave labor, would, in the short run, improve the working conditions of slaves and, in the long run, lead to the end of the internal slave trade. Another thread in this racist lineage is the set of laws that were set up by the British to prohibit Indigenous people from importing or exporting goods. With the growing importance of trade, these bans negatively impacted the economic and political position of members of the historical Nigerian oligarchy. As a result, Saro merchants, the freed Kiro slaves who migrated to Nigeria from Sierra Leone in the early nineteenth century and who were allowed to trade, gained significant power over the Indigenous peoples. Palm oil production also reinforced gender roles in Yorubaland, for men's labors were limited to harvesting and transporting, while women were responsible for producing the oil. The labor intensity of palm oil production led to the increased use of slave labor, particularly an increase in numbers of female slaves.[14]

Even after the British abandoned their practice of internal slavery, they did not abandon their vision of apartheid. Water and sanitation facilities were provided by the British administration primarily to the wealthy British enclaves (Gandy 2006). Investments in urban infrastructure similarly followed the path of these wealthy enclaves, including Victoria Island, the area being "protected" by Eko Atlantic. When communicable diseases such as influenza and bubonic plague ravaged the Indigenous enclaves between 1923 and 1939, the British responded with forced evictions from the slums and relocation of families to the mainland, a practice that continues to this day (Olukoju 1993). Apartheid by another name was enforced as "the 'hygienist' discourse which developed in tandem with new scientific approaches to public health policy in the cities of Europe and North America ... refashioned in a colonial context to produce a cultural dualism between 'modernity' and 'tradition' so that investment in urban infrastructure was disproportionately concentrated in wealthy enclaves" (Gandy 2006, 375).

With these lineages in mind and putting the lens of an ecointersectional analysis to work, let us return to contemporary Lagos. The region now known as Lagos was originally settled by members of the Ogu people. Ogu communities like Makoko and Iwaya in Lagos State now include many poor who have emigrated from and continue to emigrate from riverine communities from the coast as well as from the poorer northern areas. These communities will not benefit from the Great Wall of Lagos, but many have been and will continue to be harmed by it. Consider, for example, the fact that, as with many forms of climate change apartheid, the protection created by Eko Atlantic is built on the devastation of others, and not only human others but that of many life forms, communities, and ecosystems. Eko Atlantic rises thanks in part to the 90 million cubic hectares of sand taken from the marine shelf (Amadi 2012, 8). And as it rises, Eko Atlantic takes with it wetlands and the fish and shellfish life they sustain as well as displacing human populations. In 2012, Makoko, a predominantly Ogu community of fisher people, was dismantled by a seventy-two-hour quit notice that was handed to residents by the State Ministry of Waterfront Infrastructure Development, followed by an influx of demolition workers who set fire to homes and businesses in

---

[14] For additional details, see Mann (2007), Chapters 4 and 5: "Innocent Commerce: Boom and Bust in the Palm Produce Trade" and "Britain and Domestic Slavery."

Makoko. The notices posted by the government regarding the eviction read, "The Lagos state government is desirous of restoring the amenity and value of the waterfront ... [and] improve the waterfront/coastline to underline the megacity status of the state."[15] Many other previously "undesirable" water-based locations, such as Otodo Gbame, Ilubirin, and Ebute Ikate, are now seen as prime "waterfront" real estate opportunities and have suffered similar fates. For example, in the Otodo Gbame community in Lekki, a fishing settlement on the edge of Lagos lagoon, over thirty thousand residents were forcibly evicted by Lagos State authorities on November 9 and 10, 2016, when their homes were set ablaze and demolished by bulldozers (Amnesty International 2016). Ilubirin, another waterfront area, suffered a similar fate in 2014, when the government promised to use the land to build affordable housing for Lagos residents. That promise dissolved when the state government partnered with a private developer to construct luxury waterfront condos, condos that, no doubt, are in need of protection from storm surges. What we see in Lagos is what we saw with apartheid in South Africa: a city in which those who are already privileged enhance their privilege at the expense of those whose lack of equality is made even more severe and do so along divisions put into place by decades of racist beliefs and institutions. In this instance, this is also accomplished by directing and often exploiting climate adaptation practices. The justifying logic is complex, and in its whorl of complexity we need to take the time to trace the lineages of systemic racisms in the contours of the choices made over many years and reveal how sedimented, systemic beliefs and dispositions regarding racial superiority are at the heart of decisions about whose lives and lifeways are worth protecting and whose are expendable. Climate apartheid.

And don't forget, sea walls do not stop a storm surge; they divert it. That means the communities on either side of the sea wall upon which Eko Atlantic is erected are more likely to experience greater negative impacts from storms.[16] And the communities so disrupted will not only be human communities. Seawalls impact habitat and species distribution of many species of flora and fauna both on land and in the water, all for the sake of offering protection to those who can afford it. Once again, we see the ways in which climate adaptation fuels climate apartheid. While we might see Eko Atlantic

---

[15] Quoted in *Al Jazeera* (2012).
[16] Idowu Ajibade (2017) argues that Eko Atlantic will increase storm surges and erosion risks for communities that are to the east of the barrier wall, such as Goshen Estate and Okun-Alfa.

as an illustration of the first domain of the infusions of systemic racisms and environmental degradation I identified in Chapter 1, namely, differential distribution of harms/benefits due to systemic racisms, we find woven into this example all three of the domains, for the lives and lifeways protected are at the expense of those whose lives and habitats are less valued.[17] Remember, adaptation is designed to protect what and who is valued. The systemic racisms that permeate the design of this adaptation, that inform what is valued, are infused with ecological indifference.

While it is certainly essential to unveil the many ways climate apartheid is supported by climate adaptation, understanding the circulations of systemic racisms in the context of climate change will require digging deeper, to the root causes of anthropogenic climate change, and becoming aware of the many ways in which systemic racisms are infused in the very practices that led to and continue to contribute to the acceleration of greenhouse gases. Before turning away from Nigeria to consider the next case study, let us pause to consider the words of Dr. Owens Wiwa, whose brother, Ken Saro-Wiwa, led the Movement for the Survival of the Ogoni People (MOSOP),[18] which aimed to establish Indigenous self-determination in part by fighting against oil companies like Shell that were drilling for oil on Indigenous lands. "As an Ogoni person, I do wish that Shell never ever came to our land. They have destroyed our society, but we in MOSOP intend to see that we restore some dignity to ourselves and conserve what is left of our environment and natural resources. We intend to tell the world the real costs of the oil they are buying. People have lost loved ones for this oil. Widows have been created because of the search for oil. Orphans abound in Ogoni because people need oil in their cars in America. *Shell oil contains our blood.* It should be avoided by every person of conscience. In that way we may persuade Shell to behave responsibly. In that way we may persuade Shell to stop the practice of environmental racism, because what they do in Ogoni they don't do in Europe or in America" (Quoted in Connors 1997, 50, my emphasis).

---

[17] As a reminder, the three dimensions identified in Chapter 1 are (1) differential distribution of harms/benefits due to systemic racisms, (2) racist institutions and practices fueling or causing environmental degradation, and (3) the basic social structures that generate environmental degradation being the same ones that generate systemic oppression of certain groups of people.

[18] The Ogoni are one of the Indigenous peoples of southeast Nigeria. Ken Saro-Wiwa founded the Movement for the Survival of the Ogoni People, which fights for social, economic, and environmental justice. Saro-Wiwa was executed in 1995 by the military dictatorship of General Sani Abacha. Many believe that the charges against him and eight other members of the MOSOP who were also executed were rigged by the government with the complicity of Shell officials. There were widespread international protests against the tribunal and the executions.

Listen carefully, for the circulations of racisms have fleshly lives and lineages.

When Coal Becomes Flesh—Incorporated Racism

Remove all evidence from my verse.
—Leonard Cohen, *The Energy of Slaves* (1972)

To understand the long history of the infusions of racial exploitation and environmental exploitation requires genealogical sensibilities to trace its bloodlines and skeletal structures. Only in this way can we begin to understand the viscous porosity[19] and recognize the complexities of the infusions of systemic racisms and ecological indifference. These are histories and lineages often long buried by cultivated ignorance and habituated indifference. In order to briefly illuminate aspects of these lineages, to help cultivate an attunement to the forgetting of race in the context of climate change, I focus this section on coal mining and convict labor in the post–Civil War US South. Let me emphasize, however, that just as the history of environmental exploitation must be understood in terms of specific communities and institutional practices at different time periods and in various locations, so too the specifics of the amalgamation of systemic racisms and environmental exploitation must be thoroughly situated—spatially, historically, fleshily—in order to fully comprehend the ways the two often coalesce. The goal of all of the ecointersectional genealogies included in this book is to gesture at the importance of unburying these histories so as to become attuned to how these lineages permeate and inform contemporary beliefs and practices.[20]

My attunement in this section is animated by a pair of poems, both titled "I Threw Open the Shutters" from Leonard Cohen's (1972) book of poetry *The Energy of Slaves*. Cohen's catalyst in writing the poems was a friend who was arrested in Hydra, Greece, for drug possession, taken off the island, and tortured in a prison in Piraeus (Nadel 1996). In the first version, Cohen writes:

---

[19] I introduced the concept of viscous porosity in a paper by this name in 2007 and continue to build on this conception in Chapter 4 in my account of Hurricane Katrina's impact on the city of New Orleans.

[20] Another fascinating genealogy of coal can be found in Yusoff (2015).

> I threw open the shutters
> light fell on this poem
> It fell on the name of a man
> tortured on a terrace
> above a well-known street
> I swore by the sunlight
> to avenge his broken feet. (10)

When we turn the page to read the second version, we find the story shifts:

> I threw open the shutters:
> light fell on these lines
> (which are incomplete)
> It fell on two words
> which I must erase:
> name of a man
> tortured on a terrace
> above a well-known street
> I swore by the sunlight
> to take his advice:
> remove all evidence from my verse
> forget about his punctured feet. (11)

Cohen's title *The Energy of Slaves*, along with the coupling of these two poems that open the collection, serve as a reminder of the determined forgetting of the fleshly labors that built nations, the fortunes of both individuals and states, and, indeed, the determined forgetting that was woven into the emergence of both colonialism and capitalism.[21] The story of the inextricable enfolding of chattel slavery into the forging of the so-called New World is long and complex. As Sylvia Wynter (1971, 95) reminds us, plantation "societies were both cause and effect of the emergence of the market economy; an emergence which marked a change of such world historical magnitude, that we are all, without exception still 'enchanted,' imprisoned, deformed and schizophrenic in its bewitched reality."

---

[21] This history is being unburied by the work of historians such as Edward E. Baptist (2014), Sven Beckert (2014), Ada Ferrer (2014), Greg Grandin (2014), Walter Johnson (2017), Jason W. Moore (2015), Cedric J. Robinson (2019), Adam Rothman (2007), Calvin Schermerhorn (2015), and Ned Sublette and Constance Sublette (2015).

Here I focus on just one of the complex movements of the narrative of slavery's imprint on the infusion of systemic racisms and environmental exploitation in the US context: enforced labor in southern coal mines. This example is an instance of the third domain identified in Chapter 1, in which the basic social structures that generate environmental degradation are the same ones that generate systemic oppression of certain groups of people. The goal of this discussion is to underscore the importance of a genealogical tracing of the contours of the infusion of systemic racisms and environmental degradation. Through such an approach, what has been rendered illegible comes to light.

Let us begin with the coal itself and trace a few of its lineages. Anthropogenic climate change will have impacts upon species and ecosystems, as well as on the entanglements of the more-than-human world. These entanglements have long histories, many of which involve complex infusions of racist exploitation and environmental overconsumption. One such nexus is coal mining. Human activities such as the burning of fossil fuels, deforestation, and agricultural practices are among the largest contributors to climate change. Of these, coal is one of the largest single sources of CO_2 emissions (Union of Concerned Scientists 2017). From 1971 to 2015, burning of coal worldwide was responsible for 44.9% of global CO_2 emissions (International Energy Agency 2017, 54). Coal's efficiency and relative abundance provided the primary energy source from the eighteenth century to the middle of the twentieth and fueled the Industrial Revolution in the nineteenth and twentieth centuries. The growing demand for coal to power steam engines shifted coal extraction to deep shaft mining beginning in the late eighteenth century, a dangerous but far more efficient method of extraction.

The impacts of coal go far beyond the greenhouse gases emitted when it is burned. Human health risks are high, both from the mining itself as well as from the pollution from mine waste. Ecosystem disruption is also high, from the impacts of the mining and from the acid rain produced as coal is burned and emits sulfur dioxide. Mercury emissions from coal burning impact both human and nonhuman animal health alike.

But coal's lineages also incorporate racist lineages. In *Coal Blooded: Putting Profits Before People*, the NAACP (2012), the Indigenous Environmental Network, and the Little Village Environmental Justice organization examined 378 coal-fired power plants in the United States. The study documents the negative impact of these coal-fired plants as well as the disproportionate negative impact on Black and Latino communities due to the siting of plants in neighborhoods with high percentages of people from one or both groups. This is an instance of the first domain identified in Chapter 1, differential impacts. The study found that of the nearly 6 million Americans who live within three miles of a coal power plant, "39 percent are people of color—a figure that is higher than the 36 percent proportion of people of color in the total U.S. population. Moreover, the coal plants that have been built within urban areas in the U.S. tend overwhelmingly to be located in communities of color" (15). Jacqueline Patterson, the environmental and climate justice director for the NAACP, identified some of the consequences of these facts: "An African American child is three times more likely to go into the emergency room for an asthma attack than a white child, and twice as likely to die from asthma attacks as a white child. African Americans are more likely to die from lung disease, but less likely to smoke. . . . And these are people who are living within three miles of the coal-fired power plants" (quoted in Yale Environment 360 2013).

As I've previously argued, such effects on African Americans are one dimension of environmental racisms and constitute one lens through which we might interrogate the disproportionate impacts of climate change on people subjected to racist oppression.[22] However, while I have no intention of minimizing this aspect of the linkage of environmental harm and systemic racisms, it does not capture the full extent of environmental racisms, what Opperman (2019) called "racist environments." It does not mine the deep and long histories of the infusions of racist exploitation and environmental exploitation. Differential impacts are not an adequate lens for fully understanding the ways that the basic social structures that generate environmental degradation are linked to, indeed are often the same ones that generate systemic oppressions of certain groups of people. It does not travel deeply enough into the ways systemic racisms were and are often incorporated into institutions and social practices that degrade environments. What we need is an account of all the ways racisms are incorporated. Let us trace some of the paths of this incorporation.

To incorporate. A verb. From the late Latin, *incorporates*, past participle of *incorporare* "unite into one body, embody, include," from Latin in- "into,

---

[22] Other than its inclusion in quotes, I am intentionally avoiding the phrase "people of color" for the ways in which it flattens differences between the people so included. It is also a term that does not travel well, for who counts as a person of color in one country will not always count as such in another, which itself signals one of the reasons attention to systemic racisms is such a problematic omission from climate justice analyses. As we begin to trace the impacts of climate-induced migration, this dimension will be crucial to consider as there might be times when the very meaning of a group's racial identity shifts as they shift spatially, and given that racist practices are often location-specific, this lens will be key to identifying how racist practices might alter in target or in practice with shifts in climate-induced migration.

in, on, upon" + verb from *corpus* (genitive *corporis*) "body." Meaning: (1) To put (something) into the body or substance of (something else), blend; absorb, eat, also solidify, harden; (2) To legally form a body politic with perpetual succession and power to act as one person, to establish as a legal corporation.[23]

To give a sense of how we might travel more deeply into the infusions of systemic racisms and environmental exploitation, let us reflect on how racism and environmental exploitation were incorporated in coal mining in the US South after the Civil War. The war ended chattel slavery as a legal institution in the United States, but it did not end its influence on the hearts and minds of many White southerners or mitigate its impact on the bodies of many former slaves. The North was not immune from internalized racism, but in the South it was bred in the bone. Years of justifying the cruelties of chattel slavery created unbroken convictions in White southerners of their superiority and deep fear and resentment of freed slaves.[24] The ideology of the inherent superiority of Whites over Blacks, the often deployed justification of the enslavement and often brutal treatment of millions of people, was deeply embedded in the psyche of many southerners.[25] The legal emancipation of people who had been treated as property did little to undermine the moral order that was used to justify chattel slavery and often triggered forms of resistance to the northern effort to force a new political structure upon the South. Not only were hearts and minds not transformed by the Thirteenth Amendment; there was little transformation of the ways land would be worked, cotton picked, or coal mined. Instead, a series of willful duplicities

---

[23] Online Etymology Dictionary (2018).

[24] This example serves as a reminder of the importance of attending to what I identified in Chapter 2 as the fourth dimension of racial climates, namely, the individual and group perceptions and attitudes concerning which lives and lifeways are considered valuable and which are seen as less worthy of protection.

[25] Of the more than 12 million African people who were abducted, enslaved, and transported across the Atlantic, approximately half a million were transported to the United States between the mid-seventeenth century and the 1808 ban on importation of slaves by Congress. Approximately 18% of those who were abducted were murdered or died due to the horrible conditions of the Middle Passage. After 1808 the Black population in the United States increased from approximately 400,000 to 4.4 million in 1860, of whom the vast majority (3.9 million) were enslaved. It is important to understand that this increase was significantly affected by the practice of forced "breeding" through systematic rape of enslaved women and White slave owners. In addition, some "marriages" between enslaved men and women were forced upon them by the slave owner with the expectation that breeding would happen, producing more slaves. Slave women who did not get pregnant were at risk of being sold into what would often be worse conditions (Berlin 1992; Sublette and Sublette 2015). For studies of the legacy of slavery on pre- and post–Civil War southern sensibilities see Deyle (2005); Fox-Genovese and Genovese (2008); Genovese (1998); Genovese and Fox-Genovese (2011); Irons (2008); Robinson (2017).

created a new system of enforced labor, including exploitative sharecropping arrangements and the convict lease system. The bodies of formerly enslaved people even after emancipation continued to be treated as a source of fuel, something to be put to work and to be consumed into the work of earning a profit. It was the energy of slaves by an only slightly different name.[26]

The reincorporation of Black Americans into unfree labor in the postwar South takes many forms. My focus is on the criminalization of Black life designed to exploit it in coal mines. Vagrancy laws served this purpose. While Mississippi was the first state to enact vagrancy laws in 1865, Alabama, Arkansas, Florida, Georgia, Louisiana, North Carolina, South Carolina, Texas, Tennessee, and Virginia were not far behind. Such laws not only identified as a vagrant anyone who was deemed insufficiently employed, but included anyone whose lifestyle was deemed inappropriate: "[R]ogues and vagabonds, idle and dissipated persons, beggars, jugglers, or persons practising unlawful games or plays, runaways, common drunkards, common nightwalkers, pilferers, lewd, wanton, or lascivious persons, in speech or behavior, common railers and brawlers, persons who neglect their calling or employment, misspend what they earn, or do not provide for the support of themselves or their families or dependents, and all other idle and disorderly persons, including all who neglect all lawful business, habitually misspend their time by frequenting houses of ill-fame, gaming houses, or tippling shops, shall be deemed and considered vagrants, under the provisions of this act" (Teaching American History 2022, Vagrancy Law, Section 1).

The broadness of vagrancy laws allowed widespread misuse, which was used to arrest and fine freed Blacks. Most of these laws had a provision that failure to pay the fine could result in convict leasing. As framed in the Mississippi vagrancy law, failure "for five days after the imposition of any fine or forfeiture upon him or her for violation of any of the provisions of this act to pay the same, that it shall be, and is hereby made, the duty of the sheriff of the proper county to hire [them] out . . . to any person who will, for the shortest period of service, pay said fine or forfeiture and all costs" (Teaching American History 2022, Section 5). But whether due to forged charges like vagrancy or other wrongs like theft or assault, real or imagined, a system of forced labor ensued that benefited plantations as well as corporations such as railroad companies and ironworks. The resulting unfree labor practices

---

[26] Here I am indebted to Blackmon's (2008) *Slavery by Another Name: The Re-Enslavement of Black Americans from the Civil War to World War II*.

resulted in deplorable working conditions and in high rates of death for those so sentenced.

Alabama's convict lease program fueled the coal industry. During the Civil War, much of the coal supplied to the Confederacy came from Alabama's coal fields, the southernmost tip of the Appalachian coal field. During that time, slaves were often taken off plantations and forced to work in the mines. Forced labor in the coal mines shifted only in name and not in practice after the Civil War, when hundreds of freed Blacks were convicted of crimes like vagrancy, then leased to companies like the Tennessee Coal, Iron & Railroad Company, one of the largest exploiters of convict labor, whose headquarters moved to Birmingham, Alabama, in 1895. A report on the metal, mineral, coal, and stock market in *The Engineering and Mining Journal* from 1908, for example, reported, "Coal operations in Alabama have been quite active recently.... The Bessemer Land and Improvement Company has made a contract for the use of 200 convicts at a price that practically equals what free labor is given" (1279).

The experience of working in the mines is described in *Homegoing: A Novel* by Yaa Gyasi (2016, 161). While a fictionalized account, it provides a glimpse of such exploitation. In it we learn of the fate of H, who was arrested on the charge of "studyin' a white woman" and, when he was unable to pay the fine, was sold by the state of Alabama to work the coal mines outside of Birmingham. The daily experience of convict laborers is described as follows: H and the other prisoners traveled through tunnels of exploded rock the three to seven miles required to reach the coal face where they were to work: "H shoveled some fourteen thousand pounds of coal, all while stooped down low, on his knees, stomach, sides. And when he and the other prisoners left the mines, they would always be coated in a layer of black dust, their arms burning, just burning.... [M]ore than once, a prison warden had whipped a miner for not reaching the ten-ton quota... whipped him until he died, and the white wardens did not move him that night or the rest of the next day, leaving the dust to blanket his body, a warning to the other convicts."

Gyasi's fictionalized account reflects the harsh reality of convict labor. Indeed, in 1909 the penitentiary committee of Texas recommended the immediate cancellation of the contract between the State of Texas and the coal mines at Calvert, Texas on the grounds that the employment of convicts in the coal mines was hazardous and unhealthy. An article in *The Engineering and Mining Journal* from that year reported that based on inspections of the mines, the committee found the following conditions: "practically all the men going to and from their daily work in the mines are forced to walk through mud and water, thereby wetting their feet, in which condition they are forced to work during the day; that some of the men were required to work in water, mud and slush from shoe mouth to half-leg deep and to do their daily task of mining seven tons of coal, which mud and water appears to affect in various ways the physical condition not only of the feet but of the entire physical person of the men thus subjected" (1068). The committee concluded that the "State of Texas has no moral or legal right to force men convicted of violation of the law to labor under such conditions" (1068).

According to Douglas Blackmon (2008, 57), in Alabama nearly 20% of leased prisoners died in the first two years of their sentence, with the mortality rate rising in the third year to 35% and the fourth year to nearly 45%. Depressions scattered across the fields around the coal mines show where many hundreds, possibly even thousands of those who died in the mines were buried, their remains incorporated into the ground. And many of those who did not die before they "served out their sentence" succumbed to the diseases caused by coal dust that settled in their lungs and became flesh. Coal workers' pneumoconiosis, black lung disease, comes upon those who have breathed in coal dust. The dust would have been thick in the mines worked by convict laborers. Little if any ventilation and very narrow passages contributed to high concentrations of coal dust breathed in hour by hour, day by day. Dust that enters the lungs becomes part of the body, as it can be neither destroyed nor removed. The particles become incorporated into the tissues and structures of the lungs and pulmonary lymph nodes. So incorporated, the dust catalyzes the release of various proteins and enzymes that cause inflammation and fibrous growths. As the growths and lesions lump together, lung tissue is destroyed, leading to severe shortness of breath, chronic cough, heart problems, and premature death. Here we see racisms, both individual and systemic, incorporated into flesh.

This bodily incorporation of coal dust was one of the consequences of the incorporation of the bodily labor of Blacks into the flourishing of the postwar economy in the US South and into the wealth of corporations like the Tennessee Coal, Iron and Railroad Company, which merged with the US Steel Corporation in 1907. Systemic racisms were in this way incorporated into the environmental harms caused by coal mining, from the impacts on ground water to the release of methane and acid mine drainage. Many rivers were, and still are, polluted by runoff from the mines that carries acids, heavy metals, and sediment. Just as we cannot ignore the impact of the loss of so many Black lives to convict labor on the average family wealth of Blacks in the twentieth and twenty-first centuries, we cannot ignore the way in which corporate wealth was grounded in both systemic racisms and environmental exploitation. To ignore these lineages or understand them only as separate and separable phenomena is to overlook the long history of their infusion. No study of the causes of climate change that overlooks the complexity of such lineages will fully address what is needed for climate justice.

The incorporation of racist exploitation and environmental exploitation means that studies that consider differential impacts, whether of the siting of coal plants or of storm barriers, tell only part of the story of environmental racism. Those who fight for climate justice must begin to tell the other half of the story.[27]

Systemic Oppression as a Driver of Ecological Change

To illustrate the second domain of the infusions of systemic racisms and environmental degradation—racist institutions and practices fueling or causing environmental degradation—and detail how it interacts with the other domains noted in Chapter 1, I return to Brazil, in this case to Pau da Lima. Pau da Lima is a favela on the periphery of the city of Salvador, the capital of the state of Bahia and the country's third-largest city. Pau da Lima is the third largest neighborhood in Salvador and has a population of roughly eighty thousand. Two-thirds of Salvador's 2 million inhabitants live in favelas or unplanned parts of Brazilian cities like that of Pau da Lima (Unger, Ko, and Douglass-Jaime 2016, 105). These settlements arose in formerly uninhabited forested regions of the city. The term "favela" is thought to have originated from the favela tree or shrub (*Jatropha phyllacantha*). The first favela in Brazil, Providência, located in Rio de Janerio, was settled in the late nineteenth century when soldiers returning from the Canudos War were without housing. They named their settlement after the shrubs found at the location of their victory in Bahia (102). Following that original settlement, many new favelas were built and settled by formerly enslaved Africans. Starting in the 1940s and accelerating in the 1970s, favelas began to increase in both size and number due to migration from rural to urban areas; the majority of

---

[27] Here I am indebted to Baptist's (2014) *The Half Has Never Been Told: Slavery and the Making of American Capitalism*.

residents in the favelas were Afro-Brasileiros (both *preto*, Black, and *pardo*, mixed-race).

Housing in favelas is makeshift. Newer structures are constructed from salvaged materials, but older structures have become more durable with the gradual incorporation of materials such as sheet metal and bricks. Favelas lack typical infrastructure, having jerry-rigged electricity and plumbing. Many have no access to city water, and waste disposal options are limited. Pau de Lima includes homes in the hilly portion of the neighborhood as well as newer settlements in the three valleys of the favela. Newer settlements, particularly those at the peripheries of the favela and at the base of the valleys, have even poorer infrastructure: "At the bottom of the valley many homes were built adjacent to open sewers that carry trash from the streets and homes along the ridges of the hill as well as trash that residents discard in open areas along the base of the valley because there are no adequate places to dispose of the trash" (James 2013). Almost half of the housing structures have open sewers (Unger, Ko, and Douglass-Jaime 2016, 108). Homes in Pau da Lima often experience water damage from flooding during heavy rains caused by inadequate drainage or leaking roofs due to poor construction.

Since the 1920s various eradication campaigns have been mounted against the favelas, including Pau da Lima, with forced evictions and razing of buildings. But with little alternative housing, favelas continued to grow. In the 1970s the drug trade in the favelas marked them as sites of both poverty and crime. As of 2010 almost 12 million Brazilians live in favelas, the majority of which are located in the metropolitan regions of São Paulo, Rio de Janeiro, Belém, Salvador, and Recife (Miranda, Grottera, and Giampietro 2016).

Leptospirosis is a rat-born disease caused by the spirochete bacterium *Leptospira*. It has been identified as the most widespread zoonotic (infection from animal to human) disease in the world, with more than 1 million cases worldwide each year and responsible for roughly sixty thousand deaths per year (Sharp et al. 2016). It is often spread through exposure to the urine of infected animals either from direct contact or from contact with contaminated soil or water as the bacterium can survive in fresh water for up to sixteen days and in soil for almost twenty-four. Leptospirosis causes fevers, chills, headache, and muscle aches, and in some cases it results in potentially fatal infections such as severe pulmonary hemorrhage syndrome as well as

Weil's disease, which can lead to life-threatening renal failure, hemorrhage, and respiratory distress.

Pau da Lima has a high incidence of *Leptospira* infection (37.8 per 1,000 person-years) and of severe leptospirosis cases involving renal insufficiency and pulmonary hemorrhage (19.8 per 100,000 population; Felzemburgh et al. 2014). As outbreaks of leptospirosis are associated with flooding and heavy rainfall, the increasing frequency and intensity of extreme weather events associated with climate change will likely result in an increase in incidents (Lau et at. 2010). Leptospirosis cases have an inverse linear association with the distance of an individual's household to an open sewer and elevation of the household from the lowest point in the valley. And among those who live in Pau da Lima, Afro-Brasileiros have a significantly higher risk for contracting leptospirosis, even after controlling for factors such as socioeconomic level (Reis et al. 2008).

Studies of leptospirosis have confirmed that slum settlements in general, including the favelas in Brazil, are creating new habitats for infestation by Norway rats (*Rattus norvegicus*). Indeed, the colonization of Salvador by Norway rats is relatively recent, coinciding with the growth in favelas in the past half-century (Kajdacsi et al. 2013). A high proportion of households in Pau da Lima are infested with Norway rats. A central driver of ecosystem alteration is human rubbish dumps as waste deposit areas and open sewers function as habitats and reliable sources of food for rats (Oro et al. 2013). The Norway rat is one of the most ubiquitous pest species globally. It adversely affects agricultural productivity, ecosystem health (native species and habitats), and public health (Capizzi, Bertolino, and Mortellit 2014). Populations of Norway rats have been expanding in all major urban centers in Brazil (Costa et al. 2021).

Complex lineages of oppression in Brazil emerging from the afterlives of slavery and colonialization circulate in these favelas. The unequal distribution of land during colonial settlement permeates current inequalities of income and wealth distributions in Brazil, which is at the top of the world inequality rankings despite being classified as the ninth largest economy in the world. Almost 55 million people live below the so-called poverty line as of 2018, based on the World Bank (2017) figure of income up to US$5.50 a day. However, poverty is not equally distributed. Afro-Brasileiros (*preto* and *pardo* combined) account for more than 75% of the population with the lowest income; 15% of Brazilian Whites (*brancos*) have incomes below the poverty line, compared to 33% of Afro-Brasileiros. Afro-Brasileiro unemployment rates are typically 35% higher than those of Whites, and income per capita of Afro-Brasileiros is about 50% less than that of Whites (Instituto Brasileiro de Geografia e Estatística 2018; Pereira 2018).[28]

Land was used as a resource during the colonial period to reward colonists and ensure political loyalty. In Brazil the unequal distribution of land was further reinforced by the creation of plantation economies fueled by the labor of slaves. Cash crops such as tobacco, coffee, sugar, and rubber brought plantation owners wealth at the expense of the enslaved Indigenous people and enslaved Africans and their descendants. Large land endowments among the first colonizers were also designed to ensure that the bodies of slaves would also be used to mine the rich mineral resources—gold, silver, and diamonds—that would support the colonial state. Land inequality set in place during the colonial period infused with racist beliefs about the inferiority of Indigenous and African people is a lineage that continues to circulate in Brazil's contemporary economic inequalities. Those inequalities are undergirded by having one of the lowest rates of intergenerational educational mobility or equality of social and economic opportunities in the world (Dunn 2007). And that inequality is infused with the legacies of colonialism for the 51% of the population of Brazil that is Afro-Brasileiros, contributing to the large racial gap in household income.

The complex lineages of oppression circulating in Brazil's extreme income gaps are a central driver of the large favela population and the high incidence of leptospirosis cases.[29] But if I stopped my analysis here, at what might appear to be a discussion of differential impacts, the first domain, I would have overlooked the ways in which those complex lineages of oppression have also impacted the ecology of the cities of Brazil, particularly of the favelas. As I argued in Chapter 1, racist institutions and practices can fuel or cause environmental degradation, the second domain of the intersections between systemic racisms and ecological indifference. In the case of Pau da Lima and other favelas in Brazil, there is a complex feedback loop between the impact

---

[28] Ironically, extreme poverty rates (households living on less than the equivalent of US$1.90 per day) have fallen during the COVID pandemic, as have rates of households living below the poverty line, due to emergency aid programs. The worry is that the positive trend in poverty reduction will reverse once the pandemic benefits end (The Brazilian Report 2020).

[29] A particularly high-risk population in the favelas are the *catadores* and *catadoras*, the 300,000 to 1 million men and women in Brazil's informal labor sector who sort through trash to find items to trade for cash.

of histories and current practices of racism and harmful impacts on environments. The absence of adequate sanitary services, both trash removal and closed sewer systems, has become a uniquely anthropogenic contributor to the burgeoning populations of Norway rats. Systemic racisms have fueled rat colonialization. And that colonialization follows racist pathways. In Salvador, a citywide sanitation program (Bahia Azul) has had a major beneficial impact on health. However, the program did not provide coverage to Pau da Lima or many of the slum settlements in the city's periphery, whereas middle-class neighborhoods close to the favelas received reliable trash removal services from state-owned and private sanitation companies (Reis et al. 2008). As a result, Norway rat infestations are much higher in favelas than in wealthier neighborhoods.

The feedbacks between systems of oppression and harms to flora and fauna are a key and often missing element of analyses of environmental racism. Indifference to the lives of those in the favela has altered not only human lifeways but other animal lifeways, in particular that of the Norway rat. Poverty and systemic racisms interlock to transform the urban ecology in ways that create new habitats for the rats. Even efforts to eradicate the rats follow racist lineages, as the most intense efforts launched by the city are targeted at privileged communities rather than the favelas, which have the greatest need for persistent rodent control (Unger, Ko, and Douglass-Jaime 2016). In fact, the sporadic control efforts in favelas through the use of rodenticide can lead to immune resistance in the local rat population, which increases the infection risks for favela dwellers. And the rat population rebounds quickly, reaching pre-intervention densities within six months (Masi, Vilaça, and Razzolini, 2009). Systemic racisms contribute both to the causes of rat colonialization and to inadequate administration of poisons to kill the rats, which impacts the evolution of rodenticide immunity, which in turn increases zoonotic disease risks in the favela communities. The feedback loops of systemic racisms.

We here see the importance of an ecointersectional analysis that traces the complex ways social inequalities shape the urban ecosystem in Pau da Lima. We see again the need for highly situated, nuanced genealogies of the infusions of systemic racisms and environmental degradation. We cannot fully understand the impacts of environmental racism without following all of these feedbacks, including the ecological effects of systemic racisms. Systemic racisms, like other socially engrained systems of oppression, often have environmental impacts, shaping ecological systems through complex feedbacks. The example of Pau da Lima provides a clear yes to Hage's question: Is racism an environmental threat?

Let Us Swear by the Sunlight to Avenge These Broken Feet

In the prologue to *The Mushroom at the End of the World: On the Possibility of Life in Capitalist Ruins*, a meditation on the co-emergence of ecologies and human communities in the contours of capitalism, Anna Tsing (2015, 1–2) offers the following reflection on precarity:

> Terrors, of course, there are, and not just for me. The world's climate is going haywire and industrial progress has proved more deadly to life on earth than anyone imagined a century ago. The economy is no longer a source of growth or optimism; any of our jobs could disappear with the next economic crisis. . . . [P]recarity once seemed the fate of the less fortunate. Now it seems all our lives are precarious—even when, for the moment, our pockets are lined.

To say that all lives are precarious, that we are all vulnerable, is the kind of truism that covers over, obscures, and, willfully or not, flattens the complexities of oppressions. We might all be vulnerable to the unpredictability of fate, but we are not all equally vulnerable to the many types of violence perpetuated by systemic oppressions. To ignore how such violence is deeply woven into the textures of environmental exploitation is a form of indifference that is at the heart of the type of environmental racism to which I urge that we become attuned—*not simply the differential impacts but the layered, habituated disposabilities of certain people and certain ecosystems and their often complexly intermeshed lineages*. Not seeing these connections is part of the muting of the atrocities perpetuated on certain groups of people and the ways these atrocities are often caught up in the very mechanisms of environmental damage that environmentalists like Tsing wish to modify.

While addressing only three of the many examples of the incorporations of systemic racisms and environmental exploitation, this chapter sought to illuminate the persistent infusions of these racist and exploiting incorporations. Such illumination will come, I contend, only through detailed ecointersectional genealogical tracing of such lineages and their incorporations. We overlook too much, silence too many lineages if we look for or desire general accounts of such infusions. Our analyses must take the form of detailed, historical, spatial, situated ecointersectional genealogies of the incorporations of systemic racisms and environmental exploitation.

No simple story will do. We must throw open the shutters and swear by the sunlight.

4
Through the Eye of a Hurricane

Beta made landfall in Texas on September 22, 2020, covering streets in Houston with water and causing flooding in the low-lying southern parts of Cameron Parish in Louisiana. What distinguished Beta was not its speed or its force, but the fact that it was the ninth named storm to make landfall in the United States in 2020, tying a record set in 1916. In fact, 2020 is a record-breaking year. It exceeded previous records for activity in the early part of the season with nine named storms from May through July. September 2020 was the most active month on record in the Atlantic, its ten named storms breaking older records of eight in one month. Beta has the dubious honor of being the storm that tied the record set in 1893 of three named storms forming on the same day, but it broke the record in terms of how quickly they formed: Wilfred, Alpha, and Beta were all named in a six-hour time span. As the name Beta indicates, the National Hurricane Center had as of mid-September already used up all the twenty-one names on its list for 2020 hurricanes and had turned to the Greek alphabet, which had happened only once before since the Hurricane Center started naming storms in 1953. Beta was the twenty-third named storm of the season. It was followed by seven named storms, setting a new record for the most active Atlantic hurricane season in history, breaking the previous record set in 2005, whose twenty-seven named storms included four Category 5 hurricanes: Emily, Katrina, Rita, and Wilma.[1]

Some hurricanes pass quickly. Others remain with us for years. Hurricane Katrina, which made landfall on August 29, 2005, is one whose impact continues to echo almost two decades later. Indeed, Katrina is currently as emblematic of New Orleans as Marti Gras, jazz, or gumbo. Those who

---

[1] As I was readying this manuscript for review, the hurricane season of 2021 blew in twenty-one named storms. While certainly well below the thirty of 2020, it was, nonetheless, the third-most named storms since 1851. One of those storms, Hurricane Ida, hit the Louisiana coast as a Category 4 storm with 150 mph winds on August 29, the sixteenth anniversary of Hurricane Katrina's landfall. Ida resulted in the deaths of more than one hundred people, approximately 280 million fish from low-oxygen conditions in inland waters, and billions of dollars in damage, including destroying sixty-eight of the eighty homes in the Indigenous community of Pointe-aux-Chênes.

experienced Katrina's power will never forget it. But even those who were far away were impacted by Katrina's devastation. For days news stations replayed shots of the levee breaches and the astonishing range of the flood waters that covered more than 80% of New Orleans. Those far removed from the water's reach watched news coverage of helicopter crews pulling people off rooftops or the suffering of the thirty thousand who took refuge from the storm in the Superdome for five long days—days in which the electricity failed and food rotted inside the hundreds of refrigerators and freezers spread throughout the building, the damaged roof leaked, and every toilet and sink ceased to function. Millions were witness to the devastation and death, the suffering and loss.

Seeing through the eye of a hurricane can be destabilizing. What was once believed to be safe ground can shift and flood beneath our feet. Feats of engineering can fail. Cities can be destroyed. Climate change can be made not simply believable but palpable. And, as we saw with Katrina, the face of suffering can be given a complexion that reveals the plight of the poor and the systemic racisms that are woven into a country's economic structures.

Seeing through the eye of a hurricane serves as a reminder that the genealogical sensibilities that we deploy to understand the complexities of climate or environmental injustice cannot focus only on the weave of lineages of power constructed by humans. I introduced the concept of genealogical sensibilities in Chapter 1 and have been working to deploy it throughout the book. In this chapter my aim is to expand on this approach to underscore the importance of seeing how the lineages of injustice and ecological indifference are infused. I want to develop further the ways genealogical sensibilities can alert us to the infusions of systemic racisms into the arrangement of neighborhoods, the sacrifice zones of garbage dumps, the placement of schools, the values that are implanted in local normalcies and habitual ways of doing business, and the many ways those injustices intersect with environmental harms. All of the case studies in previous chapters are designed to illustrate the nature and importance of ecointersectional genealogies for understanding the complex nature of climate injustices and to appreciate the ways systemic racisms and harms to environments co-occur. By devoting this chapter to one case, I aim to broaden and deepen my analysis to provide more of the facets of the infusions of exploitations of some people and of some environments. My aim, as with all the examples, is not only to reveal the complexity of the problem but to begin to shift habits of thought and action by dislodging indifference.

Katrina provides a lens for understanding that our genealogical sensibilities must attend not only to local formations and practices but also to the complex exchanges of oceans, wetlands, river flows, and oil deposits as they intermesh with the actions and impacts of oil industries, the work of the US Army Corps of Engineers, and the afterlives of slavery. The actors to which we must attend are complex assemblages: life forms, economic systems, geological formations, the complex flows of water, political formations, ecosystems, the built environment. Climate injustice, indeed, racial climates, arise out of multiple lineages, multifaceted histories, and complex material exchanges. While tracing the impacts of systems of oppressive practices, beliefs, and institutions is a key component of understanding climate injustice, we overlook the complexity of the exchanges if we do not see how *environments are shaped by systems of oppression and are, in turn, crucial contributors to those systems.* Hence the importance of an ecointersectional approach informed by genealogical sensibilities.

As we have seen in previous chapters, attunement to habits of indifference to the flourishing of some lives and lifeways reveals the intricate infusions of human institutions and ecological systems. Witnessing Katrina through the lens of ecointersectional genealogies provides paths for tracing infusions of ecological indifference and systemic injustices, paths for seeing the ways human choices and environmental processes co-emerge.

Viscous Porosity—Katrina

Katrina is a natural phenomenon that happens in part because of human social structures and practices. Seeing through the lens of Katrina reveals the complex infusions of that which we refer to as "natural" or "human-made," "social" or "biological." Such demarcations were seamlessly swept together in Katrina's counterclockwise rotation. Katrina came into being because of a concatenation of phenomena; low-pressure areas, warm ocean waters, and swirling in that classic cyclone pattern were also the phenomena of deforestation and industrialization.

A hurricane pulls its strength from the heat of the ocean's surface waters. Katrina swirled into a Category 5 hurricane thanks to surface waters in the Gulf of Mexico that were 2 degrees warmer than normal for the time of year.[2] Does it make sense to say that the warmer water or Katrina's power was

---

[2] The National Oceanic and Atmospheric Administration reported in 2000 that ocean waters had warmed to a depth of two miles in five years (Levitus et al. 2000). The scientists who reported these

socially produced, thus rendering Katrina a nonnatural phenomenon? No, but the problem is the framing of the question. We cannot sift through and separate what is "natural" from what is "human-induced." The issue here is not simply epistemic. Weather on Earth is affected by heat from the sun, the movement of air, and atmospheric pressure. The weather is also affected by how we build our cities, by what we cover with concrete or asphalt and what we keep as green spaces, and even by the crops we grow in our farmlands and our farming methods (Cotton and Pielke 2007). Weather and climate are also affected by the buildup of greenhouse gases, primarily carbon dioxide, methane, and nitrous oxide, which retain heat and raise global surface temperatures. As I write, NASA reports that global temperature has risen over 1.8 °F since 1880.[3] That shift in global temperature is the result of human activities such as fossil fuel combustion and deforestation, which are in turn fueled by social beliefs and structures. In the United States we have hammered home the unwavering belief that economic success and independence are determined in part by access to and consumption of goods. Consider just two examples. In the past century, floor space per person in homes, whether owned or rented, houses or condos, has almost doubled (from approximately 400 to 800 square feet). The size of homes, particularly their floor space, is "a direct driver of energy demands and associated environmental impacts" (Moura, Smith, and Belzer 2015, 2). Moreover, the average household sports two vehicles, with the number of minivans and SUVs significantly rising since 1990. Personal vehicle use is another significant driver of climate change (Energy Information Administration 2005).

The Intergovernmental Panel on Climate Change (2013b) forecasts a global temperature rise of 2.5 °F to 10 °F over the next century. Even at the lowest projection, such a shift will cause significant weather-related changes that will impact lives and lifeways. In asking whether Katrina was a natural or human-caused event, we are trapped by the false choice of framing human

findings argued that the worldwide ocean warming is probably caused by a combination of natural variability and human-induced effects.

[3] Each time I've addressed this topic, even if my edits are only six months removed from the previous draft, the numbers shift. To compare this measure of 1.836 °F noted during the summer of 2021 to the current measure, visit the Climate page of NASA's website: https://climate.nasa.gov. We also have to factor in the impact of the coronavirus pandemic on recent emissions. While acknowledging that the analysis was uncertain, a recent Carbon Brief study indicated that the pandemic could result in emissions cuts in 2020 in the region of 2 billion tons of CO_2, or the equivalent of about 5.5% of the global total in 2019 (Evans, 2020). However, the expectation is that once the pandemic is controlled by a vaccine and that vaccine is widely available globally, the emissions will quickly rebound.

impacts as somehow separate and separable from environmental impacts. Katrina is emblematic of what I call the *viscous porosity* between humans and environments, between social practices and natural phenomena. I speak of "porosity" to signal the myriad ways so-called social orders and so-called natural orders are infused. There is no sharp ontological divide here but rather complex infusions of phenomena. This does not mean that we cannot attempt to determine the extent to which certain human actions increased the intensity of a hurricane or some other weather-related phenomena.[4] Indeed, issues of distributive justice may require that such a distinction be made in order to determine how to apportion responsibility across nations for harm from human-induced climate change, as may be done if we adopt a "polluter-pays" principle of responsibility. We can make distinctions, even between "nature" and "culture," to clarify or identify differences for particular purposes and in particular situations. But it is important to avoid viewing these distinctions as having autonomous, ontological status and deny the dynamic infusions, the porosities, that characterize phenomena of which the distinctions are a part. In other words, we cannot simply "read" such distinctions from the "natural" joints of things. We must instead take responsibility for the distinctions we employ and be attentive not only to what we can learn from such distinctions but also to their limits and to who and what is silenced by deploying them.

Attention to the viscous porosity of the happening of things helps to remind us of the complexity and abstraction involved in making distinctions such as "human contributions to global temperature," with its nature/culture implication. "Viscosity" signals the importance of attention to the complex ways of material agency; hence the phrase "viscous porosity" rather than "fluidity." Viscosity is neither fluid nor solid, but intermediate between them. Viscosity signals the ways phenomena often work to maintain their form or movement: a form of resistance to change in the midst of change. Genealogical attentiveness to the porosity of interactions helps to undermine the notion that distinctions, as important as they might be in particular contexts, signify a natural or unchanging boundary, a natural kind that does not exist outside of particular perspectives, discourses, and social practices. At the same time, viscosity retains an emphasis on resistance to changing

---

[4] The science of attribution of extreme weather events has grown exponentially over the past fifteen years. An overview of approaches is covered in the 2016 National Academies of Sciences, Engineering, and Medicine report *Attribution of Extreme Weather Events in the Context of Climate Change*.

form and is a more helpful image than fluidity, which is too likely to promote a notion of open possibilities and overlook the resistance and opposition as well as the propensities and attractions among identities and forms of existence. The viscous porosity of things signals the complex infusions of human embodiments and environments, the continuous happening of the more-than-human. Katrina gathered strength and force in the viscous porosity of fossil fuel consumption and ocean waters, the melting of ice sheets and industrialization. To put flesh on these theoretical bones, let us turn to New Orleans.

New Orleans

While it began with Katrina, attention quickly shifted to New Orleans. The city is surrounded by water: the Gulf of Mexico, the Mississippi River, and Lake Pontchartrain. It is a city built on land that was subject to regular flooding from the Mississippi. Much of the city now lies below the level of the river that helped to create it. Half of the city is currently below sea level, an average of six feet below, though there are points at which the land is a staggering ten feet below sea level.

Part of the psychology of living in New Orleans, a city in which cargo boats on the river are at times sailing on waterways significantly *higher* than street level, is believing that human agency will win out over other forms of material agency. That belief was not warranted in 2005 and arguably is not warranted today, but it makes living below sea level palatable. Numerous scientific studies were produced by the Army Corps of Engineers before Katrina that provided computer simulations predicting the devastation that such a hurricane could bring. But denial is a powerful force. Even President George W. Bush and Michael Chertoff, secretary of the Department of Homeland Security, practiced it. In an interview with Diane Sawyer on *Good Morning America* on September 1, 2005, Bush said he did not think that anyone could have anticipated the breach of the levees. And Chertoff (Chertoff et al. 2005) justified the slow disaster response rate as being due to what he called the "second catastrophe," namely, that the breach of the levees "really caught everybody by surprise."[5] Denial indeed functions in complex ways.

---

[5] The complete quote from Chertoff is as follows: "Well, I think if you look at what actually happened, I remember on Tuesday morning picking up newspapers and I saw headlines, 'New Orleans Dodged The Bullet,' because if you recall the storm moved to the east and then continued

One need not practice this type of denial to live below sea level. Approximately 26% of the Netherlands is below sea level,[6] an area that supports over 60% of the country's population of almost 16 million people. After a serious flood in 1953, the Netherlands inaugurated the Delta Commission to build a system of dikes, dams, and other structures to provide flood safety at a far higher storm level than the New Orleans system. While no technology is foolproof, the confidence of New Orleanians prior to Katrina had to be based either on denial or on ignorance of the risks, while Dutch confidence has a more solid foundation. Not that there is no denial at work even in the Netherlands. To wall off major sea arms means destroying ecosystems and losing coastline (almost four hundred miles of coastline). Living below sea level can be done, but it requires what Andrew Pickering (1995, 78) calls a "dance of agency" among the more-than-human agents: engineers and oceans, concrete and water, marshland and live oaks.[7]

New Orleans emerged out of complex infusions. The Mississippi and its coursing into the Gulf were the transit by which wealth in the form of grain and lumber from the North and cotton and sugar from the South were transported for shipment east or oversees. Its transit gave birth to the city. The Mississippi carried wealth, but given the particulars of the land, it also carried death. Flooding has been a commonplace of the city of New Orleans, not to mention the illnesses the swampy land bred.[8] Efforts to control the waters of the Mississippi were equally commonplace.

---

on and appeared to pass with considerable damage but nothing worse. It was on Tuesday that the levee—may have been overnight Monday to Tuesday—that the levee started to break. And it was midday Tuesday that I became aware of the fact that there was no possibility of plugging the gap and that essentially the lake was going to start to drain into the city. I think that second catastrophe really caught everybody by surprise. In fact, I think that's one of the reasons people didn't continue to leave after the hurricane had passed initially. So this was clearly an unprecedented catastrophe. And I think it caused a tremendous dislocation in the response effort and, in fact, in our ability to get materials to people" (Chertoff et al. 2005).

[6] Approximately 50% of the land in New Orleans is currently below sea level.
[7] Pickering's (1995) *The Mangle of Practice* provides a helpful model of the dance of material agency, in which agency is often, but not always, human agency. His essay "Asian Eels and Global Warming" extends this work to develop what he calls a posthumanist alternative to realism/social constructivism that emphasizes the coupled becomings of humanity and the environment. He argues that traditional disciplines necessarily obscure such "heterogeneous assemblages" (Pickering 2005, 34).
[8] While the swamp was referred to in the nineteenth century as "a fountain of death," it was not the swamp itself that was to blame but the mosquitoes that were transported across oceans by ships and who took up residence in and thrived in the swamp. It was their bites that transmitted illnesses like yellow fever (Campanella 2008).

A city is a complex material-semiotic interaction reflective of the viscous porosity of things. New Orleans rests at the heart of multiple interactions. Consider the levees: they emerged from the viscous porosity of more-than-human forces. The city sits on the banks of the Mississippi where sediment from the river created areas of elevated land called "natural levees" approximately ten to fifteen feet above sea level. New Orleans' earliest buildings sat on top of these levees. But the natural levees—the raised land at the sharp bend in the river where French colonists built La Nouvelle-Orléans, the land feature from which the "Crescent City" nickname would arise—those levees were subject to frequent flooding. Labor was needed to fortify the levees, but when mortality rates proved to be too high for the original criminals and contract laborers who were imported from Europe, the French turned to African captives to dig ditches and reinforce the levees—a labor pool that had an equally high mortality rate, but where "supplies" were higher. As the population grew, the labor of slaves was used to clear land and build houses farther inland. But the land that was not on the levees was at lower elevations and thus more prone to flooding. To create usable land, water had to be pumped out of the area, which caused the ground to sink even lower.

Remember, half of New Orleans currently lies below sea level—an average of six feet below sea level. But when the French colonials established La Nouvelle-Orléans none of it was below sea level. The levees transform the local geology and hydrology and are in turn shaped by them. Remove runoff water and build levees to stop the river from flooding, and soils dry out and the land subsides. Keep doing that, and the land will drop below sea level. As the land drops further below sea level, levees that once were adequate can no longer hold back the coursings of the Mississippi. This is the dance of agency Pickering (1995) refers to, an ongoing and sometimes inelegant dance between the local geology and hydrology in the New Orleans area and the values and politics of the US Army Corp of Engineers.

Before turning to the extensive levee system that makes New Orleans what it is today, we need to recognize that not all the reclaimed land of the area was crafted by modern engineering technologies. I pick this complex interaction as a reminder, a caution to avoid positing an Edenic time before colonialization and industrialization or falling prey to the persistent myth of passive Indigenous people who simply lived in but did not transform "nature." The people who lived in the area that was to become New Orleans actively shaped its land. The land was rich in resources, including shellfish. Shellfish were such a prevalent food source that shell middens or debris mounds accumulated. From these emerged a new ecozone in the marsh, one that materialized from the viscous porosity of more-than-human agency. The middens contributed to the emergence of significantly different plants and alteration of the distributions of plants in the marshes. They provided the dry land needed for human habitation (see Kidder 2000). The cypress trees that are the hallmark of the eastern marshes took root because of the middens, as did the oak trees that lent their name to the islands. These oak stands provided the economic promise that, in the eighteenth century, catalyzed colonization of the area. These same middens would become the literal foundation of buildings in New Orleans, for their contents were used to create the material of houses and the lime that plastered the walls of the buildings of the emerging city.

As is often the case, human agency, though not always human intentionality, is infused with the agency of other lifeways and environments. Human consumption and refuse practices altered flora habitats, which in turn altered human interests—the viscous porosity of things. The point is that material agencies in their heterogeneous forms infuse in complex ways. Agencies in all these instances emerge out of such entwinings; they are not antecedent to them. Our genealogical sensibilities must be attuned to such manifold agencies and their emergent interplay. To separate human forces from natural forces or see systemic oppressions as separable from environmental degradation creates divides that will impede our efforts to fully understand and effectively respond to climate injustice.

We often view nature as subdued by technology, the story of human agency impacting the so-called natural order. But we often forget to reverse the interaction, for the Mississippi and Katrina and those shell middens have agency too, agency that impacts the so-called social order. Should we choose for pragmatic reasons to make a division between what is "natural" and what is "social," as I have here, it behooves us to remember the viscous porosity of these phenomena, a porosity that undermines any effort to make an ontological division into kinds—natural and cultural—where the edges are clean and the interactions at best additive. In other words, "social orders" do not happen—do not exist—as phenomena separate from "natural orders." Systemic racisms, to take just one example, are not separable from "a natural world." Environments are pervaded with systemic oppressions as well as with "natural" disasters. Oppressions and poverty are permeated by storms and floods as well as by standards of normalcy, educational systems, and systems of justice. Storms and floods are permeated by consumption patterns, city design, and zoning ordinances. *Viscous porosity* describes all formations, the inevitability of change, and the at times agonizing slowness of forms of suffering to disperse, porously, into other phenomena. Our ecointersectional genealogies must be nimble and attuned to these complex and shifting infusions.

The River and the Swamps

The land along the lower Mississippi floods. Those who live there live with the flooding in different ways. Long before the land was "explored" by Europeans and long before settler-colonialism, many villages were built along the firm ground of the banks of the Mississippi. The original inhabitants of the land that is now called New Orleans were the Chitimacha; the Atakapa, Caddo, Choctaw, Houma, Natchez, and Tunica inhabited other areas throughout what is now called Louisiana. It was a land of abundance: fruit, vegetables, nuts, fish and shellfish, migrating game birds, as well as large game like deer. Choctaw, Houma, and Chitimacha peoples lived with the flooding of the Mississippi. They too would at times shore up the land by building earthen levees, but they also adjusted to the river rather than trying to adjust the river to them and would move to higher ground when the floodwaters rose. Those early levees were only a hint of what was to come.

The levee system in Louisiana has been shaped by numerous forces: technology, economics, weather, colonization, sedimentation patterns, slavery, the Mississippi River, to name a few. To understand the complex exchanges between systemic oppressions and environmental degradation our genealogical sensibilities must be attuned to their viscous porosity. The swirling waters of the Mississippi and year upon year of its seasonal surges created the rich soil that, as colonialists took over the land, fueled a corridor of plantations in Louisiana. From Baton Rouge to New Orleans, plantations bordered both sides of the river. The labor that would farm those plantations came from the bodies of people kidnapped from the continent of Africa as well as from Indigenous people who were forced into slavery.[9] But what the

---

[9] The story of slavery in the United States too often occludes practices of enslaving people of Indigenous descent. According to a recent study by Leila Blackbird (2018, 13), "Native and mixed-race Black-Native people comprised approximately 20 per cent of Louisiana's slave population." For accounts of what has been called "the other slavery," see Reséndez (2016); Gallay (2009); Shefveland (2016).

waters of the Mississippi nurtured, it could also destroy. To protect their sugar cane crops from the flooding, plantation owners forced the people they had enslaved to build levees along the river. Such levees were basically hills of rocks and dirt. The work, dubbed "mud work," was both arduous and dangerous and was a continuous battle as the flood waters and quickly growing vegetation continuously undermined the levees. Slaves packed clay and sand, dirt and rock into ever eroding hills. By 1858 there were over one thousand miles of levees in Louisiana, in some cases as high as thirty-eight feet, built with the labor of enslaved people (Barry 1997).[10]

Not content with the narrow strips of higher ground, in 1849 the US Congress passed an act to drain the swamp lands of Louisiana (U.S. Congress). Congress ceded nearly 10 million acres of federal land[11] to the state, "all the swamp lands therein which are subject to overflow and unfit for cultivation," on the condition "that the proceeds of said lands shall be applied exclusively, as far as necessary, to the construction of the levees and drains . . . to reclaim the swamp and overflowed lands therein" (352–353). The bill allowed logging to generate revenue for such reclamation. As a result, virtually all of the old-growth cypress forests were logged for profit, though relatively little of the land was reclaimed. The loss of the cypress forests accelerated the flooding, as the cypress trees had stored flood waters and held the spongey soils of the marshland together.

Almost half a century passed before the Orleans Levee Board placed value on the swamps. When it became clear that building higher and higher levee walls to control the river would not be sufficient, the Board proposed using the swamp as a spillway by removing levees at strategic spots to reduce flood levels. When the city outgrew its elevated footprint, construction was pushed farther and farther into swampland. That expansion required even more drainage projects with more pipelines and pumping stations to move the water. By the 1930s over thirty thousand acres of swampland had been reclaimed and turned into suburbs. But the reclamation project sank the land even further below sea level. Thanks to redlining practices, most of those who moved to the reclaimed and now lower-lying land were White middle-class families.[12] One of the exceptions to this rule was the Lower Ninth Ward,

---

[10] After the Civil War, convict labor, the slavery by another name discussed in Chapter 3, was deployed to rebuild the levees damaged by the war and by neglect.

[11] This was land that had been taken from the original inhabitants first by the Spanish, then ceded to the French in 1800, land which the United States bought from the French in the Louisiana Purchase soon thereafter.

[12] Ironically, with the exception of the Desire and Florida projects, public housing in New Orleans had been built on relatively high ground less susceptible to flooding.

whose development was fueled by the federal GI Bill, which helped to subsidize loans to returning veterans and became one avenue for middle-class Blacks to move into better neighborhoods and own their homes. Thanks in part to those loans, lower-lying areas, those farther from the river and more recently drained, were turned into suburbs. While middle-class Blacks began to move into the Lower Ninth, middle-class White families began to move to suburbs such as the St. Bernard Parish, where the land was often as low-lying as in the Lower Ninth (Horowitz 2020).[13]

Black Gold

The swamps and marshes hid other wealth: oil and gas. The first successful oil well in Louisiana was drilled in 1901 in Jennings. Over the next fifty years, the oil industry would take a firm hold in the state and, as it did, impact both people and the land. Oil and gas reserves attracted companies who invested in mineral leases and exploration. All that exploration and drilling and transporting brought new residents, and previously small towns boomed. Accessing and transporting the oil and gas required laying new pipelines. Indeed, the Louisiana Department of Natural Resources boasts that the state currently has close to fifty thousand miles of pipeline, approximately one-fifth of which run through wetlands (Louisiana Department of Natural Resources n.d.). The oil and gas industries dredged over ten thousand miles of wetlands for the canals needed to lay pipelines and to access wells. These canals often become pathways for salt incursion, which damages freshwater vegetation. As the marsh plants died, the canals that were dredged became wider, and the salt water intruded all the more. Without anchoring plants, the marsh soil disintegrated, and what was once wetland became open water. The oil and gas industry was not the only factor, but the viscous porosity of wetlands, levees, invasive species, sea level rise, hurricanes, and those dredged canals resulted in extensive wetland loss in Louisiana—about 1,883 square miles of land from 1922 to 2010 (Couvillion et al. 2011, 1).

Consider the US Energy Information Administration map of pipelines in Louisiana (Figure 4.1). It is a crazy cat's cradle of pipelines crisscrossing the land, reaching out to the Gulf and back, as well as lines connecting to the

---

[13] In 1960 93% of the population of St. Bernard was White. Between 1940 and 1960 the population of the Lower Ninth shifted from 69% White to 68% Black (Horowitz 2020, 48).

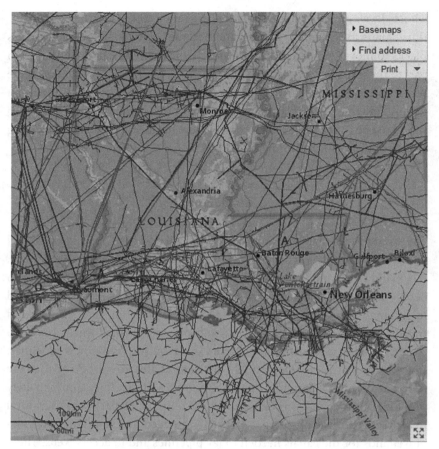

Figure 4.1 The US Energy Information Administration map of pipelines in Louisiana.

Source: US Energy Information Administration, "Energy Disruptions," accessed June 22, 2022, https://www.eia.gov/special/disruptions/.

adjacent states of Texas and Mississippi. Each traces a path of interaction. Along with risks of salt water intrusion, cutting through wetlands to install pipes often alters flooding patterns for adjacent wetlands. Navigation canals for petroleum exploration and other boat traffic contribute to wetland loss. And these losses combine with a high rate of soil subsidence and lack of sediment reaching the wetlands due to the levee effects of the Mississippi. Hurricanes can cause erosion that permanently alters the wetlands. The combined force of Hurricanes Katrina and Rita in 2005 and Gustav and Ike in 2008 caused approximately 328 square miles of costal land loss in

Louisiana (Barras 2009). The viscous porosity of so-called social and natural orders.

Ecointersectional genealogies help to attune us to the complex infusions of more-than-human agency; they also remind us to attend to whose land is being washed away and why. The land those pipelines crisscross is Houma land. Though Houma lifeways often involved moving during seasonal changes or to adjust to times of flooding, the Houma's first settlement was on Ouiski Bayou, high ground north of the area currently known as the city of Houma. The Houma were granted land on Bayou Terrebonne in the late eighteenth century by the Spanish. The French honored the land grant when Spain transferred the land now known as Louisiana to them. When the French sold the land to the United States the purchase agreement required honoring the land grant.

The United States, however, denied the Houma's claim in 1817. When settler-colonizers made their lifeways difficult, the Houma moved deeper into the bayous (Dardar 2000). Due to the relatively small size of the tribe as well as their location in "undesirable land," the Houma were overlooked in the nineteenth century, during the time of the Indian Removal Act. Then, in the early twentieth century, much of the Houma ancestral land was stolen by oil companies, which filed various "legal" claims against the Houma to expropriate the land, such as not having documented proof of birth, not paying taxes, and failing to file a deed. Some non-English-speaking Houma were convinced or coerced into signing papers to "lease" their land; in reality, these were quitclaim deeds through which the Houma lost their land (Williams 2009; Crepelle 2018).

Colette Pichon Battle, director of the Gulf Coast Center for Law and Policy, explains, "[W]e need Federal recognition for the United Houma Nation. . . . They've always existed where we are. But our federal government doesn't recognize them. The problem when the federal government doesn't recognize you when you're the largest tribe in South Louisiana is that you don't get royalties when your land sits on a lot of oil and gas. You also don't get a say in how disasters are cleaned up in your community, with your tribe" (Shah et al. 2015, 102). As the wetlands erode, the land that is lost is Houma land, but land they cannot legally protect, for while the Houma have been recognized by the state of Louisiana, the federal government, perhaps influenced by a strong oil lobby, refuses to recognize the United Houma Nation as a tribe.

Hurricanes like Katrina and the suffering they inflict catch the media's attention. But what is often overlooked are the more subtle and often slow-onset violences. Genealogical sensibilities help us become attuned to what Brian Klopotek, Brenda Lintinger, and John Barbry (2008, 57) refer to as "ordinary trauma," such as "the slow but ongoing trauma of being a poor person of color in the urban United States."[14] It is only by understanding the intricate interactions between such ordinary traumas and extraordinary traumas like Hurricane Katrina that we can truly appreciate the complexity of racial climates. "Comparing the ordinary and extraordinary," they explain, "allows us to compare and contrast the experiences of racialized groups with experiences of indigenous groups" in order to understand the convergences and divergences (56). They compare the extraordinary trauma of the devastation of Katrina, which displaced almost 200,000 Black residents, more than 75,000 of whom did not return, with the efforts made to relocate the Tunica-Biloxi people in the 1930s. Comparing the two situations helps us see that extraordinary traumas, like a hurricane that strikes quickly and leaves newsworthy devastation in its wake, are much easier to identify. But underlying such traumas are often the particulars of ordinary traumas; in the case of the Tunica-Biloxi people and the Houma, "it was the slow, ordinary trauma of racism and colonialism, constantly grinding away at their resources, strength, and traditions," which is far less newsworthy, far more difficult for those not in its midst to recognize, yet just as destructive as a hurricane (59). While acknowledging the importance of culture and place for Black New Orleanians who were displaced by Katrina, Klopotek, Lintinger, and Barbry remind us of a significant difference between their displacement and the displacement of the tribal families who had lived in the area. Alongside the ordinary trauma of being a poor person in the United States, tribal members like the Houma who were displaced had also experienced the subtle ordinary violence of the gradual but relentless loss of their land. The difference, the authors argue, is that their "right to the land might be alienated forever if they were to abandon it, unalterably changing their collective identity. Blacks and whites will be blacks and whites wherever they go, but when a tribe leaves its homeland in the United States, its indigenous status does not necessarily follow to its new home" (59).

Colonialism, salt water, profit, wetlands, levees, hurricanes, the movements of oil and gas, and sea level rise all interact in complex, shifting ways. These infusions not only fuel environmental degradation but are also

---

[14] The concept of ordinary and extraordinary trauma anticipated Rob Nixon's (2011) concept of slow violence.

intimately entwined with the racist exploitation of the Houma, exploitation that denied them their rights to their ancestral land. The ordinary trauma of this exploitation includes the loss of their land as it floods, sinks, and in many cases slips away into the Gulf, as well as the cheating, fraudulent contracts, and land grabs, and the willful ignoring of these actions by both the government and businesses. Black gold, tens of thousands of flooded homes and businesses, huge corporate profits, the hurricane-caused deaths of thousands of Louisianans, the destruction of one-quarter of Louisiana's wetlands, and the merciless exploitation of the Houma are all inseparable and infused in the area currently known as New Orleans.

Toxic Flesh

The dance of agency also happens at a more intimate level. The boundaries between our flesh and the flesh of the world we are of and in are porous. While that porosity is what allows us to flourish—we breathe in the oxygen we need to survive and metabolize the nutrients out of which our flesh emerges—this porosity often does not discriminate against what can kill us. The viscous porosity of the water and food we need to survive often binds itself to strange and toxic bedfellows. Our genealogical sensibilities must be attuned to such porosities for environmental injustices often occur at these ecointersectional moments of exchange.

Hurricane Laura made landfall near Cameron, Louisiana, on August 27, 2020, as a Category 4 hurricane with wind gusts up to 150 mph. As Laura cut its path north across the state, storm damage in the town of Westlake caused a fire in a Biolab plant near Lake Charles that manufactures trichloroisocyanuric acid, a product that is prepared from cyanuric acid via a reaction with chlorine gas and sodium hydroxide. The Biolab plant also manufactures chlorinating granules and other specialty blends for cleaning products (White 2017). John Bel Edwards, the governor of Louisiana, warned residents of the Westlake, Moss Bluff, and Sulphur area to shelter in place with their windows and doors closed and air conditioners turned off as the fire in the Biolab plant was a chemical fire caused by a chlorine leak from the facility and was releasing chlorine gas into the air.[15]

---

[15] Exposure to chlorine gas can cause serious respiratory problems.

As hurricanes move over the land, the high winds, storm surges, and flood waters they bring with them put toxic sites as well as industries that use or produce hazardous substances at considerable risk. The Union of Concerned Scientists identified forty-nine hazardous sites that could be affected by Hurricane Laura, including proposed and currently listed Superfund sites: "A total of 9 sites lie within the predicted extreme storm surge area [of Hurricane Laura] that are currently designated by the EPA as official Superfund sites currently listed on the National Priority List" (Carter 2020).

Chemical fires and floods compromising superfund sites are those extraordinary traumas that make the news. But the ordinary traumas, those day-to-day heightened risks due to the entwining of systemic racisms and ecological indifference, often get ignored. Many in Louisiana live with the ordinary trauma of air pollution, industrial leaks, and other potentially toxic exposures. According to Barbara Allen (2003, 1), "the chemical industry in Louisiana annually reports the equivalent of sixteen thousand pounds of hazardous waste for every citizen in the state," the equivalent of "12.5% of all hazardous waste reported nationally." One of the more infamous areas of Louisiana is the seventy-mile stretch of the River Road that lines both sides of the Mississippi from Baton Rouge to New Orleans. Petroleum and chemical plants as well as landfills dot the river between these two cities. The wastes and pollutants these industries produce has led to the area being labeled Cancer Alley. Many residents refer to it as Death Alley.

Long before modern industries started dotting the River Road, it was bound on both sides by sugar plantations. One of these, Bon Séjour plantation, now called Oak Alley Plantation, in St. James Parish, is a sightseeing destination for tourists who are seldom reminded of the labors of the hundreds of slaves who built the house, planted and tended the sugar cane and the gardens, and lived and died at the whim of the owners. Some of the land around those sugar cane fields transitioned after the Civil War to Black-owned farmland, but in the twentieth century much of the land of Bon Séjour and other large plantations was sold to petrochemical companies.[16] The creation of Cancer Alley arguably began at the turn of the century, when in 1909 Standard Oil opened a refinery in Baton Rouge. Over time, sugar

---

[16] Dow Chemical, to cite just one example, explains that it began with the purchase of four plantations: "Dow came to Louisiana in 1956, drawn by the state's abundant natural resources, excellent transportation network, deep water port, easy access to the Mississippi River, dedicated workforce and available land. With the purchase of four plantations in Iberville and West Baton Rouge parishes, Dow established Louisiana Operations—its first site in the state" (Dow in Louisiana n.d.).

cane fields and farms were replaced by oil-refining and chemical-processing plants. There are now almost 150 plants along the River Road. In St. James Parish alone there are thirty-two petrochemical plants, or one for every 656 residents. And twelve of those thirty-two petrochemical plants are located in the parish's Fifth District, a district—which is 86% Black.

Blacks constitute 40% of those who live along Cancer Alley.[17] If we focus our ecointersectional lens more sharply we uncover an even greater disparity, namely, that many of the census tracts at highest risk for developing cancer from toxin exposure are in Black-dominated neighborhoods: "Eleven of the thirteen high risk tracts in East Baton Rouge Parish have at least 75% black population, and most are well above 90%. As a collective, the high risk tracts in this parish are 84% black. . . . Overall, high risk tracts in Orleans Parish are on average 60% black, compared to approximately 50% black in the remainder of tracts. A significant cluster of low risk tracts is found in three parishes adjacent to Orleans; Jefferson, Plaquemines, and St. Bernard. Nearly all of these tracts range from 75% white to more than 90% white. This provides clear evidence for racial disparities in cancer risk throughout Cancer Alley" (James, Jia, and Kedia 2012, 4373–4374).

For those who live along the River Road the risk of developing cancer is significantly elevated: "The mean cumulative cancer risk was 45.8 per million, meaning that up to 46 individuals out of one million could potentially develop cancer over a lifetime exposure to all carcinogenic air toxics in ambient air" (James, Jia, and Kedia 2012, 4369). The corresponding cancer risk in Louisiana is 37.1 per million and US-wide 30.3. But aggregating often occludes the complex infusions between race and class. Along the River Road those in the lowest income groups (less than $25,400 annually) bear a cumulative cancer risk 12% higher than those in the highest income group (more than $41,600). The most highly polluting industries along the River Road typically cluster in the lowest income tracts: "High risk tracts in Orleans Parish have a combined median household income of $29,600 per year" (4372). Because of the all-too frequent correlation of race and class, those who live in Black-dominated areas along the River Road have a 16% higher cumulative risk compared to those who live in White-dominated areas. But again, aggregating can flatten specifics. People living in the little town of Reserve, Louisiana—a town with a population of less than ten

---

[17] The racial makeup of Cancer Alley is 55% White. The racial makeup of Louisiana is 62.4% White and 33% Black, and national averages are 75.8% White and 13.6% Black (US Census 2021).

thousand, where 64% of the population is Black—are fifty times more likely to get cancer than someone living elsewhere in the United States (Lartey and Laughland 2019).

The toxicity of Cancer Alley manifests in many ways, from toxics like formaldehyde and benzene to heavy metals like mercury that bioaccumulate in flesh. The Noranda Alumina plant on the border of St. John and St. James parishes has been emitting mercury into the air for decades. In 2015, plant officials alerted the Louisiana Department of Environmental Quality of having exceeded safe emission standards and asked for permission to continue running the plant despite this. According to Gordon Russell (2019), a Louisiana journalist, the Department "in late 2017 granted the request, giving Noranda a permit that allowed it to send 1,500 pounds of mercury into the air each year—a bit more than the plant's owners estimated it had already been emitting. The permit called for the company to reduce that, over five years, to a maximum of 1,200 pounds" and pay a fee of $95,750. A Department official explained that "the social and economic benefits of Noranda Alumina outweigh its adverse environmental impacts."[18]

We see clearly represented in these examples the ways that ecological indifference and systemic racisms intermesh in complex and compounding ways. *Economic concerns are placed above environmental health.* Mercury seeps into the flesh of those living along the river—humans and other mammals, fish, and birds. Mercury can cause physiological, neurological, behavioral, and reproductive harm in us all. Reduced fertility and abnormal development have been documented in many animal species, including humans (Evers 2018). Birds lay fewer and smaller eggs and feed their chicks less. Song abilities are impacted for some species of songbirds in ways that negatively impact their reproductive success. Mercury kills toad eggs and tadpoles. Fish and salamanders become sluggish and less responsive to predators. *Ecological indifference intersects with systemic racisms, resulting in some groups of people as well as other life forms being at higher risk from such toxins.* Chronic exposure to mercury, for example, through regular consumption of fish with elevated mercury levels can lead to cognitive impairment and higher risk of fatal diseases in humans and other mammals. The lifetime risk of cancer

---

[18] This facet of the case study could be greatly expanded. So many towns along Cancer Alley have narratives that provide insight into the intermeshing of ecological indifference and systemic racisms. As just one example, *The Guardian* offered a year-long series about the town of Reserve, home to the Pontchartrain Works facility, in which the risk of cancer is fifty times the national average (Laughland and Lartey 2019).

in St. John the Baptist Parish, a town with a population of about forty-three thousand, is eight hundred times higher than the US average.[19]

Ecological indifference places wealth above ecosystem well-being. Systemic racisms place Blacks at higher risk from toxins due to ecological indifference. The interaction between ecological indifference and systemic racisms involves more than mere coincidence. It emerges from a commitment to profit over the safety of lives, or at least some lives. Genealogical sensibilities enable us to see, in locations as disparate as the River Road of Louisiana and Yanomami land in Brazil, how the basic social structures that generate environmental degradation are the same ones that generate systemic oppressions of certain groups of people—the third domain in which the intermeshing of systemic racisms and ecological indifference are manifest.

If we return to St. James Parish and track the polluting industries, we can literally map the ways systemic racisms place Blacks in harm's way—the first domain of the intermeshing of systemic racisms and ecological indifference, namely, differential distribution of risks and harms due to systemic racisms. In St. James Parish 85% of the polluting industries are located in the primarily Black census districts of the towns of Covent and Uncle Sam, which are 61% Black, and the town of St. James, which is 91% Black (Mullin 2020, 31). That intersection is not simply a vestige of past racist practices; it is also a product of current racist practices influencing the siting of polluting industries.

In 2019, the Formosa Plastic Group, a conglomerate headquartered in Taiwan, proposed building a $9.4 billion plastics complex, one of the largest in the world, in northern St. James Parish. Once again, the facility is sited in a majority-Black district. The company requested air permits to release up to 1.6 million pounds of toxic chemicals annually as well as permits to fill in or modify approximately sixty-two acres of wetlands. With the promise of over a thousand permanent jobs and over $350 million in state and local taxes, the parish's planning commission approved the land use permit. In January 2020 Louisiana state regulators issued the needed air permits despite active opposition from local residents.[20] What we see as we travel River Road is that

---

[19] The racial demographics of St. John the Baptist Parish as of 2019 are 56.1% Black, 34.3% White, 5.26% Latino (Data USA 2019).

[20] Formosa Plastics broke ground in March 2020. RISE St. James, a faith-based grassroots organization founded by Sharon Lavigne to advocate for racial and environmental justice, unsuccessfully petitioned the Louisiana Department of Environmental Quality to deny air permits. However, a petition submitted by the Center for Constitutional Rights on behalf of RISE St. James to halt the construction on the grounds that the company did not disclose cemeteries on the land use application was more successful. Formosa has agreed to delay construction activities until February 2021 as a result of the lawsuit filed in July to halt the project until the impact on historic grave sites of enslaved

ecological indifference and systemic racisms have been and continue to be infused.

Black Trash

Arguing for the need to rethink and reframe environmental questions in the context of politicized race and space, Charles Mills (2001) focuses on the standpoint of *black trash*.[21] Arguing that "for centuries in the United States, Blacks *themselves* have been thought of as disposable, an excrescence in the body politic" (74), Mills traces a genealogy in which Blacks are seen as a threat to the White body politic, a threat that had to be contained, controlled, and kept out of sight. "Blacks do not have free range over the topography of the body politic. Rather, they are restricted to second-class spaces, as befitting their second-class, subperson status: N[-]town, Darktown, Bronzeville, the black belt, the ghetto, the inner city, in housing arrangements" (87).[22] Arguing that spaces designated Black neighborhoods are already seen as "polluted" by racial identifiers, "it is only appropriate that the waste products of industrialization should be directed toward them" (89).[23]

One approach to controlling a threat is to contain it, to locate it where it can be surveilled and policed. One way to do this is to incarcerate people, and the state of Louisiana is indeed vested in this approach. Louisiana has an incarceration rate of 1,094 per 100,000 people, compared to a national average of 664 per 100,000; 60.6% of those incarcerated in Louisiana are Black, and

---

Blacks as well as its environmental impacts can be more carefully examined. As of April 2021, construction on the plant remained on hold as the US Army Corps of Engineers had yet to make a decision on the permit that they suspended for reevaluation in November 2020.

[21] Carl Zimring's (2015) *Clean and White* offers a lens similar to that of Mills (2001) in tracing the association of White racial identity with cleanliness and Black racial identity with waste and contamination.

[22] Out of respect and with attention to the impact of the N-word on some people, I have elected to abbreviate the term in quoting Mills (2001).

[23] The complex exchange between systemic racisms and ecological indifference I detail deploying Mills's (2001) concept of Black trash is paralleled in many other locations/exchanges, though differences in detail are essential to understanding how the two are infused in particular locations and during specific time periods. One powerful example is Traci Brynne Voyles's (2015) analysis of the legacy of uranium mining in the Navajo Nation. Voyles examines what she refers to as "wastelanding," the Euro-American construction of Indigenous lands in the American Southwest as wasted and useless. Her analysis traces the intermeshing of colonialism, wastelanding, and environmental injustice. She argues, "The power exerted over environmental resources, and the ways in which those in power construct knowledge about landscapes, are a central part of how what we now call social injustices are produced" (ix).

24.5% Latino.[24] Only 14.9% of those incarcerated are White in a state where 62.4% of the population is White (Prison Polity Initiative 2021).[25]

Imprisonment is not the only way to contain people. Housing is another method. From redlining to the siting of public housing, this approach has been a linchpin of de facto segregation in New Orleans. The siting of schools was one of the mechanisms of de facto segregation. Walter Stern (2018) in *Race and Education in New Orleans* traces the role of the siting of educational facilities in New Orleans before desegregation as one of the ways the city segregated neighborhoods. As Stern explains, cities were intentionally segregated by placing Black public schools in older, racially mixed neighborhood. As just one example, Stern notes how New Orleans' first public high school for Blacks, McDonogh 35,[26] was sited strategically by the School Board in 1917 with the understanding that it would likely transform an economically and racially mixed neighborhood into one that was predominantly Black. Basically, the racial mixing allowed city officials to designate the area as Black and build a Black school knowing it would likely lead to White flight. And leave they did.

Another approach to contain people is to create a new community and create it as Black by building public housing and siting a Black school in the neighborhood. This is the story of Desire. In 1949, New Orleans leaders picked what was then a remote location to build a public housing development. The Desire Housing Project was in a part of the Upper Ninth Ward originally intended as an industrial zone. It was bounded by train tracks on two sides and an industrial canal on a third.

I focus on Desire to show the literal intersections of ecological indifference and systemic racisms. Desire was built adjacent to land that had been a city dump. Desire is Mills's (2001) concept of "black trash" made flesh. The area was used as a dump starting in 1909 and became one of the main dumps for both residential and industrial waste. Situated near the intersection of

---

[24] According to the US Census, in 2021, 33% of the population of Louisiana is Black and only 5.6% is Latino (US Census 2021).

[25] The Prison Policy Initiative's omission of statistics on incarceration rates of Native Americans in Louisiana and in the United States is explained as due to complications with data collection (Daniel 2020). However, they note that based on the 2010 Census the incarceration rate of Native Americans in the United States was 1,291 per 100,000 people, more than double that of Whites.

[26] A complex controversy has arisen over the name of the school, as John McDonogh was a wealthy shipping magnate and plantation owner who both bought and sold slaves. When he died, he left his large estate to the two cities in which he had lived, Baltimore and New Orleans, for the purpose of setting up schools for poor children regardless of gender or race. The city of New Orleans used the money they received to build more than forty schools, including McDonogh 35. Stern (2018) documents how many of them resulted in greater segregation of the city.

Agriculture Street and Almonaster Avenue, what came to be known as the Agriculture Street Landfill was in fact an open, ninety-five-acre dump. Over the years it was filled with thousands of tons of garbage, including industrial and medical waste. Well into the 1950s, when the majority of the garbage from the city was being incinerated, the Agriculture Street Landfill continued to receive refuse. To counter a state law passed in 1948 to prohibit open-air landfills in highly populated areas, city officials designated the Agriculture Street Landfill a "sanitary landfill" by regularly applying DDT (dichloro-diphenyl-trichloroethane) to the surface as well as spraying Diazinon to control the heavy fly infestations—chemicals that have been found to have carcinogenic capacity and are outlawed for residential or environmental use (O'Dwyer 2020b).[27] The collected debris often caught fire, resulting in the dump being called "Dante's Inferno."

Looking for cheap land for public housing, the city turned to Desire in 1949 and by 1956 had built what was then one of the largest public housing sites in the country.[28] And they built it next to an active dump. The city closed the dump in 1958, likely due primarily to the need for residential land rather than to the protests that had been ongoing for over a decade because of the noxious odors and other impacts. The first of the public housing units opened in 1956, two years prior to the closing of the dump. Once complete, the complex had over 260 two-story brick buildings with over eighteen hundred units housing thirteen thousand residents. The city spared every expense in building the complex. Rather than pouring foundations, the structures were built directly on top of the wet swampland. To cut costs, the city built with wood and brick veneer. Wood foundations on swampland soil: even before Hurricane Betsy hit New Orleans in 1965 and flooded the bottom-floor apartments of the Desire Housing Project, the structures had started to sink and structural damage was commonplace.

Betsy hit New Orleans as a Category 4 hurricane. The floodwalls along the Industrial Canal collapsed and the flood waters stretched from Gentilly into St. Bernard Parish. More than six thousand houses in the Lower Ninth,

---

[27] DDT was banned in the United States in 1972 due to evidence of environmental and toxicological harms. Diazinon was outlawed for household use in 2002 and for lawn and garden use in 2003, as well as for various agricultural practices. Diazinon is highly toxic to birds as well as to fish and bees. Chronic exposure has been shown to lower neurobehavioral scores in humans (Anderson and Wexler 2005, vol. 1).

[28] The Desire area was not unpopulated. In the 1940s it was a Black community with a population of nearly eight hundred and included twenty businesses and nine churches. Perhaps the most famous business was the Hideaway Club, where Fats Domino played.

houses belonging primarily to Blacks, stood in flood water for more than a week.[29] The devastation from Betsy had a huge impact across the region, with estimates of $1 billion in property damage (Horowitz 2020, 58). All that debris had to go somewhere, so despite the proximity of the public housing units, the city reopened the Agriculture Street Landfill. Every day approximately three hundred truckloads of trash and waste were dumped in the landfill and burned. Every day for nine months. No restrictions were placed on the debris; much of the refuse contained lead and arsenic (O'Dwyer 2020a).

The Agriculture Street Landfill closed again in the summer of 1966. The city once more seized the opportunity to add more housing units to the now "vacant" land adjacent to the Desire Housing Project. Thanks to a federal program designed to encourage homeownership for lower-income families, the Housing Authority of New Orleans began construction of the Press Park Townhouses in 1969. Over two hundred "lease to own" residences were advertised in the local paper as real estate for "coloreds." In 1975, the Orleans Parish School Board purchased land in the area to build the Moton Elementary School. The School Board knew the area was a landfill and conducted soil testing. While the testing identified numerous toxic substances, including lead, arsenic, and mercury, the Board decided that "remediation" through adding new soil on top of the landfill would be sufficient. It wasn't.

In the late 1970s the Housing Authority began construction of Gordon Plaza, which would include sixty-seven single-family homes. None of the residents of either the Press Park or the Gordon Plaza housing developments were informed that their homes would sit on top of a former dump. In the mid-1980s residents and local environmentalists recommended testing the soil and air in the subdivision when "testing performed at the site of the new Moton Elementary School in 1983–1984 revealed high levels of toxic chemicals in the soil" (O'Dwyer, Loyacano, and McIntire 2020). They were assured by the EPA that of the over 130 toxic chemicals identified, only one, lead, was found in levels high enough to generate health concerns.

---

[29] Many people living in the Lower Ninth believed that city officials had bombed the floodwall, repeating a decision that was made during the flood of 1927 to dynamite the levee at Caernarvon to protect the city's economic center. While no one has found evidence supporting this belief, there is evidence that city officials did close the floodgates along the Industrial Canal, causing the water to gather in the Lower Ninth and thus sacrificing those who lived in the area (cf. Colten, 2007; Horowitz 2020).

Residents successfully fought for retesting, and in 1993 the EPA declared both the residential area and Moton Elementary a Superfund site. In the mid-1990s residents filed class-action lawsuits against the city, its housing authority, and the local school board for knowingly putting their houses and the elementary school in a contaminated area and causing elevated rates of cancer and various respiratory problems.[30] The Agriculture Street Landfill is contaminated with over 140 toxic materials, including arsenic, lead, and polynuclear aromatic hydrocarbons, at least 49 of which are associated with cancer. As one of the cleanup actions the EPA installed a permeable geotextile mat and covered it with two feet of soil to form a barrier against the toxic land. A barrier that was washed away by flooding during Hurricane Katrina. According to a 2018 story in *The Louisiana Weekly*, "Environmental scientist Wilma Subra worked as a community advisor for Gordon Plaza and tested the site after the storm, finding a sediment sludge containing polynuclear aromatic hydrocarbons and heavy metals, as well as high levels of dioxins. A 2013 [Federal Emergency Management Agency] report confirmed toxic chemicals in the area, surveying the Press Park site and finding that toxins persisted under homes and driveways" (Holmes 2018). After Katrina, the community was largely abandoned, though a few residents who owned single-family homes in Gordon Plaza returned after the storm. For financial reasons they had no other options.

Desire is a case study of the infusions of ecological indifference and systemic racisms, of the ways climate and environmental injustices intermesh with histories of harms to ecosystems. The indifference to the health and well-being of those who lived in the neighborhood rests on the same foundation of indifference that resulted in years of toxic contamination of the area's ecosystem. The lineages of that indifference are now placing Blacks in New Orleans at a much higher risk of death from COVID-19. A study published in June 2020, well before the fall peak of virus deaths, found that "Black New Orleanians account for nearly 88 percent of all non-[long-term care] deaths, whereas white New Orleanians account for a much lower 9 percent," a trend that the authors argue is largely consistent with national studies (Weinstein and Plyer 2020).

Indifference is deadly.

---

[30] In March 2022, the residents won a $75.3 million judgment.

Beyond Indifference

"Hurricane Katrina," explain Klopotek, Lintinger, and Barbry (2008, 57), "was, among many other things, a teachable moment, an event that helps us talk about race, poverty, and power. The extraordinary trauma of Katrina briefly exposed the slow but ongoing trauma of being a poor person of color in the urban United States in ways that shocked some observers, but merely confirmed the harsh reality of life for many people of color."

The news coverage after Katrina echoed the refrain "How could this happen in this country?" The theme of "shock" was prevalent in the first few weeks. A story with the headline "Shock Snaps US Media Out of Its Long Trance" in *The Observer* (2005) included a reporter's eyewitness account of the conditions in New Orleans: "There are, I estimate, 2,000 people living like animals inside the city convention centre and around it. They've been there since the hurricane. There's no food. There's absolutely no water. There's no medical treatment. There's no police and no security. And there are two dead bodies lying on the ground and in a wheelchair, both elderly people, both covered with blankets now." Such reports and video footage of conditions in the convention center led to claims like that in *Newsweek*: "It takes a hurricane. It takes a catastrophe like Katrina to strip away the old evasions, hypocrisies and not-so-benign neglect. It takes the sight of the United States with a big black eye—visible around the world—to help the rest of us begin to see again. For the moment, at least, Americans are ready to fix their restless gaze on enduring problems of poverty, race and class that have escaped their attention" (Alter 2005, 42).

Have we indeed begun to see again? And if we do see, do we care? How do we, in our caring, avoid "old evasions, hypocrisies and not-so-benign neglect"? Indifference to lives and lifeways are woven throughout my account of the histories of the area that came to be known as New Orleans. Indifference has histories, and these histories trouble the distinctions we like to make between natural disasters and human-made disasters, between systemic racisms and environmental degradation, between the wreckage from hurricanes and the violence of ordinary trauma, between environmental injustice and climate injustice. In this chapter, I have focused on some of the lineages of indifference and their complex infusions. We need to see disasters for what they are and to carry out scholarship and activism inspired by ecointersectional genealogical sensibilities that can—in the face of the many lineages of those disasters—interrupt willful blind spots and habits of ignoring, provide ways to disclose what is hidden, and interfere with business-as-usual ways of proceeding. Perhaps what we need to move beyond indifference and evasions is the kind of disorientation and rude questioning that is a hallmark of attunements and actions motivated by genealogical sensibilities. And this alongside a determined commitment to the incompleteness of solutions and the need to continuously reexamine and respond.

By refusing forms of forgetting of past injustices or denial of current injustices, genealogical sensibilities provide opportunities to see and attend with the weight of histories and experience their circulations in the present. To learn to see the complex viscous porosity of "social" orders and "natural" orders and to appreciate the intricacies of their infusions. To cultivate activist, lineage-informed, and assertive dissatisfaction wherever oppression is found. To be oriented in the world by questioning and at the same time to be open to being affected by the weight of histories, with their complex reverberations in the present, rather than being affectively indifferent. Those are *the* issues. The cultivation of ecointersectional genealogical sensibilities can incite people to create breaks and openings through unhesitating efforts to question habituated narratives. This is part of what it means to see through the eye of a hurricane, to see in ways that inspire liberatory action toward transformations and reorientations that engender breathing room to live and to live differently.[31] This is the preparation needed to respond to climate injustices.

One such reorientation is articulated by Michelle Roberts, national co-coordinator of the Environmental Justice and Health Alliance for Chemical Policy Reform. She views George Floyd's cry "I can't breathe" as emblematic of the continuing treatment of Blacks and one of the afterlives of slavery. " 'I can't breathe,' " Roberts argues, "predates the United States of America. For us, it came when the first person came from the shores and was shackled to the bottom of that ship" (quoted in Mullin 2020, 29). Robert D. Bullard, a founder of the environmental justice movement, similarly argues that "I can't breathe" is a sign not only of police brutality but also of the greater environmental health burdens carried by Blacks. "Whether we can't breathe because of toxic pollution or policing," says Bullard, "it's the same systemic racism that is killing us" (quoted in Lerner 2020). The Black Lives Matter protests. Genealogical sensibilities. Breathing room.

How do we live, act, think, desire, theorize in ways that create breathing room?

---

[31] I am indebted to the work of Alia Al-Saji (2018) for the concept of breathing room.

5
Weathering the Climate

The weather affects us all. It has bodily impacts as the summer heatwave makes our body glisten with fine sweat or we feel the lining of our nose crinkle in the subzero temperature of a winter cold wave. We may have to live with the stench of smoke from drought-caused forest fires that permeates our homes and lingers for weeks or the musty smell of the mold that saturates our homes after floods from heavy rains or storm surges. We undergo its impacts when we experience the loss of the familiar landscapes that make up our homelands. I have felt those impacts when I see the wide swath of dead trees in my home state of Pennsylvania as the warmer winters allow the hemlock woolly adelgid to destroy stands of hemlocks across the state. Such changes often have affective dimensions, feelings of loss or depression, or anxiety and stress, and can lead to higher rates of interpersonal violence, especially gender violence (Whittenbury 2013; Castañeda Camey et al. 2020; Tuana 2017).

We experience weather in all its immediacies and fluctuations. We pull our coats more tightly around us as clouds cover the sun and the afternoon temperatures drop, or we dash for cover as the skies erupt in a sudden rainstorm. In addition to the sensory experience of the weather—the warmth of the sun or the rain on our skins—the weather can have affective dimensions. Our spirits are buoyed by the brightness of a sunny morning, or we find ourselves disheartened by the day-after-day of overcast skies.

Climate is not the same as weather. The Intergovernmental Panel on Climate Change (2013a, 1450) offers this definition: "Climate in a narrow sense is usually defined as the average weather, or more rigorously, as the statistical description in terms of the mean and variability of relevant quantities over a period of time ranging from months to thousands or millions of years. The classical period for averaging these variables is 30 years, as defined by the World Meteorological Organization. The relevant quantities are most often surface variables such as temperature, precipitation and wind. Climate in a wider sense is the state, including a statistical description, of the climate system."

Climate is not static. It shifts seasonally due to various factors, including the tilt of the Earth. Even average global temperature is variable from year to year due to factors such as the natural fluctuations of the El Niño Southern Oscillation. Global climate change refers to those variations that persist for decades or more. We know from geological evidence that global climate change can be a naturally occurring phenomenon, as we know that the world was warmer in the long distant past.[1] The modifier "anthropogenic" is significant even though often silent in current discussions of climate change as it refers to a persistent shift in the climate due primarily to human activities that are causing an unprecedented rate of global warming. According to NASA's *Vital Signs of the Planet*, "the planet's average surface temperature has risen about 2 degrees Fahrenheit (1 degree Celsius) since the late 19th century, a change driven largely by increased carbon dioxide emissions into the atmosphere and other human activities."[2]

Although global average temperatures are rising at unprecedented rates, not all parts of the Earth are impacted by climate change in the same way. The poles are warming faster than any other region. While the Earth has warmed about 1.8 °F during the past forty years, the Arctic has warmed by more than 2.7 °C, or an astonishing 4.86 °F during the same time period (Box et al. 2019). Precipitation impacts will also vary by region, with some regions experiencing greater rates of precipitation than normal while others will experience higher levels of drought conditions. The point is that assuming that anthropogenic climate change will impact all regions in the same way is a mistake that will lead to ineffective and potentially unjust strategies to address its impacts. Effective adaptation strategies, for instance, must take into account the likely climate risks relevant to a region as well as understand the types of vulnerabilities relevant to that community. Responses to climate impacts must be carefully tied to regional climate risks and vulnerabilities.

Weathering Racial Climates

We experience weather, but we don't experience climate.[3] But racial climates *are* a matter of experience. As Christina Sharpe (2016) illustrates in *In the*

---

[1] In the Cretaceous period, a hundred million years ago, the world was significantly warmer than it is today.
[2] See NASA (n.d.b.).
[3] While we don't experience climate, we do have expectations about it, ideas of how it "should be." When I lived in Oregon, I expected it to rain most days until July, when I would look forward to three

Wake: On Blackness and Being, in the United States anti-Blackness is "the total climate." Sharpe critiques the view of slavery as a "singular event": "In the United States, slavery is imagined as a singular event even as it changed over time and even as its duration expands into supposed emancipation and beyond. But slavery was not singular; it was, rather, a singularity—a weather event or phenomenon likely to occur around a particular time, or date, or set of circumstances. Emancipation did not make free Black life free; it continues to hold us in that singularity. The brutality was not singular; it was the singularity of antiblackness. . . . [A]ntiblackness is pervasive *as* climate" (106). For Sharpe, anti-Blackness in the United States is an *ecology*, a way organisms relate to one another and to their physical surroundings.

The racial climate in the United States involves many different phenomena. Some of us can shop in stores without being followed around; others of us cannot. Patricia Williams (1991) in *The Alchemy of Race and Rights* narrates her experience at a New York Benetton when a young White clerk refused to allow her to enter the store, claiming it was closed despite the fact that it was 1:00 p.m. during a holiday shopping period and there were a number of White shoppers in the store. Or consider the phenomenon of "driving while Black," which refers not only to the experience of Blacks being stopped more often by police but the myriad ways the mobility of individuals seen as Black are restricted and circumscribed. The movements of certain groups of non-White people in the United States are often policed both literally and metaphorically. "Stop and frisk" efforts by police, for example, disproportionately impact Blacks and Latinos.[4] In New York City, to note just one site, Blacks and Latinos make up more than 80% of individuals stopped, even though they constitute approximately 50% of the city population (Goel, Rao, and Shroff 2016). White people in the United States often call the police on Black people who are in public spaces but have not done anything wrong. While there was the well-publicized incident in Central Park of a White woman calling 911 because a Black man asked her to follow park rules and leash her

---

months of gloriously sunny and rain-free days. Now that I live in Pennsylvania, I expect snow in the winter and dearly hope that the snowstorms hold off until all the leaves have dropped from the trees.

[4] I struggled here with the choice of term—Latino, Latina/o, Latinx. I started with Latina/o, but quickly realized that it was undermined in the very next statement because the Latina/os who are disproportionately stopped and frisked are men. Later, when I discuss how Latinos are treated as unwelcome foreigners, the reference is to both women and men. If we reserve the term "Latinx" for nonbinary or trans individuals, the racial climate shifts yet again. I settled on "Latino," both here and throughout the book, but with a clear recognition that it is one of a number of imperfect choices as gender is always implicated.

dog (Stewart 2020), thousands of other incidents each year illustrate a climate in which Whites often see Blacks as threatening and Whites' greater willingness to use the police as a threat, as well as the greater willingness of police to take reports from Whites seriously.[5] Even when the police are not involved, White people in the United States often act as if they are threatened by a Black person, locking their car doors, clutching their handbag more tightly, or moving to the other side of the street (cf. Yancy 2008).

Racial climates are experienced. People live in them, and they live in people. They have bodily impacts, shape communities, leave marks on psyches. Coping with the persistent and repeated stresses of living in racist climates leads to a different type of *weathering*, a constant "wear and tear" on the body caused by repeated exposures to stressors. Studying the impact of systemic racisms in the United States, the public health researcher Arline Geronimus coined the term "weathering" to refer to the effects of what I call "racial climates." "The stress inherent in living in a race-conscious society that stigmatizes and disadvantages Blacks," Geronimus explains, "may cause disproportionate physiological deterioration, such that a Black individual may show the morbidity and mortality typical of a White individual who is significantly older. Not only do Blacks experience poor health at earlier ages than do Whites, but this deterioration in health accumulates, producing ever-greater racial inequality in health with age through middle adulthood" (Geronimus et al. 2006, 826). Racial climates can have a profound effect on health.

Dealing with the afterlives of slavery, what Sharpe (2016) refers to as the climate of anti-Blackness, involves chronic stressors. These stressors are at times linked to poverty and include exposure to chronic stress caused by food insecurity, substandard housing, and greater exposure to violence. However, numerous studies have supported the finding that in the United States, racial disparities in mortality persist even after adjustment for socioeconomic status and health behaviors. Such studies document that systemic racisms, apart from any magnification or muting due to economic status, are a significant component of health and mortality disadvantages for Blacks in the United States (Duru et al. 2012; Geronimus et al. 2001; Tomfohr, Pung, and Dimsdale 2016; Williams and Mohammed 2009).[6] The repeated exposure to

---

[5] For more on this phenomenon, see Ari Shapiro's (2018) interview with Jason Johnson and Henderson and Jefferson-Jones (2020).

[6] The concept of "allostatic load" has been developed to refer to "the accumulation of physiological perturbations as a result of repeated or chronic stressors in daily life," and studies have documented

racist climates leads to physical stress responses, releasing neuroendocrine hormones that build up over time and can lead to health burdens, in particular immune system issues, cardiovascular issues, diabetes, stroke, and cancer (Howard and Sparks 2016).

Just as anthropogenic climate change does not impact all regions of the globe in the same way, racial climates do not follow a singular pattern. The racial climate in the United States for Latinos is not identical to that for Blacks. While both are more likely to be subjected to police profiling than Whites, Latinos are more often treated as unwelcome foreigners despite how many generations of their families have lived in the United States. They are often criticized for speaking Spanish and are told to "go back to their home country" (Lopez, Gonzalez-Barrera, and Krogstad 2018). Racial climates are often impacted by complexly different histories; hence the singular importance of genealogical sensibilities. Anti-Black racism in the United States is permeated by the afterlives of slavery and its many legacies in law and habit, from Jim Crow to incarceration rates. Anti-Latino racism in the United States carries legacies of conquest and brutality. The Mexican-American War, for example, resulted in the forceful capture of Alta California and Santa Fe de Nuevo México, both territories of Mexico. The war resulted in the Mexican cessation of the present-day US states of California, Nevada, Utah, most of Arizona, the western half of New Mexico, the western quarter of Colorado, and the southwest corner of Wyoming. There has been and is currently strong anti-immigration sentiment in some of these states regarding the very people whose ancestors' land was invaded. A long history of violence against Mexicans, including a complex history of lynching and other forms of murder by citizens and state troopers alike, color current instances of anti-Latino racism in the United States (Muñoz Martinez 2014). Racism toward Indigenous people in the United States carries the afterlives of genocide, removal from and loss of homeland, enslavement, and the persistent view of Indigenous people as "savages" without "civilized" religion, government, or familial relations (Bialuschewski and Fisher 2017; Rifkin 2011). The Chinese and subsequently other Asians were seen as dangerous to the peace and security of the country and classified alongside other undesirable aliens, including paupers, criminals, and anarchists. That legacy continues to

---

allostatic load differences by race (Duru et al. 2012, 89). These include levels of hormones secreted in response to stress or biomarkers that signal the effects of such hormones.

permeate contemporary anti-Asian racism in the United States, despite the myth of Asian Americans as the "model minority."[7]

Racial climates contain histories, but they are also informed by contemporary events. Trump's anti-immigration policies and racist rhetoric about Latinos contributed to a 24% increase in hate crimes against Latinos, as documented in a 2017 report by the FBI on hate crimes (Federal Bureau of Investigation 2017). Anti-Asian racism in the United States soared in 2020 as Asians were "blamed" for the pandemic. As important as it is to understand the histories and complexities of shifting racial climates within a country, it is equally important to understand that racial climates are not identical across countries. Anti-Chinese racism in South Korea is not identical to anti-Chinese racism in the United States, which is different from anti-Chinese racism in Australia. Despite those differences, Human Rights Watch (2020) has documented increases in hate crimes against Chinese individuals in all these countries since the discovery of the coronavirus.

The point is that although racial climates impact people's experiences, they do not follow a simple logic and often vary across time and region. While it is my contention that the basic social structures that generate environmental degradation are the same as those that generate systemic oppressions of groups of people, how that link occurs both historically and in the present is complex and variable. To understand how racial climates impact communities and environments requires carefully situated examinations of the lineages of oppressions and practices of environmental exploitation and the ways they are entwined. Hence the importance of the different case studies that I have offered in this book. Sweeping claims about racial climates or efforts to identify universal patterns in the way systemic racisms intersect with environmental degradation will not only be inadequate but will risk ineffective and potentially unjust approaches to addressing either climate/environmental justice or racial climates. Cultivation of ecointersectional genealogical sensibilities is thus an essential component of efforts to address racial climates and the complex ways in which they are linked to environmental degradation. This cultivation requires alertness to the situated lineages of oppressive practices and the often ignored or obscured ways relations of power function. The specifics that entwine oppression and power are found

---

[7] There were a series of anti-Chinese immigration acts, including the Chinese Exclusion Act of 1882. The 1924 Johnson-Reed Act excluded from immigration Chinese, Japanese, Indians, and other Asians on the grounds that they were racially ineligible for naturalized citizenship (Ngai 2004).

in social structures, systems of justice, standards of normalcy, deeply bred dispositions and emotional responses, and current conceptions of the more-than-human world. This cultivated alertness is essential to appreciating the complex infusions of systemic racisms and ecological indifference. It is also the first step toward putting in question the oppressive relations of power and transfiguring them with the goal of developing more just racial climates.

The work of understanding racial climates, as I have said, is thus far larger a project than can be accomplished in one book or by one author. Just as understanding the complexity of anthropogenic climate change and its shifting impacts requires the collaboration of large numbers of analysts who study both the past dynamics and the ongoing impacts of increases of greenhouse gases on the climate, so too understanding the complexity of racial climates requires a scholarly community that pays careful attention to the ways systemic racisms differentially occur for different groups of people and in different countries and regions. Doing so requires attention to the historical legacies and afterlives of past histories of oppressive practices specific to that group and in that region, attention to how they are shaped by contemporary habits, beliefs, and practices of normalization, as well as analyses of the intersections between such lineages of racism and those of ecological indifference. This is the work of genealogical sensibilities.

Such studies require an ecointersectional lens in order to attend to the various ways in which other differences circulate in racial climates. Just as the impacts of climate change on individuals or communities can be affected by economic resources or by gender dynamics, so too the impacts of racial climates can be eased or intensified depending on a community's or individual's economic resources or a region's gender expectations. Tracing the lineages of such differences often reveals complex and frequently uneven imbrications in the systems that link racism and other forms of systemic oppressions and environmental degradation.

Genealogical sensibilities can provoke scholarship and activism that aims to disclose the lineages of racism specific to regions and groups of people within those regions. They incline people to work to reveal how those histories continue to circulate in current beliefs and habits. To be effective in developing more just racial climates, genealogical sensibilities must also be sensitive to the ways histories of systemic oppression of some groups can intersect with and affect other groups, as well as being attentive to the often subtle ways racial climates can shift and change. Efforts to address racial climates must also be grounded in an ecointersectional perspective attentive to the ways racism is intermeshed with other dimensions of systemic oppression such as sexism, ableism, heterosexism, and other forms of normalization, including habits of treating environments as fungible, as consumable. Genealogical sensibilities in this context not only habituate people to disclose racist beliefs, practices, and institutions but they can also habituate people to interrupt and recast the ways people recognize and inhabit the world, to incite change in the ways people think and feel, and predispose them to expect that beliefs and values that once felt inalienable are in processes of transformation.

When Justice Wears a Blindfold

The need for historically and regionally situated ecointersectional genealogies is glaringly evident in the field of climate justice. Over the past two decades, there has been a burgeoning recognition of the need for a climate justice perspective that attends to the ethical dimensions of anthropogenic climate change. Philosophers, geographers, and political theorists have examined how best to respond to inequalities in impacts both in terms of regions (spatial inequalities) and in terms of the impacts on future generations (temporal inequalities); (see, for example, Adger et al. 2006; Gardiner 2006; Lowe and Paavola 2005; Müller 2001; Page 2005; Weston 2008). There has also been a growing literature concerning historical responsibility in which analyses of a country's contributions to current emission totals are considered in light of that nation's moral responsibility for negative impacts and correlated duties regarding mitigation and adaptation efforts (representative examples include Baatz 2013; Caney 2006; Halme 2007; Kronlid 2014; Meyer 2004). The notion of historical responsibility is often part of the climate justice and climate ethics literature that attends to the fact that those regions least responsible for the greenhouse gas emissions that contribute to anthropogenic climate change are often those that now and will continue to experience the highest negative impacts (e.g., Broome 2012; Gardiner 2011; Gardiner et al. 2010; Gardiner and Weisbach 2016; Garvey 2008: Harris 2010; Heyward and Roser 2016; Kasperson and Kasperson 2001; Posner and Weisbach 2010: Preston 2016; Roser and Seidel 2016; Stern 2007; Tremmel and Robinson 2014; Vanderheiden 2008; Williston 2019).

Both a race and a gender justice perspective are almost always absent from these accounts. These omissions are a fascinating study in a form of denial that is kept in place by a persistent valuation of certain types of lives and certain types of experiences as those that count or count more. In this way, the lives and experiences of certain groups of people can be ignored without those in privileged positions even realizing that they are doing so. This is an example of what Charles Mills (1997) labeled an "epistemology of ignorance." He argues that the racial contract in Europe and the United States is held in place in part due to the active production of ignorance, a "pattern of localized and global cognitive dysfunctions (which are psychologically and socially functional), producing the ironic outcome that whites will in general be unable to understand the world they themselves have made" (18).

I contend that this same willful ignorance is at work in the absence of attention to systemic racisms and systemic sexism (and their intersections) in current work on climate ethics and climate justice. Focusing, for example, on gender justice perspectives in the field of climate justice reveals a shocking disconnect between the prevalence of literature on gender and climate change and the almost total absence of this perspective in the climate justice or climate ethics texts previously mentioned. Over the same two decades that have witnessed an exponential rise of literature in the fields of climate justice and climate ethics, there has been a virtual explosion of literature examining the ways in which gender roles, the gendered divisions of labor, and systematic sexism, as well as underlying economic, social, and political factors, can result in gender differences in the impacts of climate change.[8] Research on gender and climate change has also become increasingly more regionally specific, echoing my earlier admonition that when we study racial climates or, in this case, gendered climates, the work be focused on particular regions and attentive to the shifting and complex dynamics of that region.[9] What we

---

[8] A representative but hardly complete sample includes Aguilar (2009); Ahmed and Fajber (2009); Alston (2010, 2015); Alston and Whittenbury (2013); Brody, Demetriades, and Esplen (2008); Cannon (2002); Cuomo (2011); Dankelman (2010); Denton (2002); Glazebrook (2011); Goldsworthy (2010); Hemmati and Rohr (2009); Hunter and David (2009); Lambrou and Piana (2006); MacGregor (2010); Masika (2002); Nagel (2016); Nelson (2007); O'Brien, St. Clair, and Kristoffersen (2010); Robinson (2011); Salleh (2009); Seager (2009); Sen Roy (2018); Terry (2009); Tuana and Cuomo (2014); United Nations Development Program (2009); Women's Environment and Development Organization et al. (2008).

[9] A representative but incomplete sample of work on gender and climate change specific to selected regions includes Allwood (2020); Alston (2015); Anderson, Verner, and Wiebelt (2017); Bhadwal et al. (2019); Boetto and McKinnon (2013); Dougherty et al. (2016); Mainlay and Tan (2012); Mensah, Vlek, and Fosu-Mensah (2020); Ogra and Badola (2015); Omolo (2011); Van Aelst and Holvoet (2016); Venkatasubramanian and Ramnarain (2018).

know and do not know about the gender dimensions of climate change can impact how we respond, and fail to respond, to climate impacts.[10]

Despite the virtual explosion of work on gender and climate change and a vocal and visible activist movement calling attention to the fact that climate justice requires gender justice (e.g., see the websites of the Women's Environment and Development Organization and GenderCC), there is a shocking absence of a gender justice perspective in books published on the general topic of climate ethics or climate justice since 2010.[11] While perhaps not a conscious denial of the importance of the experiences and lives of individuals who are negatively affected by systemic oppressions due, in this example, to systemic sexism in the context of a changing climate, there is, nonetheless, in the very literature that aims to identify and address climate injustices a persistent and willful attention to only certain types of lives and to a limited set of experiences, interests, and concerns. Given the wealth of literature clearly documenting the need for a gender justice perspective in the field of climate justice, the ignoring of gender in the context of analyses of climate justice concerns is too systematic to simply be an innocent oversight or omission. It reflects an emphasis on certain types of lives and certain types of experiences over others, as well as on aggregate impacts without attention to how differences, in this case gender differences, affect such impacts.

This absence is significantly more glaring in work on racial climates. While the omission of attention to gender dynamics within the very literature that

---

[10] While granting the importance of examining and understanding the complex ways in which women and men are, or are not, differentially affected by climate change impacts such as droughts, sea level rise, shifts in vector-borne diseases, or extreme weather events, such studies on their own are not sufficient to fully disclose the role of gender in the context of climate change. We also have to understand all the domains in which gender is relevant to our responses to climate change, from the affective dimensions of how women and men respond to climate change (Alston 2006; Alston and Kent 2008; Larson et al. 2018; Tschakert, Tutu, and Alcaro 2013) to gender differences in the perception of risks related to climate impacts (Assan et al. 2020; Lawson et al. 2020; Mishra and Pede 2017; Owusu, Nursey-Bray, and Rudd 2019; Partey et al. 2020; Quandt 2018; Showalter, López-Carr, and Ervin 2019). Such studies have shown that reactions to and perceptions of climate change risks can diverge due to gender differences and that these differences, in turn, can impact attitudes concerning how best to respond to climate change and thus have an impact on climate justice. Even more complex are the ways in which values embedded in the climate sciences, including studies of mitigation, adaptation, and geoengineering responses to climate change, can have a gender dimension (e.g., Boyd 2002; Buck, Gammon, and Preston 2014; Lee and Zusman 2018; Sikka 2018).

[11] Engagement with literature on gender justice and its relevance to climate justice and climate ethics is absent from the following: Arnold (2014); Broome (2012); Brown (2012); Gardiner and Weisbach (2016); Heyward and Roser (2016); Kanbur and Shue (2018); Kronlid (2014); Moellendorf (2014); Moss (2018); Shue (2014); Thompson and Bendik-Keymer (2012); Tremmel and Robinson (2014); Williston (2019). The exception to this lack of attention to a gender justice perspective is the *Routledge Handbook on Climate Justice* (Jafry, Helwig, and Mikulewicz 2018), which includes a full section (four articles) on climate justice and gender as well as an article on Indigenous perspectives on development.

alleges to be examining issues of climate justice is appalling, there is an even more serious absence when it comes to racial climates in that there has been no similar burgeoning of literature on the topic of what I am calling racial climates. Work on this topic is beginning and we will likely see a similar "explosion" in this literature in the next decade.[12] However, there is a lesson to be learned from the persistent ignoring of the links between climate injustice and systemic oppression due to sexism and due to gendered differences in climate justice literature *despite* a robust literature on this topic. That lesson is that the fight to include the dimension of racial climates within the field of climate justice and climate ethics will take persistence, insistence, and, very likely, transformation of the field.

Racist Conceptualizations

In interrogating the ways systemic racisms are entwined with environmental harms—both harms to certain groups of people and harms to other life forms and to habitats—I have focused on systemic racisms regarding groups of people or communities. But systemic racisms also circulate in our ways of conceptualizing countries and regions. One salient dimension of the racial climate can be found in a mode of classification that is central to discussions of climate justice and the domain of climate policy as well as international relations in general, namely, the distinction between the "Global North" and the "Global South."[13] The United Nations Development Programme (2004) explains that the distinction "rests on the fact that all of the world's industrially developed countries (with the exception of Australia and New Zealand) lie to the north of its developing countries." They explain that while not all

---

[12] In addition to the previously mentioned work of Hage (2017), Vergès (2017), Yusoff (2018), Whyte (2017), and the special issue of *Critical Philosophy of Race* (Tuana and Bernasconi 2019), a recent issue of *Environment and Planning D: Society and Space* is devoted to the topic "Race and the Anthropocene" (Baldwin and Erickson 2020). The enfoldings of racism and ecosystem harms in South Africa is the subject of Lesley Green's (2020) *Rock | Water | Life: Ecology and Humanities for a Decolonial South Africa*. In addition, there has been a growing interest in the work of Sylvia Wynter (Wynter and McKittrick 2015; Kline and Cole 2017; Parker 2021) and Achille Mbembe (Lykke 2019 and Reyes and Chirindo 2020) as providing frameworks for conceptualizing a new form of humanism with crucial implications for understanding and combating anthropogenic climate change.

[13] Any set of terms that aggregates and then divides the world, such as East/West, First World/Third World (with or without the addition of the Second World), developed countries/least developed countries, modern/traditional, high-income economies/low-income economies, are problematic from a number of dimensions. While I will use the designation Global North/Global South (reflecting rankings on the Human Development Index), I do so throughout with quotes in recognition that distinctions like this embed values in ways not always fully transparent.

developing countries are the same, "they all share a set of vulnerabilities and challenges," hence the value of the distinction. This terminology has been deployed in a variety of contexts, but my focus here is on examining the distinction's role in climate policy debates and in literature on gender and climate change.

The distinction between the "Global North" and the "Global South" has gone through numerous figurations over the years. Nour Dados and Raewyn Connell (2012, 13) explain that, given its use in decolonial studies, "the term Global South functions as more than a metaphor for underdevelopment. It references an entire history of colonialism, neo-imperialism, and differential economic and social change through which large inequalities in living standards, life expectancy, and access to resources are maintained." Dados and Cornell's optimism that scholars and policymakers who use the term "Global South" are in fact aware of such "histories of colonialism, neo-imperialism, and differential economic and social change" may not be warranted. Even when the distinction is deployed to advance feminist or decolonial efforts, it is not clear that it can escape its histories and lineage of meanings. The histories of polarizations such as that of the "Global North/Global South" carry lineages of systemic racisms and historical undertones from fields such as sociology and anthropology that described global differences in social progress by drawing broad distinctions between "advanced" and "primitive" societies and lifeways. The lineages of these efforts often circulate in the use of distinctions such as "Global North" and "Global South" even when the distinction is designed to emphasize geopolitical power relations, colonialism, or historical responsibility. Analogous to Edward Said's (1978) reminder that "orientalism" functions through the unshakable assumption of Western superiority and the exaggeration of difference, we find shadowing the distinction between the "Global North" and the "Global South" undertones and historical lineages of conceptions of progress, agency, and modernity on the one side and stasis, vulnerability, and tradition on the other. As Sandra Harding (2008, 1) has argued in *Sciences from Below*, distinctions such as the "Global North" and the "Global South" that are used to divide the world are "haunted by anxieties about the feminine and the primitive, both of which are associated with the traditional." Harding underscores that all that is deemed valuable, "objectivity, rationality, good method, real science, social progress, civilization—the excellence of these and other self-proclaimed modern achievements are all measured in terms of their distance from whatever is associated with the feminine and the primitive" (3). While demonstrating that "the feminine" and "the primitive" are constructed by practices of modernity and its deep connection to empire and colonization, Harding contends that these lineages continue to inform what is valued as conceptions of progress, of technological development, indeed even of science are shaped by a Eurocentric model that is both gendered and racialized. And this so-called progress of Western scientific and technological development is built on the exploitation of people as well as widespread environmental degradation. Dados and Connell (2012) are correct in saying that the distinction between the "Global South" and the "Global North" references histories of colonialism and exploitation. What is less clear is whether the distinction can be deployed without reanimating those very same lineages. Amy Piedalue and Susmita Rishi (2017, 554) argue that it is imperative "we recognize the colonial logic operative in a contemporary geographic imagination of the global South as a category able to contain and delimit a diverse set of places by virtue of appealing to their association with an incomplete modernity—with poverty, ill health, poor sanitation, ethnic conflict, corrupt governance, cultural backwardness, gender inequality, and so on."

Harding's (2008) insights provide a powerful lens through which to appreciate the ways narratives surrounding anthropogenic climate change are informed by and reinforce the framework she labeled "Western modernity." Policy efforts, for example, typically assume that a central goal is to transfer to the "Global South" scientific and technological expertise so that these regions can "modernize." Such policies assume that models of progress and modernization from the "Global North" are the only valuable ones: "Modernization means Western modernization, and 'science' refers only to Western science" (10). What Harding's work so clearly reveals is that the interests that structure knowledge and determine what is known as well as what is ignored are the interests of the more powerful nations and those issues that matter to powerful organizations and corporations. She documents how science "from above" enacts and reinforces a linked set of dualisms in which the first term is privileged: objective/subjective, science/folk wisdom, civilized/savage, modern/primitive, agency/passivity, masculine/feminine.

The "Global North"/"Global South" polarization animates such dualisms in ways that engage complex lineages linked to race as well as to gender. Gail Bederman (1995, 25) argues in *Manliness and Civilization*: "[I]n the context of the late nineteenth century's popularized Darwinism, civilization was seen as an explicitly racial concept. It meant more than simply 'the west' or 'industrially advanced societies.' Civilization denoted a precise stage in human racial evolution—the one following the more primitive stages of 'savagery' and 'barbarism.' Human races were assumed to evolve from simple savagery, through violent barbarism, to advanced and valuable civilization. But only white races had, as yet, evolved to the civilized stage. In fact, people sometimes spoke of civilization as if it were itself a racial trait, inherited by all Anglo-Saxons and other 'advanced' races."

In the nineteenth century, says Bederman, the distinction between "civilized manliness" and "primitive masculinity" was used to link male dominance to White supremacy. "Savage" men were seen as unmanly, incapable of the agency or achievements of "civilized" men. "Savage" women, lacking the refinements of civilization, were forced into lives of labor and drudgery—carrying heavy burdens, doing difficult farm labor—and were without the physical delicacy or spiritual refinements of "civilized" women. The psychologist G. Stanley Hall (1916), to take just one of many examples, insisted that the world's non-White races were children who needed the supervision and protection of the "civilized" world. The alleged weakness and dependency of "primitive" races were often used to justify racial violence, including enslavement and genocide.

Of particular import for debates about anthropogenic climate change are the lineages of beliefs prevalent in the eighteenth and nineteenth centuries concerning how "civilized" races improve on and "cultivate" nature, while "primitive" races simply lived in nature without any effort to improve or master it. The eighteenth-century French naturalist Georges-Louis Leclerc, Comte de Buffon, for instance, refers to how civilized races assist and improve nature. Seeing humans as divinely appointed stewards of God's creation, Buffon believed it was "man's" duty to improve and perfect it, and argued that a key signature of civilization is the modification and enhancement of nature (Glacken 1960, 3). Comparing what he referred to as "brute nature" to cultivated or civilized nature, Buffon (2018, 125) argued that a sign of uncivilized people was the poor condition of their environments: "Compare in effect brute Nature with Nature cultivated," Buffon asserted, "compare the small wild nations of America with our great civilized peoples; compare even those of Africa, which are only half civilized. See at the same time the state of the lands that these nations live in: you will easily determine the small worth of these men by the slight impression that their hands have made on the soil. Either stupid, or lazy, these half-brute men, these unpoliced nations, large or small, only weigh down the globe without comforting the Earth, starve it without nourishing it, destroy without building, using all and renewing nothing."

Such conceptualizations, though now different in tone, haunt debates concerning "the geological agency of humans" and inform arguments proposing a new geological epoch, what has come to be called "the Anthropocene." Michael Simpson (2020, 55), for example, in "The Anthropocene as Colonial Discourse," argues that the conceptual antecedents of the Anthropocene concept date back to views such as those of Buffon's of "civilizing" nature and, as a result, are bound up with and reproduce "Eurocentric and colonial understandings of modernity and its colonial Other that were inherited from European Enlightenment."[14] Legacies of the justifications for colonialism, such as "the ideology of use that casts both land and its native inhabitants as in need of improvement," are identified by Brenna Bhandar (2018, 26) in *Colonial Lives of Property: Law, Land, and Racial Regimes of Ownership*. These legacies continue to circulate in many of the uses of "Global North"/"Global South" distinction. Countries included within the "Global South" are depicted as being at a less advanced stage of cultural and technological development, and those living in the "Global South" are often described as vulnerable and in need of assistance.

These same lineages that link civilization to manliness, progress, control, and the improvement of nature, and which are informed by racial and gender biases, saturate climate discourses. As Cedric Robinson (2019, 22) so clearly articulated in his essay "Notes toward a 'Native' Theory of History," "it was not by chance that the dominated, whether they be classes (the poor, the peasantry, and the working class), ethnic groups and peoples (the Irish, Slavs, Jews, and Blacks), or civilizations (Africans, Asians, New World Indians, etc.), were 'reduced' in those histories to prehuman beings." In ways that echo colonialist efforts to bring "civilization" to "primitive" societies, climate policy often assigns agency to the "Global North," insisting that it bears the responsibility to bring to the supposedly vulnerable "Global South" the technological and policy solutions they are lacking. Such a position assumes that quality of life is to be measured by "northern" standards, what Dipesh

---

[14] It is fascinating to note, and in support of Simpson's claim about conceptual antecedents, that the translators of Buffon's (2018) *The Epochs of Nature*, Jan Zalasiewicz, Anne-Sophie Milon, and Mateusz Zalasiewicz linked its significance to current debates about the term "Anthropocene." As they explain, "the meaning of concepts such as eons, eras, and epochs will undoubtedly continue to develop with future knowledge, but the long shadow of Buffon's original construction of the first of them, *Les Époques*, remains crucial to the scientific and moral arguments for and against a recognition of human traces in the strata of the Earth" (xvi).

Chakrabarty (2000, 7) refers to as "historicism," namely, that the histories of all societies are "variations on a master narrative that could be called 'the history of Europe.'" This "northern" quality of life is thus to be delivered by the "North" to the "South."[15] In this conceptualization, the "Global South" is viewed as vulnerable and less able to act. Gendered tropes of this same dualism often depict women in the "Global South" as victims. In many of the discourses about the responsibility of the "Global North" to the "Global South," we often find lineages of the "contradictory gestures" Alfred López (2001, 208) refers to: "The history of imperialism; that is, of the colonizing impulse, like the history of the West itself, is the history of these contradictory gestures, of the simultaneous desire to apprehend/civilize/assimilate, and suppress/vanquish/exterminate that which is experienced as alien: as other."

Let me be clear, a justice perspective *does* require acknowledging the differential impacts of climate change on regions, as well as recognizing that some groups have more resources for adaptation than others. While not intending to deny either of these points, the repeated trope of conceptualizing the "Global South" through a "deficit" model—as vulnerable, without adequate resources, less able to act in the face of climate impacts—repeats and is informed by centuries of discourses regarding these countries as lesser: less developed, less modern, less technologically advanced, less stable, less capable of self-governance. The problem is that while the rhetoric reflects certain truths, it plays into and perpetuates systemic racist prejudices about these countries embedded in the sensibility of Western modernity and, in so doing, fuels racial climates.

This dual trope of the "Global South" as victim of climate change in need of the resources of the "Global North" to survive is prevalent in climate policy as well as in the climate science literature. The Paris Agreement that became part of the United Nations (2016) Framework Convention on Climate Change, for example, "reaffirms that developed countries should take the lead in providing financial assistance to countries that are less endowed and more vulnerable." This same trope circulates in the climate science literature. Stephen H. Schneider and Janica Lane (2006, 28), in "Dangers and Thresholds in Climate Change," tell us that "the uneven distribution of climate change impacts leaves the hotter, poorer nations—the countries that have less adaptive capacity—more vulnerable and more in need of adaptation. These

---

[15] It goes almost without saying that this is the same logic that has been used to justify the colonization of the "South" in order to advance civilization.

countries are not well equipped to deal with natural disasters such as storms, flooding, and droughts that exact high tolls in lives, fractions of GDP, and quality of life in developing countries. It will be difficult enough for them to cope with moderate and gradual climate change: 'surprises' could devastate them in both absolute and relative terms." Schneider and Lane's aim is well-intentioned: to encourage scientists and policymakers to attend to justice and equity challenges and to provide resources for doing so. In both instances and despite good intentions, the same discourse that Harding (2008) warns us about haunts these texts. The "less developed" are framed as less modern, less capable, less technologically advanced. The next step is that the "more developed" nations are responsible to assist the "less developed" and to do so in such a way that they can be on a path to becoming developed, where the image of "developed" is that provided by the "Global North." Though perhaps not intended, the racist lineages of the "Global South" as backward and unable to help itself reverberates in such accounts. The assumption is that solutions to the climate crisis are not to be found within the cultures and lifeways of the countries that are included in the "Global South." The "Global North" is framed as the norm and the source of reason, science, and technology needed to address the very problems that it itself has created.

Racial climates haunt discussions of climate change impacts in the "Global South." Even feminist efforts to call attention to the impact of climate change on women risk repeating the same tropes of lack and passivity. Consider an early essay on gender and climate change written by Fatma Denton (2002). In what would serve as a field-defining essay, Denton delineated the various reasons why gender matters to climate change impacts, vulnerability, and adaptation. She pointed to women's absence from decision-making and the harmful impacts of ignoring gendered relations in designing adaptation policies. She demonstrated how these omissions would lead to inequitable solutions to climate impacts. Her essay helped to shift attention in the climate domain to the harms caused by the various forms of systemic sexism, including the exclusion of women from climate change science and policy. Denton concludes her analysis by arguing that the inclusion of women and attention to issues of gender equity are essential to successful adaptation projects because "women are at the centre of sustainable development, and ... ensuring greater gender equalities in all sectors would mean that society as a whole will benefit" (17).

Despite the importance of Denton's (2002) analysis, her framing of the problem of gender and climate change is enmeshed in a wider symbolic structure that is at once gendered and racialized. Consider this pivotal quote: "[C]limate negotiations could be seen as a parody of an unequal world economy, in which men, and the bigger nations, get to define the basis on which they participate and contribute to the reduction of growing environmental problems, while women, and smaller and poorer countries, look in from the outside, with virtually no power to change or influence the scope of the discussions" (10). The passage reiterates the common discursive depictions of women as passive and vulnerable and symbolically associates passivity and vulnerability with the "Global South," which is discursively feminized through this trope. Men and "bigger nations" are active and in control; women and "smaller and poorer countries" are virtually powerless. While clearly wanting to bring about positive changes, framing the problem in ways that engage lineages of racialized and gendered discourse risks further entrenching the very issues one is fighting to change. As Saidiya Hartman warns, it risks becoming "the site of the re-elaboration of that condition, rather than its transformation" (Hartman and Wilderson 2003, 185).

Such dualisms are hardly unique to Denton's work; they circulate widely in climate discourses to link agency with the "Global North" and vulnerability with the "Global South," often reanimating linkages between agency, capability, and "civilization" as well as those between manliness and "civilization." Understanding such framings of the problem of climate change is an important component of understanding and addressing racial and gender climates. While valuable research has investigated the gendered dimensions of climate discourse (e.g., Arora-Jonsson 2011; MacGregor 2009; Swim et al. 2018), it is important to address their co-occurrences with systemic racisms to understand how gender bias can be linked to the afterlives of conquest and colonialism that instituted conceptions of non-Western countries as uncivilized, primitive, and vulnerable and in need of protection from the "North." The feminine and the masculine are not simply polarized; the feminine, and all that is linked to it, is seen as lesser, in the sense of less agential, less knowledgeable, less capable. The "Global South" is at once "feminized" and depicted as lesser, namely, less capable of responding, less able to adapt, which animates racial climates. This view in turn intensifies the image of passivity and vulnerability of the women from the "Global South."

It is important not to see this as a critique of a particular theorist. This form of gendered and racialized discourse, with its depiction of women and men in the "Global South" as the victims of climate change, is a common trope throughout the literature on climate change. It frames how we represent climate injustice, as well as the images that are used to depict the gendered impacts of climate change, often by the very organizations whose aim is to call attention to the importance of including gender in climate impact or adaptation studies.

The subtitle and cover image of Henry Shue's (2014) collection of essays, *Climate Justice: Vulnerability and Protection*, for instance, repeats the trope of the "Global South" as vulnerable and in need of protection (Figure 5.1). Despite

Figure 5.1 The cover of Henry Shue's (2014) collection of essays, *Climate Justice: Vulnerability and Protection*.

130 RACIAL CLIMATES, ECOLOGICAL INDIFFERENCE

the complexity of Shue's position, the cover animates the common association of those who are vulnerable as racialized. Viewers are unlikely to see the hand depicted on the cover as representing those who will be protecting the vulnerable; rather, they will see that hand as representing those who are in need of protection. The geographical location of the image is nowhere specified, but the all-too-common association of vulnerability with the "Global South" is likely to trigger the assumption of needed protection from the "Global North."

Analogous to the image on Shue's volume, literature on the gendered impacts of climate change includes myriad images of women suffering from climate change induced drought or floods. The women are always located in what can be clearly read as a "less developed nation" and marked via their activities as poor, often rural laborers (Figure 5.2). Through such images gender, race, class, and nation are linked together to trigger the many connotations of the deficit model of the "Global South" as primitive, undeveloped, not technologically sophisticated, passive, vulnerable. Tina M. Campt (2017, 3) asks in *Listening to Images*, "How do we contend with images intended not to figure black subjects, but to delineate instead differential or degraded forms of personhood or

Figure 5.2 An example of the type of image typically found in publications focusing on the impacts of climate change on women.
Source: United Nations Women Watch (2002); photograph ©Tim McKulka

subjection—images produced with the purpose of tracking, cataloging, and constraining the movement of blacks in and out of diaspora?"

I do not contest the importance of identifying those countries most responsible for anthropogenic climate change. Attention to historical responsibility for the rise in atmospheric greenhouse gas concentrations requires making such distinctions, given that developed countries were the main contributors to this increase in the twentieth century. However, such distinctions must be made with care and caution. There are significant differences even within the categories of developed and developing countries. To aggregate and make claims about responsibility or vulnerability risks flattening the issues.[16] These problems are amplified when using the "Global North"/"Global South" label; as I have argued, doing so risks the imposition of a deficit model in which Western views of progress become the standard by which the "Global South" is measured and found wanting. The racial climate writ large.

Greening the Racial Climate—Population Matters

In the previous section I focused on the ways discourses surrounding the "Global North" and the "Global South" carry racist lineages. These lineages also permeate debates about population control, which in turn feed into racial climates. The phrase "population control" in the context of climate change is relevant to two often interrelated domains. The first involves concerns about overpopulation and the perceived need, in the face of the impact of population on climate change, to control population growth. The second involves concerns about population migration and the perceived need to control the movements of (particular) peoples. The distinction between the "Global North" and the "Global South" informs discussions of population—both overpopulation and population migration—as crucial factors in global climate change. What we find in many of these discourses is another domain in which systemic racisms as well as systemic sexism permeate climate discourses, again at the level of nations.

---

[16] Even in the context of historical responsibility the calculation is complex, and the specific situation of countries must be taken into account. Some developing countries, like Brazil, have made a large contribution to greenhouse gases due to deforestation. Other developing countries, like China, have rapidly increasing energy-related emissions. Yet others, like Indonesia, have low energy-related CO_2 emissions but relatively large land-use emissions (den Elzen et al. 2013). Add to this the distinction between luxury emissions and subsistence emissions and the calculation becomes even more complicated.

The deficit model of the "Global South" is prevalent in debates concerning overpopulation as a key contributor to environmental degradation. In *Reproductive Rights and Wrongs: The Global Politics of Population Control*, Betsy Hartmann (2016) notes that despite changing demographics that have ended the era of rapid global population growth, overpopulation ideology is still common, in part because it is so politically useful.[17] She argues that it is often used to explain and justify economic inequality and as a scapegoat to obscure the root causes of environmental degradation. As just one example, Hartmann references the image-filled book *Overdevelopment, Overpopulation, Overshoot* (Butler 2015), stating that "it blames most every ecological crisis on population growth. The book's lurid photographs of dark-skinned crowds, starving African children, and close-up pregnant bellies rob people of their identity and dignity. That such images are deemed acceptable—the book was featured in a number of major media outlets—is a testament to how deeply racism, like a major river, continues to carve and shape the population landscape. Misogyny follows closely behind" (Hartmann 2016, 9).

The specter of poverty and conflict in the "Global South" haunts population control debates. In "The Tangled Web: The Poverty-Insecurity Nexus," Lael Brainard, Derek Chollet, and Vinca LaFleur (2007, 1) assert that "extreme poverty exhausts governing institutions, depletes resources, weakens leaders, and crushes hope—fueling a volatile mix of desperation and instability. Poor, fragile states can explode into violence or implode into collapse, imperiling their citizens, regional neighbors, and the wider world as livelihoods are crushed, investors flee, and ungoverned territories become a spawning ground for global threats like terrorism, trafficking, environmental devastation, and disease." While recognizing that untangling the poverty-insecurity web is difficult, the authors underscore the urgency of the problem by describing the coming population explosion in those "poor, fragile states." "Over the next four decades," they warn, "the population of developing countries will swell to nearly 8 billion—representing 86 percent of humanity. Addressing poverty—and clearly understanding its relationship to insecurity—needs to be at the forefront of the policy agenda. The world simply cannot afford to wait" (2). Declaring that global security is in the balance, the authors call for a partnering of NGOs, private-sector representatives, governments, and activists to effectively address the

---

[17] The average global family size is about 2.5 children.

poverty-population nexus in developing countries. While certainly acknowledging the need for sound business and effective governance in developing countries, the authors depict the catalysts of this change coming from developed countries, citing the Bill and Melinda Gates Foundation, the Brookings Institution's Wolfensohn Center for Development, and the U.S. Millennium Challenge Corporation, once again repeating the trope of the "Global North" as agential and the "Global South" as vulnerable and in need of assistance.

While the active/passive trope is a problematic component of the distinction, an even more pernicious aspect is identified by Susan E. Rice (2007, 31) in her essay in the same anthology, namely, the belief that poverty is the destiny of certain groups of people. As she puts it, in the United States "global poverty [is] dismissed by many as the inevitable fate of the black, brown, and yellow wretched of the earth," resulting in the majority of Americans being "variously, tired or ignorant of, or indifferent to, a scourge that kills millions across our planet every year." Racial climates are often at the fore of discussions of both global poverty and overpopulation.

Overpopulation in the "Global South" is a continuing refrain in literature on climate change. In *The Urban Fix: Resilient Cities in the War against Climate Change, Heat Islands and Overpopulation,* Douglas Kelbaugh (2019, xii) insists that "another mega-narrative lurking in the background is global population growth, that other hockey-stick curve of the last several centuries." Kelbaugh is clear that overpopulation is only one side of the problem, referencing excessive consumption in developed countries on the other side. However, it is to the "Global South" that he turns to identify the challenge of what he calls "explosive population growth." While recognizing the importance of tailoring strategies to reduce consumption in developed countries, he focuses on reducing birth rates in developing countries, lamenting, for example, that "too few Sub-Saharan African countries have had aggressive birth control and family planning programs" (69).

The linkage of overpopulation and environmental problems is a common refrain. The organization Population Matters (2022), based in the United Kingdom, explains its motivation as follows: "We believe that population is one of the most important, but neglected, contributors to almost all of the major problems facing us today. In particular that means the multiple environmental threats our planet faces, but an unsustainable population also contributes to poverty, conflict, resource depletion and a poorer quality of life for many people." They acknowledge that addressing population is not the only solution, but insist that "adding ever more people to the billions already here makes each of those other solutions harder to achieve." Their bottom line is that "if we are to succeed in preventing the worst effects of climate change, we must take action to address population size."

While the trope of overpopulation in the "Global South" is often repeated, racial climates are particularly intense in discussions of immigration. Most environmental anti-immigration stances embrace a version of Garrett Hardin's (1974) "lifeboat ethic," a position fueled by racial climates, which likely also accounts for its lasting influence. Hardin's explicit aim of shifting beliefs and attitudes about foreign aid and immigration was initially developed in his influential 1974 commentary in *BioScience*, "Living on a Lifeboat," a position he continued to develop in his later publications. In "Living on a Lifeboat" he advocates a Malthusian concept that poverty, conflict, and environmental degradation are mutually reinforcing processes that, unchecked, will spiral out of control. According to Hardin, what is at stake is no less than human survival. Not concerned about anthropogenic climate change, his worry about global-level impacts and potential environmental catastrophe gave rise to a mindset that continues to impact current responses to climate change.

Hardin's (1974) position is based on the concept of "carrying capacity" and his belief that humans may have already exceeded the limited carrying capacity of the land, or, to put it more precisely, each nation may have done so. He illustrates what he calls "the ethics of a lifeboat" as follows: "Approximately two-thirds of the world is desperately poor, and only one-third is comparatively rich. . . . [M]etaphorically, each rich nation amounts to a lifeboat full of comparatively rich people. The poor of the world are in other, much more crowded lifeboats. Continuously, so to speak, the poor fall out of their lifeboats and swim for a while in the water outside, hoping to be admitted to a rich lifeboat, or in some other way to benefit from the 'goodies' on board. What should passengers on a rich lifeboat do?" (561). Hardin argues that any response other than turning away those who wish to be admitted to a rich lifeboat will lead to catastrophe, for the carrying capacity of the land would thereby be compromised.

Hardin's (1974) simplistic metaphor and analysis provide a frame for understanding many of the dynamics currently at play in the discourses of population control. There are various components of this discourse. It begins with the view of overpopulation as a central issue of our time. It then attributes the source of overpopulation to the "Global South," where population growth is allegedly "out of control." In a third step, the link between population growth and poverty, referenced above, is embraced. To this is added the firm belief that the poor of the world, finding limited resources in their own countries, wish to be admitted to the richer countries, where they will have more opportunities. Hardin's position is that even semi-open borders would lead to ultimate carrying capacity collapse, so that "our grandchildren—everyone's grandchildren—would have only a ruined world to inhabit" (567). The fifth step in this discourse is the assumption of a causal link between population growth and environmental degradation: "[E]very human being born constitutes a draft on all aspects of the environment—food, air, water, unspoiled scenery, occasional and optional solitude, beaches, contact with wild animals, fishing, hunting—the list is long and incompletely known" (565). From this follows the ultimate conclusion: that population growth, or even extending the lives of those currently born through food banks or other humanitarian care, will have a negative impact on those nations that have already reached or exceeded their carrying capacity. As Hardin callously phrases it, "*every life saved this year in a poor country diminishes the quality of life for subsequent generations*" (565, italics in original).

The persistence of linkages between the "Global South," overpopulation, and environmental degradation reverberates in anti-immigration sentiments in environmental discourses. Infused in many of those discourses are the racist stereotypes that are a component of racial climates. In a widely read, albeit controversial article in *The Atlantic*, Robert Kaplan (1994) forewarns of what he calls "the coming anarchy" caused by scarcity, crime, overpopulation, tribalism, and disease. "It is time," he explains, "to understand 'the environment' for what it is: the national-security issue of the early twenty-first century. The political and strategic impact of surging populations, spreading disease, deforestation and soil erosion, water depletion, air pollution, and, possibly, rising sea levels in critical, overcrowded regions like the Nile Delta and Bangladesh—developments that will prompt mass migrations and, in turn, incite group conflicts—will be the core foreign-policy challenge from which most others will ultimately emanate, arousing the public and uniting assorted interests left over from the Cold War" (58). Focusing his discussion on West Africa, Kaplan insists that these countries provide a microcosm of "the coming anarchy" in much of what he refers to as "the underdeveloped world." In addition to referencing widespread poverty and disease, Kaplan's position is bolstered by numerous racist descriptions of people in West Africa as embracing "animist beliefs not suitable to a moral society" and as having "loose family structures" (46); young men in Abidjan drinking and gambling during the day and committing crimes at night (49); the Sierra Leone national army as "unruly rabble" (46); children "as numerous as ants" (53); governments throughout the African continent that "show little ability to function, let alone to implement even marginal improvements" (59). Kaplan asserts that "in Africa and the Third World, man is challenging nature far beyond its limits, and nature is now beginning to take its revenge" (53).

In support of his anti-immigration stance, Kaplan (1994, 60) offers a version of Hardin's lifeboat ethic that he attributes to Thomas Homer-Dixon:[18] "Think of a stretch limo in the potholed streets of New York City, where homeless beggars live. Inside the limo are the air-conditioned post-industrial regions of North America, Europe, the emerging Pacific Rim, and a few other isolated places, with their trade summitry and computer-information highways. Outside is the rest of mankind, going in a completely different direction." Kaplan offers his own racist version of the world outside the limo: "a rundown, crowded planet of skinhead Cossacks and *juju* warriors" (62). His environmentalist stance is laced through and through with racist imagery, a trend all too frequent in the United States when environmental concerns are used as justifications for anti-immigration policies.

The concept of "carrying capacity" is frequently deployed by environmentalists to promote racist anti-immigration positions. Some, like the writer and environmentalist Edward Abbey, deploy this conception in an overtly racist manner. In "Immigration and Liberal Taboos," Abbey (1988, 43) argues that "it might be wise for us as American citizens to consider calling a halt to the mass influx of even more millions of hungry, ignorant, unskilled, and culturally-morally-generically impoverished people ... especially when these uninvited millions bring with them an alien mode of life which—let us be honest about this—is not appealing to the majority of Americans. Why not? Because we prefer democratic government, for one thing; because we still hope for an open, spacious, uncrowded, and beautiful—yes, beautiful!—society, for another. The alternative, in the squalor, cruelty, and corruption of Latin America, is plain for all to see."

Other environmentalists deploy the concept of carrying capacity but cloak their racism by insisting that they are working to preserve a way of life. The nonprofit advocacy group (Carrying Capacity Network n.d.), for example, after focusing on the fact that immigration is the cause of approximately 80% of the

---

[18] In his book *Ends of the Earth* Kaplan (1996) references an interview with Homer-Dixon as the source of this quote.

population growth in the United States, explains that they are committed to dramatically limiting immigration "to conserve the best of America—before it's developed, overrun, consumed, and polluted by runaway population growth."

Californians for Population Stabilization (2020b), a nonprofit organization founded in 1986, makes a link between environmentalism and nativism by advancing a quality-of-life argument for limiting immigration. Their lead motto is "Out-of-control population growth threatens the California dream." The argument is that unless the population of California and the country at large is stabilized, we will see "the California dream slipping away and along with it, the American dream." They justify their anti-immigration stance by maintaining that their members simply wish to "save some California and some America for their grandchildren." Insisting that population growth in California is a product of mass immigration, they argue for reduced immigration (approximately 300,000 per year) in order to "meaningfully uphold and nurture the American Dream for people who want to come to the U.S." Here they insist, "[D]on't blame immigrants, blame our government's antiquated immigration policy." Their clear message is that care for "the environment" means limiting immigration. Their 2020 Earth Day ad tells us that "population growth is an environmental problem for the world and for the US." They follow this claim with the statement "And we know why our population has grown by 100 million since [the original] Earth Day." The unspoken answer is depicted in the accompanying image of long lines of people standing in the immigration line of an airport, with the "Welcome home" line for citizens literally empty. The ad ends with a quote from the founder of Earth Day, Senator Gaylord Nelson: "The bigger the population gets, the more serious the problems become.... In this country, it's phony to say 'I'm for the environment but not for limiting immigration'" (Californians for Population Stabilization 2020a).

Immigration anxieties turn on an axis of racialized otherness. As Hartmann (1998, 114) explains, "building an image of an overpopulated, environmentally degraded and violent Third World is politically expedient, especially as it feeds on popular fears that refugees from this chaos will storm our borders."[19] Linking anti-immigrant policies with environmentalism

---

[19] Hartmann's (1998) paper was part of a special issue of *Environment and Urbanization* on the topic of "Sustainable Cities Revisited." The essay was anthologized in *Dangerous Intersections: Feminist Perspectives on Population, Environment, and Development* (Silliman and King 1999), a collection of essays authored by members of the Committee on Women, Population, and the Environment. The Committee aims to expose the racial and class politics behind the anti-immigration movement in the United States.

in ways that disguise systemic racisms and racial privileges is clearly documented in recent studies such as Lisa Sun-Hee Park and David Pellow's (2011) *The Slums of Aspen: Immigrants vs. the Environment in America's Eden* and John Hultgren's (2015) *Border Walls Gone Green: Nature and Anti-immigrant Politics in America*.

As climate change became a dominant theme in policy and in the media, its impacts were added to those of overpopulation and scarcity. Climate change–related impacts aggregated by overpopulation and scarcity were seen as leading to an era of international instability and conflict caused by population movements and failed states.[20] Adding fuel to the fire was the specter of so-called climate refugees, those forced to migrate due to environmental issues caused by climate change. Christian Aid (2007), a British charity, warned of what they called "the human tide" of millions of climate migrants. Comparing the current situation to that of the 66 million people displaced at the end of the Second World War, they warn that "unless urgent action is taken . . . a further 1 billion people will be forced from their homes between now and 2050" (1). While not attributing all such forced migration to climate change, they argue that the effects of climate change will "join and exacerbate the conflicts, natural disasters and development projects that drive displacement" (1).

One influential representation of climate refugees is in the Michael Nash film by the same name which was released in 2010 and claims to represent "the human face of climate change." *Climate Refugees* is designed as a warning. Starting from the assertion that at the time of the release of the film there were 25 million climate refugees, Nash insists that the number will double by 2011, one year later, with the clear implication that the numbers will swell exponentially over subsequent years. These numbers are presented against the backdrop of Senator John Kerry's admonition that "climate change is on a complete collision course with civilization as we know it," followed by the warning that many civilizations have collapsed in the past due to environmental causes. The image of migrating hordes is heightened by over two dozen bright red arrows depicting the inevitable flow of migration from the African continent, South America, and the "Global South" in general inexorably leading to the bullseye of North America, an image guaranteed to fuel already vociferous anti-immigration sentiments in the United States.

---

[20] See, for example, Campbell (2008); CNA Military Advisory Board (2014); Dyer (2008); Manzo (2010).

Hardin's lifeboat ethics remain a key component of racial climates. The image of boat- or plane-loads of immigrants fleeing to the United States to escape climate-induced disasters turns on the racial climate. Populations from the "Global South" are figured as threats to environments and to the "American" way of life. Given that the majority of people displaced by climate change will very likely move within their own country, the fearmongering of films like *Climate Refugees*, which present those in the "Global South" as invading hordes threatening the United States, simply feeds into anti-immigration sentiments, whether intentionally or not. Racial climates can even inform what seem to be neutral concepts like carrying capacity and sustainability. In an oddly perverse twist, racial climates can at times even permeate what appear to be efforts to address racial justice. Roy Beck (1996, 485), an anti-immigration activist who founded NumbersUSA, offers as an argument against immigration what he calls "equal opportunity for the descendants of slavery." While acknowledging that immigration is not the cause of what he labels the "pathologies of the black underclass," he states that immigration "has helped eliminate the best economic friend black Americans had: a tight labor market."

Cloaking racial climates in environmentalism or protectionism is just one of the many mechanisms of the ecology of racial climates. Becoming alert to the shifting lineages and impacts of racial climates, engaging genealogical sensibilities in order to appreciate their complex situatedness in histories and geographical locations call for a community of researchers whose aim is to address these complex issues. Perhaps what is needed is something akin to the Intergovernmental Panel on Climate Change, but in this case to provide policymakers and the general public with regular assessments on racial climates, their implications and potential future risks, as well as to put forward adaptation and mitigation options.[21]

---

[21] Modified from the mission statement of the Intergovernmental Panel on Climate Change (n.d.).

Conclusion

Cultivating Anthropocenean Sensibilities

As I have demonstrated throughout this book, ecointersectional analyses informed by genealogical sensibilities reveal the deep infusions of racial climates and ecological indifference. Such an approach can help us see the ways that our current environmental disasters—from anthropogenic climate change to soil depletion and water pollution—are linked to histories of and continuing practices of overconsumption for some and unfree labor for others; to histories of treating oceans, forests, waterways, and meadows, as well as their inhabitants, as resources for consumption; to histories of indifference in exposing living beings to toxicity; to the insistent separation in dominant sensibilities of humans from other life forms and the persistent structures of domination that animate that separation—nature/culture, mind/matter, savage/civilized.

What I've offered is not a global solution or a set of guidelines for contesting racial climates but rather the recognition that racial climates and ecological indifference happen in placed-based, complexly lineage-informed ways that undermine any search for a single definition of the problem or any type of universalizable "fix." Genealogically informed ecointersectional analyses provide tools for understanding and acting differently *in particular locations*. In other words, these are historically and geographically situated approaches. Such analyses are and must be specific to particular locations and their distinct histories and intricate systems of power. Like Anna Tsing's (2015, 37) "rush of stories" in *The Mushroom at the End of the World*, such analyses "cannot be neatly summed up. Its scales do not nest neatly; they draw attention to interrupting geographies and tempos. These interruptions elicit more stories. This is the rush of stories' power as a science." Like Tsing's ethnographies of how entities make worlds together, genealogically informed ecointersectional analyses do not search for global accounts but work to identify grounded and place-based examinations of systems of power. They do not provide simple solutions; instead they offer insights and attunements that can open us to new ways of living, to new—and to other—ways of world-making.

I came to this study from the context of anthropogenic climate change and the ways in which both gender and racial formations have been obscured in mainstream approaches. In the context of climate change and the myriad ways in which human activities have shaped and been shaped by the world we are of and in, there is another resource to be found in the midst of this crisis, another resource to combine with ecointersectional genealogies. This is a resource that could augment efforts to shift dominant sensibilities, a resource I call "anthropocenean sensibilities."[1] As I will illustrate, this is a paradoxical tool that, when it functions well, does so in such a way as to undo itself from within itself. But it is also a dangerous tool, for if it miscarries, it reinforces that which it attempts to undo. Rather than trying to remove the risk in order to resolve the paradox, I argue that remaining with the paradox, indeed, animating it, opens possibilities for living otherwise.

While anthropocenean sensibilities derive some of their attunements from current discussions of the so-called Anthropocene, its meanings deviate as well as inherit from that perspective. I begin with inheritance and with the recognition that, like most lineages, it is neither simple nor without danger. There can be found in the emerging debates about the Anthropocene a potential turning, a shift in sensibilities, an opportunity to loosen the hold of dominant Western sensibilities that impose what Val Plumwood (1993, 2009) referred to as a hyperseparation of humans from the rest of nature, a structure of dominance in which one side of the binary is valued and the other side is relegated to an inferior position. As I have argued throughout this book, the divide between humans and nature in dominant sensibilities is a racialized divide, a way in which disposability of certain groups of people and certain environments have been woven together.

The promise of the Anthropocene is that it offers opportunities for finding paths beyond the racialized nature/culture divide. As Dipesh Chakrabarty (2021) argues in *The Climate of History in a Planetary Age*, the human as a geological agent cannot be understood from within a purely humanocentric framework but requires a shift to the planetary, a shift that decenters the human. "The globe," Chakrabarty writes, "is a humanocentric construction; the planet, or the Earth system, decenters the human. The doubled figure

---

[1] I originally developed this term in "From a Lifeboat Ethic to Anthropocenean Sensibilities" (2020). My reason for not capitalizing "anthropocenean" will become clear. I am referencing neither geochronologic units nor a global phenomenon.

of the human now requires us to think about how various forms of life, our own and others', may be caught up in historical processes that bring together the globe and the planet both as projected entities and as theoretical categories and thus mix the limited timescale over which modern humans and humanist historians contemplate history with the inhumanly vast timescales of deep history" (4). For Chakrabarty the Anthropocene demands a more capacious understanding of the political that goes beyond humanocentrism, beyond indifference to the biosphere. He contends that the Anthropocene requires us to extend the ideas of politics and justice to the "earthbound," that is, to the agent of history "that is more than human and necessarily includes the human" (210). Following Chakrabarty's gesture, anthropocenean sensibilities can encourage us to attend to relationality and do so in ways that trouble conceptual systems and ways of living that hyperseparate humans from nature. Amplifying this promise is the potential of "the Anthropocene concept," as Gabrielle Hecht (2018a) phrases it, "to bring together researchers across the natural, social and human sciences—as well as the arts—in order to better understand the complex dynamics that put our species at risk" and to clarify "connections between planetary and individual suffering."

But the promise of the Anthropocene is linked to its danger. The danger lingers in Hecht's quote. While insisting on better appreciating the connections between "planetary and individual suffering," it is, for Hecht, risks to "our" species that drives the shift in attention. The danger of the Anthropocene is that the emphasis on the anthropos—on the human as a "geological agent" who is disrupting, accelerating, or refashioning natural processes—rather than decentering the human, will more forcefully center it, binding it with images of mastery, looking yet more insistently for ways to control Earth systems.[2] Consider the opening salvo of the *Ecomodernist Manifesto*: "To say that the Earth is a human planet becomes truer every day. Humans are made from the Earth, and the Earth is remade by human hands . . . [in] the Age of Humans" (Asafu-Adjaye et al. 2015, 6). If attention to the Anthropocene moves in this direction, it will not go beyond humanocentrism. Rather, this kind of attention risks reinforcing all the lineages from which hyperseparation is animated—modernity, colonialization, extractivism—and from which ecological indifference and systemic racisms

---

[2] Climate engineering, particularly solar radiation management via sulphate aerosol injection, is just one of many such proposals for how humans might take yet more control of the climate. See, for example, David Keith's (2013) *A Case for Climate Engineering*.

co-emerge. Here lies the paradox of anthropocenean sensibilities. It is a doubled paradox, for woven into conceptions of the Anthropocene are the very lineages—colonialization, racial capitalism, self-interested individualism—that must be undermined if we are to move beyond hyperseparation.[3] Anthropocenean sensibilities must thus be attentive to the ways lineages of the past are reanimated even in the most seemingly promising transformation. Moving beyond those lineages animates the other dimension of the paradox, namely, that anthropocenean sensibilities aim to move beyond themselves, to destabilize the animating subject, the anthropos.

Anthropocenean sensibilities thus begin with *anthropos* and its myriad meanings. We are told that the Greek word *anthrōpos* can be used for individuals or as a generic term. It has often been translated as "man" or "men" or "mankind" or "humankind." Like the term "mankind" "anthropos", has a masculine sense. When used as a collective noun, it can be gender-inclusive; when used to refer to a particular person, that person is always male. It is set apart from the Greek *gynaika*, which refers to an individual woman or a group of women. An inclusion in the midst of such a separation remains, nonetheless, an implicit exclusion. We hear the term "mankind," and it is unclear who is included.

Paul Crutzen (2006, 16, my emphasis), who first popularized the term "Anthropocene," after providing a long list of activities—population growth, industrialization, urbanization, fossil fuel emissions, land use changes, wetland and forest destruction—phrases it this way: "Considering these and many other major and still growing impacts of human activities on earth and atmosphere, and at all, including global, scales, it thus is more appropriate to emphasize *the central role of mankind* in geology and ecology by using the term 'Anthropocene' for the current geological epoch." Again the allegedly universalizing term "mankind." But is it so clear who has contributed to what has been called "the great acceleration"? The response that has resonated within the literature is a resounding no. Only some groups of humans—groups often differentiated by power and wealth, as well as by race and gender—are responsible for "the great acceleration."[4] This is part of

---

[3] Kathryn Yusoff's (2018) discussion of proposals for the "golden spike" of the Anthropocene, the geological marker used to indicate a shift in geologic time, analyzes the infusions of systemic racisms in three of the possible material beginnings for the Anthropocene.

[4] In addition to studies that demarcate the differential responsibility of global corporations as well as the "developed" countries of the North (see Malm and Warlenius 2019 for an overview of this literature), a different perspective is offered by those who interrogate how certain groups were not included within the category human, as well as delineating the afterlives of being seen as less than

what I mean by anthropocenean sensibilities—not accepting universalizing formations but following the systems of power and the lineages of meanings that continually make and remake who counts as anthropos.

Just as many have interrogated the questionable inclusiveness of the term "mankind," we have seen a growing and vocal body of critique centered on the inclusiveness of the "anthropos" of the Anthropocene. Among the many alternatives to the purportedly inclusive Anthropocene are the Capitalocene (Moore 2016, 2017, 2018), the Chthulucene (Haraway 2015), the Plantationocene (Haraway et al. 2016; Haraway and Tsing 2019), Racial Capitalocene (Vergès 2017), and White Supremacy Scene (Mirzoeff 2018). Such efforts at once critique and build on the notion of large-scale human modification of the earth system, but do so with a critical lens concerning which anthropoi are implicated and how. This attentiveness is a feature of what I refer to as anthropocenean sensibilities. As we consider how social systems and Earth systems infuse, we come to see ever more clearly how it is that not all humans or all lifeways are implicated in such global systems shifts as "anthropogenic" climate change. We begin to understand the force of particular lifeways. We begin to examine and better understand how colonialism, extractivism,[5] and forms of systemic oppressions are at the heart of such shifts. We begin to think from concrete situations and examine the histories of particular practices and their situated impacts. Indeed, current critical interrogations of the concept of the Anthropocene have often arisen from and heightened genealogical sensibilities to reveal the ways discourses of the Anthropocene reify racialized and colonialist biases. Michael Simpson (2020, 64), to take just one example, critiques "the way discourses of the Anthropocene [that] center the role of Western modernity often [remain] bound up in, and [reproduce], deep-seated narratives about the progressive development of European societies through stages of cultural advancement marked by greater social and technological complexity, and greater mastery over nature, which elevated these societies above non-Western peoples and thereby justify the entrenchment and furthering of Western colonial modernity."

---

fully human (e.g., Bennett 2020; Jackson 2020). Bringing these perspectives together would provide a richer response to this type of query.

[5] Gómez-Barris's (2017) study of extractivism in South America provides a rich illustration of how territories in South America have been deemed "extractive zones" by agents of colonial capitalism, and also how local knowledges and what she calls "submerged perspectives" challenge and invert the colonial extractive view.

Accompanying such attention to the often shifting and complex lineages that disrupt the assumption that it is humans as a species that are responsible for shifts in Earth systems is another "Which?" query that is a component of anthropocenean sensibilities. Too often when we query *which* humans are responsible for climate change, we forget to ask another question, namely, "Which *human*?" "Human" is not understood in the same way in all places. Nor is the difference between human and nonhuman similarly framed. As Mark Jackson (2018, 9) illuminates, "There is a geography to what is meant by 'human' and what is meant by 'not-human' or 'other.' When compared to a modern European, an Amazonian Achuar person will have a very different understanding of how the human differs from the non-human. An Ojibwa person might have a very different understanding of the distinction between living and non-living." Anthropocenean sensibilities attune us to the happening of many worlds and the realization that not all of them posit humans via hyperseparation from nature or animate a divide between humans and nonhumans.

Marisol de la Cadena (2019), for instance, draws our attention to what she calls the "anthropo-not-seen" and in doing so animates the paradox of anthropocenean sensibilities. She discusses the protests of the Awajún and the Wampis, two related Indigenous groups in the country currently known as Peru. In 2009 the Awajún and Wampis were part of an Amazonian-wide strike against new laws in Peru that would open their territory to corporate oil exploration, laws that were enacted without their consultation and were thus in violation of international agreements. At the heart of the conflict, Cadena argues, is that the police and the Awajún and Wampis belong to different worlds. The Peruvian state sees the territory as a parcel of land that is under its jurisdiction. The Awajún and Wampis see the land as "an entity that emerges through the Awajun Wampis' practices of life that may, for example, make people the relatives of rivers . . . and kinship between people and water and forest may transform territory into Awajun Wampis, as in a recent public declaration by their leaders in which they said, 'Territory is the Awanjun Wampis'" (37). Here, Cadena argues, we see a historical disagreement over *"what territory is and what kind of relations make it"* (37–38, emphasis in original). She calls this situation "the anthropo-not-seen," which she conceptualizes as "the world-making process through which heterogeneous worlds that do not make themselves through practices that ontologically separate humans (or culture) from nonhumans (or nature)—*nor necessarily conceive as such the different entities in their assemblages*—*both* are obliged into that distinction (and thus willfully destroyed) *and* exceed it. The anthropo-not-seen would thus be *both* the will that requires the distinction (and destroys whatever disobeys the obligation) *and* the excesses to that will: the collectives that, like the Awajun Wampis, are composed of entities that *are not only* human *or* nonhuman because they are also with what (according to the obligation) they should not be: humans *with* nonhumans, and the other way around" (40).

Cadena's work functions as a twofold reminder. On the one hand, we come to better appreciate that colonialism and imperialism not only worked through the lens of race and gender (Lugones 2007, 2010), they also aimed at erasing worlds that did not fit the invader's ontologies. On the other hand, we recognize that other worldings persist despite the force and violence of these efforts.

Anthropocenean sensibilities attune us to world-making processes that do not make themselves through hyperseparation, do not order things according to hierarchies based on race or gender, do not animate ecological indifference, and in which the ground for coupling the exploitation of "humans" and the exploitation of "nature" is undone. Such worldings happen in many different ways and locations. Such sites include but are not limited to Indigenous worldings like those of the Awajún and Wampis or the many Indigenous peoples who have fought against often forced assimilation into dominant sensibilities.[6] They also include many whose lineages give rise to alternatives to dominant sensibilities while yet living in the weave of those very sensibilities. Melanie L. Harris (2017, 53), for example, in *Ecowomanism: African American Women and Earth-Honoring Faiths*, argues that the experiences of African and African American women offer resources for understanding not only the intricate links between earth justice and social justice but also the ground for an alternative vision that embraces the infusings of humans with the earth, "a way of being in community with all others in the earth community." Ecowomanism, Harris explains, "honors its African cosmological roots as a valid and authentic epistemology of how to be an ethical earthling, living on the planet today. As many African peoples' values are shaped by their religion and religious practice, so, too, are ecowomanism's values shaped by their identity as descendants of Africa, carrying embodied and actual indigenous

---

[6] A small sample of this literature includes Bird-David 2017; Cadena 2015; Cusicanqui 2019; Fujikane 2021; Hughes and Barlo 2021; Kimmerer 2013; Simpson 2017; Tallbear 2011; Tangwa 2000; Todd 2015a; Tosam 2019; Viveiros de Castro 2007, 2015.

roots. To honor African cosmologies—and the theories and practices of environmental justice that are informed by them—is an act and method of resistance in that it joins the postcolonial move to expose the remnants of colonial ecology and dismantle this by infusing the field with true ecowomanist epistemology" (76).[7] As Cadena (2019, 40) phrases it, while such lifeways "are obliged into" dominant sensibilities, they yet "exceed" them.

Cadena's anthropo-not-seen is a reminder that the anthropos posited in debates about the Anthropocene, including many of the critiques, is a dominant but not an exhaustive conceptualization. Other conceptions and lifeways of "humans" currently exist and have always existed alongside and at times in the midst of what are now "dominant" sensibilities. Modes of relationality and views of life and nonlife that depart from or are incommensurable with Western sensibilities may offer new paths for addressing racial climates. It is for this reason that Kyle Whyte (2017, 159) argues that the concept of the Anthropocene is "not precise enough." It is a term, Whyte contends, that is incapable of distinguishing between the "reciprocal relationships" of Indigenous peoples "with thousands of plants, animals, and ecosystems," on the one hand, and colonial interventions that disrupt these reciprocal relationships, on the other (159). In a similar vein, Macarena Gómez-Barris's (2017, 4) work aims "to decolonize the Anthropocene by cataloging life otherwise, or the emergent and heterogeneous forms of living that are not about destruction or mere survival within the extractive zone, but about the creation of emergent alternatives."

Cadena's anthropo-not-seen is also a warning to be alert to how lifeways that do not include hyperseparation are at risk of being assimilated or annihilated. As Juanita Sundberg (2014) reminds us, even theories that are or should be open to such lifeways, such as posthumanist theories,[8] occlude and even erase non-European ontologies. They do so initially by "continuously refer[ing] to a foundational ontological split between nature and culture *as if it is universal*" (35). Then in efforts to "think anew" by providing an alternative to this ontological split, such theorists overlook lifeways that have never

---

[7] In *Being Property Once Myself: Blackness and the End of Man*, Joshua Bennett (2020, 4) argues that "the black aesthetic tradition provides us with the tools needed to conceive of interspecies relationships anew and ultimately to abolish the forms of antiblack thought that have maintained the fissure between human and animal."

[8] With "posthumanism" Sundberg (2014, 34) is referring to "a diverse body of work rooted in Anglo-European political philosophy that refuses to treat the human as 1) an ontological given, the privileged if not the only actor of consequence and, 2) disembodied and autonomous, separate from the world of nature and animality."

embraced such a division. We see this occlusion all too frequently in writing that heralds the "promise" of the Anthropocene. To take just one example, Rory Rowan (2014, 447) in "Notes on Politics after the Anthropocene" contends that the Anthropocene cannot "be accommodated within existing conceptual frameworks, including those within which policy is developed, but signals a profound shift in the human relation to the planet that questions the very foundations of these frameworks themselves." He suggest that the Anthropocene instead has triggered "a crisis in our fundamental conceptual categories and our relations to the planet" (449) and in doing so "creates opportunities to cast the planet itself as a key player in the drama of human politics rather than simply its stage" (447). Here we see the assumption of a singular conceptual framework shared by all, "our fundamental conceptual categories." This framework is then posited as one that separates the planet from humans, "the social and the natural, the human and the inhuman," in a typical human/nature divide. The Anthropocene is then seen as creating an opportunity to "think anew" as it reveals that these divides are "muddied by way of their mutually constitutive intrusions" (449). The implication is that there is a universally shared foundational ontological split between nature and culture that the Anthropocene is calling into question. Worlds that do not make themselves through practices that ontologically separate humans and nature are, as Cadena noted, continuously overlooked.

Cadena's (2019) anthropo-not-seen is also a call. As lifeways defend themselves, "stories emerge that may bring into existence a public that does not yet exist" (45). Such stories might disrupt the habit of hyperseparation and open sensibilities to new entities and new forms of relationality—not nature here and human there, but perhaps sensibilities in which the more-than-human both encompasses and exceeds human worlding. These are sensibilities in which a nature/culture hyperseparation is meaningless. Sensibilities in which anthropos is a wholly other thing than that posited in worlds that hyperseparate. While those of us who have inherited dominant Western sensibilities are likely to find such sensibilities unintelligible, anthropocenean sensibilities offer paths to appreciation of such lifeways. Just as debates about the Anthropocene have led to a wealth of critiques concerning which anthropoi are in fact responsible for global transformations, anthropocenean sensibilities are opening those of us caught up in Western sensibilities to *possibilities and actualities of other worlds, to possibilities and actualities of other anthropos.* Anthropocenean sensibilities resist and perhaps exceed the flattening and occlusions that the concept of the Anthropocene cannot avoid creating.

Anthropocenean sensibilities attune us to the particularizing effect of the definite article "the" of *the* Anthropocene in ways that destabilize it. Not *the* Anthropocene, which, as Zoe Todd (2015b, 250) argues, "erases the differential histories and relationships that have led to current environmental crises," but rather sensibilities that call our attention to the many ways and myriad locations in which systemic oppressions and ecological indifference have been infused. This is in the spirit of Kathryn Yusoff's (2018, 2) *A Billion Black Anthropocenes, or None* in which she argues that geology as a racialized epistemic regime is implicated in the dominant classifications and relations of humans to non- or inhuman matter and "the legacy of racialized subjects that geology leaves in its wake." Anthropocenean sensibilities work alongside genealogical sensibilities to encourage attention to the lineages and ongoing legacies of practices of extraction and dispossession that have already resulted in innumerable anthropocenes for those who have been subjected to systemic racisms. From plantations to so-called Indian boarding schools, precious metals to coal mines, there are numerous sites and complex lineages of anthropocenes that arise from the intermeshing of systemic oppressions and ecological indifference. "Imperialism and ongoing (settler) colonialisms," writes Yusoff, "have been ending worlds for as long as they have been in existence" (xiii).

As with the insistent plural of Yusoff's Anthropocenes, anthropocenean sensibilities orient us to scale and location. They resist the prevailing conception that *the* Anthropocene is a unified phenomenon or identifies a specific origin for human intervention in Earth systems. In a similar vein, Hecht (2018b, 112) argues for "putting the Anthropocene in place." Insisting on the indefinite article, Hecht focuses on *an* African Anthropocene as one of "many possible points of departure, many stories to tell, and many ways of telling them" (112). She reminds us that "while the Anthropocene continually inscribes itself in all our bodies—we all have endocrine disruptors, microplastics and other toxic things chugging through our metabolisms—it manifests differently in different bodies. Those differences, along with the histories that generated them, matter a great deal—not just to the people who suffer from them, but also to humanity's relationship with the planet" (Hecht 2018a). Hecht's case studies of uranium and gold mining in various regions and communities in Africa are designed to illustrate how the impacts of such planetary phenomena as climate change, biodiversity loss, and pollution become etched into the bodies of those in these regions who mined or lived with contaminated air and water, and the persistent indifference of those who benefit from the profit of such labor. Hecht's admonition to put the Anthropocene in place is an enactment of the genealogical dimensions of anthropocenean sensibilities, the importance of understanding, in the absence of one, universal Anthropocene, the differing histories *and* geographies of specific places.

Racial climates and ecological indifference similarly require the indefinite article. Systemic racisms and the particularities of ecological indifference happen differently in different locations and time periods, and those differences are often crucial to the ways racial climates are infused with ecological indifference. No grand story will do. What is needed are grounded, place-based analyses with attention to histories and afterlives of systemic oppressions and interrogation of the specific manifestations of ecological indifference woven into that history. With each indefinite article, each time we recognize *a* racial climate and trace the ways it interacts with *a* form of ecological indifference, we get closer to forms of understanding that can offer new ways of seeing and being. Seeing *from* specific locations as well as learning to understand the entanglements *among* locations provide openings to the liberatory promise of anthropocenean sensibilities. In this way we can begin to understand the particular forms of violence often hidden by the planetary scale of the Anthropocene, and we can appreciate the lives and lifeways that are impacted by those particular violences.

The promise of anthropocenean sensibilities is the ability to attend differently and to attend to differences. But this does not mean that the differences to which we each attend are predetermined. In this book I've called attention to the particularities of some of the infusions of systemic racisms and ecological indifference. But attunement to how systemic racisms entwines with the many ways in which power operates—such as speciesism, class, gender, sexuality, systems of education, institutions of justice—is needed to fully appreciate, and transform, the problems we . . . and not just human we's . . . face together. A conception or practice of climate justice that does not do this will inevitably miss its mark.

Debra Bird Rose (2009) calls for new forms of writing in the Anthropocene that will be "capable of shaking up our culture, and awakening us to new and more enlivened understandings of the world, our place in it, and the situated connectivities that bind us into multi-species communities." Attention to the particular has been my response to her call. A response that aspires not only to shift forms of scholarship but also to cultivate shifts in sensibilities needed to live together differently. In the words of Donna Haraway (2016, 101), "we need stories (and theories) that are just big enough to gather up the complexities and keep the edges open and greedy for surprising new and old connections."

Acknowledgments

Tracing the lineages of influence that culminate in any piece of writing is difficult; in the case of *Racial Climates, Ecological Indifference* it is practically impossible as so many different influences have contributed to my current understanding of the complex infusions of systemic racisms and climate change. Having worked in the field of gender and climate change since the early 2000s, my attunements to the complexity of this field were enhanced by working with scholars like Petra Tschakert, Asuncion Lera St Clair, Margaret Alston, Kerri Whittenbury, Carolyn Sachs, Bettina Koelle, Jennifer Wagner-Lawlor, Shaheen Moosa, and Chris Cuomo. My understanding of climate science and climate risk assessment has benefited from over a decade of partnering with an amazing group of climate scientists, including Klaus Keller, Robert Lempert, Richard Alley, Rob Nicholas, Erica Smithwick, and Chris Forest. My thinking on systemic racisms and climate change was richly influenced by work that arose from a partnership with Achille Mbembe, Sarah Nuttall, and Robert Bernasconi, which led to a series of talks and a conference on race and climate change cosponsored by the Wits Institute for Social and Economic Research and the Rock Ethics Institute that culminated in a special issue of *Critical Philosophy of Race*. The insights that emerged from this partnership were enhanced by working with a group of amazing graduate students whose thoughts inform my work on systemic racisms in myriad ways: Romy Opperman, Eyo Ewara, William Paris, Axelle Karera, Emma Velez, Tiffany Tsantsoulas, and Desiree Valentine. My attention to issues of colonialism have been influenced by the opportunity to work with and learn from decolonial scholars like María Lugones, Alejandro Vallega, Omar Rivera, and Eduardo Mendieta. The opportunity to engage in dialogue with an interdisciplinary group of graduate students on the infusions of racial climates and ecological indifference while polishing the final version of this manuscript enhanced my thoughts in ways difficult to describe. My thanks to Hanan Al-Alawi, Kathleen Blackwood, Müge Gedik, Rebecca Haddaway, Kayla Huxford, Jessica Klimoff, Su Young Lee, Julianne Mann, Hannah Matangos, Michelle Meeks, and Merve Sen.

My great good fortune in working over many years with Del McWhorter on topics relevant to this book circulates throughout my writing.

Particular thanks to Charles Scott, who has served as my muse throughout the writing of this book. No one inspires frenzy or awakens lyric quite like he.

I thank the generosity of several editors and publishers for permission to incorporate into this book revised versions of ideas I first tried out in articles published in their journals and anthologies:

- The first two sections of Chapter 3 are reprinted in a revised version from "Climate Apartheid: The Forgetting of Race in the Anthropocene," *Critical Philosophy of Race* 7, no. 1 (2019): 1–31 with permission from Penn State Press. The discussion of Brazilian charcoal production in Chapter 2 is substantially revised from an earlier discussion of that topic in this article.
- Some material in the first and second sections of Chapter 4 appear in an earlier form in "Viscous Porosity: Witnessing Katrina," in *Material Feminisms*, edited by Susan Hekman and Stacy Alaimo (Durham, NC: Duke University Press, 2007).
- Earlier and significantly different versions of some of the material in Chapter 5 appeared in "Climate Change through the Lens of Feminist Philosophy," in *Meta-Philosophical Reflection on Feminist Philosophies of Science*, volume 317 of *Boston Studies in the Philosophy and History of Science*, edited by Maria Cristina Amoretti and Nicla Vassallo (Dordrecht: Springer Press, 2016); "Gendering Climate Knowledge for Justice: Catalyzing a New Research Agenda," in *Research, Action and Policy: Addressing the Gendered Impacts of Climate Change*, edited by Margaret Alston and Kerri Whittenbury (Dordrecht: Springer Press, 2013); and "From a Lifeboat Ethic to Anthropocenean Sensibilities," *Environmental Philosophy* 17, no. 1 (2020): 101–123.

References

Abbey, Edward. 1998. "Immigration and Liberal Taboos." In *One Life at a Time, Please*, 41–44. New York: Henry Holt.

Abram, David. 1996. *The Spell of the Sensuous: Perception and Language in a More-Than-Human World*. New York: Pantheon Books.

Abram, David, with Tema Milstein and José Castro-Sotomayor. 2020. "Interbreathing Ecocultural Identity in the Humilocene." In *Routledge Handbook of Ecocultural Identity*, ed. Tema Milstein and José Castro-Sotomayor, 5–25. Abingdon: Routledge.

Adger, W. Neil, Paavola Jouni, Saleemul Hug, and Mary Jane. Mace. 2006. *Fairness in Adaptation to Climate Change*. Cambridge, MA: MIT Press.

Aguilar Revelo, Lorena. 2009. *Training Manual on Gender and Climate Change*. International Union for Conservation of Nature and the United Nations Development Programme in partnership with the Gender and Water Alliance, ENERGIA International Network on Gender and Sustainable Energy, United Nations Educational, Scientific and Cultural Organization, Food and Agriculture Organization, and the Women's Environment and Development Organization as part of the Global Gender and Climate Alliance. San José, Costa Rica: Masterlitho S.A.

Ahmed, Sara. 2008. "Imaginary Prohibitions: Some Preliminary Remarks on the Founding Gestures of the 'New Materialism.'" *European Journal of Woman's Studies* 15(1): 23–39.

Ahmed, Sara, and Elizabeth Fajber. 2009. "Engendering Adaptation to Climate Variability in Gujarat, India." In *Climate Change and Gender Justice*, ed. Geraldine Terry, 39–56. Oxfam Working in Gender and Development Series. Rugby, UK: Practical Action Publishing.

Ajibade, Idowu. 2017. "Can a Future City Enhance Urban Resilience and Sustainability? A Political Analysis of Eko Atlantic City, Nigeria." *International Journal of Disaster Risk Reduction* 26: 85–92.

Ajibade, Idowu, and Gordon McBean. 2014. "Climate Extremes and Housing Rights: A Political Ecology of Impacts, Early Warning and Adaptation Constraints in Lagos Slum Communities." *Geoforum* 55: 76–86.

Alaimo, Staci. 2012. "Insurgent Vulnerability and the Carbon Footprint of Gender." *Kvinder, Køn & Forskning* 18: 11–22.

Alipour, Yasi. 2021. "Allison Janae Hamilton with Yasi Alipour." *Brooklyn Rail*, April. https://brooklynrail.org/2021/04/art/Allison-Janae-Hamilton-with-Yasi-Alipour.

Al Jazeera. 2012. "Nigeria Forces Thousands from Floating Slum." 29 July. https://www.aljazeera.com/news/2012/7/29/nigeria-forces-thousands-from-floating-slum.

Allen, Barbara. 2003. *Uneasy Alchemy: Citizens and Experts in Louisiana's Chemical Corridor Disputes*. Cambridge, MA: MIT Press.

Allwood, Gill. 2020. "Mainstreaming Gender and Climate Change to Achieve a Just Transition to a Climate-Neutral Europe." *Journal of Common Market Studies* 58: 173–186.

Al-Saji, Alia. 2018. "Hesitation as Philosophical Method—Travel Bans, Colonial Durations, and the Affective Weight of the Past." *Journal of Speculative Philosophy* 32(3): 331–359.
Alston, Margaret. 2006. "'I'd Like to Just Walk Out of Here': Australian Women's Experience of Drought." *Sociologia Ruralis* 46(2): 154–170.
Alston, Margaret. 2010. "Gender and Climate Change in Australia." *Journal of Sociology* 47(1): 53–70.
Alston, Margaret. 2015. *Women and Climate Change in Bangladesh*. New York: Routledge.
Alston, Margaret, and Jennifer Kent. 2008. "The Big Dry: The Link between Rural Masculinities and Poor Health Outcomes for Farming Men." *Journal of Sociology* 44(2): 133–147.
Alston, Margaret, and Kerri Whittenbury, eds. 2013. *Research, Action and Policy: Addressing the Gendered Impacts of Climate Change*. Dordrecht: Springer Netherlands.
Alter, Jonathan. 2005. "The Other America." *Newsweek*, September 19, 42–48.
Alvarez, Alex. 2017. *Unstable Ground: Climate Change, Conflict, and Genocide*. Lanham, MD: Rowman & Littlefield.
Amadi, Ako. 2012. "Eko Atlantic City—A Sustainable Development Project for Coastal States? Best Practices from Other Countries." In *Eko Atlantic Project—Opinion Papers*. Africa Portal. https://www.africaportal.org/publications/eko-atlantic-project-opinion-papers/.
Amazon Watch. 2019. "Amazon Deforestation Is Driven by Criminal Networks." https://amazonwatch.org/news/2019/0917-amazon-deforestation-is-driven-by-criminal-networks-report-finds.
American Lung Association. 2020. "State of the Air." http://www.stateoftheair.org/.
Amnesty International. 2016. "Nigeria: Fire and Demolitions That Left 30,000 Homeless Must Be Urgently Investigated. November 11. https://www.amnestyusa.org/press-releases/nigeria-fire-and-demolitions-that-left-30000-homeless-must-be-urgently-investigated/.
Andersen, Lykke E., Dorte Verner, and Manfred Wiebelt. 2017. "Gender and Climate Change in Latin America: An Analysis of Vulnerability, Adaptation and Resilience Based on Household Surveys." *Journal of International Development* 29(7): 857–876.
Anderson, Bruce D., and Philip Wexler. 2005. *Encyclopedia of Toxicology*. San Diego, CA: Academic Press.
Appiah, Kwame Antony. 2020. "The Case for Capitalizing the B in Black." *The Atlantic*, June 18. https://www.theatlantic.com/ideas/archive/2020/06/time-to-capitalize-blackand-white/613159/.
Arnold, Denis. G., ed. 2014. *The Ethics of Global Climate Change*. Cambridge: Cambridge University Press.
Arora-Jonsson, Seema. 2011. "Virtue and Vulnerability: Discourses on Women, Gender and Climate Change." *Global Environmental Change* 21(2): 744–751.
Asafu-Adjaye, John, Linus Blomqvist, Stewart Brand, Barry Brook, Ruth DeFries, Erle Ellis, Christopher Foreman, David Keith, Martin Lewis, Mark Lynas, Ted Nordhaus, Roger Pielke Jr., Rachel Pritzker, Joyashree Roy, Mark Sagoff, Michael Shellenberger, Robert Stone, and Peter Teague. 2015. "Ecomodernist Manifesto." www.ecomodernism.org.
Assan, Elsie, Murari Suvedi, Laura Schmitt Olabisi, and Kenneth Joseph Bansah. 2020. "Climate Change Perceptions and Challenges to Adaptation among Smallholder

Farmers in Semi-Arid Ghana: A Gender Analysis." *Journal of Arid Environments* 182: 104247–104252.
Baatz, Christian. 2013. "Responsibility for the Past? Some Thoughts on Compensating Those Vulnerable to Climate Change in Developing Countries." *Ethics, Policy and Environment* 16(1):94–110.
Balbus, John, and Cecilia Jeanne Sorensen, eds. Forthcoming. "Impacts of Climate Change on Women's Health." Special issue of *International Journal of Environmental Research and Public Health*.
Baldwin, Andrew, and Bruce Erickson, eds. 2020. "Race and the Anthropocene." Special issue of *Environment and Planning D: Society and Space* 38(1).
Bales, Kevin. 2012. *Disposable People: New Slavery in the Global Economy*. Berkeley: University of California Press.
Bales, Kevin. 2016. *Blood and Earth: Modern Slavery, Ecocide, and the Secret to Saving the World*. New York: Spiegel & Grau.
Baptist, Edward E. 2014. *The Half Has Never Been Told: Slavery and the Making of American Capitalism*. New York: Basic Books.
Barad, Karen. 2007. *Meeting the Universe Halfway: Quantum Physics and the Entanglement of Matter and Meaning*. Durham, NC: Duke University Press.
Barras, John A. 2009. *Land Area Change and Overview of Major Hurricane Impacts in Coastal Louisiana, 2004–08*. U.S. Geological Survey Scientific Investigations Map 3080. Pamphlet. Reston, VA: U.S. Dept. of the Interior.
Barry, John M. 1997. *Rising Tide: The Great Mississippi Flood of 1927 and How It Changed America*. New York: Simon & Schuster.
Baxter, Brian. 2005. *A Theory of Ecological Justice*. London: Taylor and Francis.
Beal, Frances M. 1969. *Black Women's Manifesto: Double Jeopardy: To Be Black and Female*. New York: Third World Women's Alliance. http://www.hartford-hwp.com/archives/45a/196.html.
Beck, Roy. 1996. *The Case against Immigration: The Moral, Economic, Social, and Environmental Reasons for Reducing U.S. Immigration Back to Traditional Levels*. New York: W. W. Norton.
Beckert, Sven. 2014. *Empire of Cotton: A Global History*. New York: Alfred A. Knopf.
Beckert, Sven, and Seth Rockman, eds. 2016. *Slavery's Capitalism: A New History of American Economic Development*. Philadelphia: University of Pennsylvania Press.
Bederman, Gail. 1995. *Manliness and Civilization: A Cultural History of Gender and Race in the United States, 1880–1917*. Chicago: University of Chicago Press.
Bennett, Jane. 2001. *The Enchantment of Modern Life: Attachments, Crossings, and Ethics*. Princeton, NJ: Princeton University Press.
Bennett, Joshua. 2020. *Being Property Once Myself: Blackness and the End of Man*. Cambridge, MA: Belknap Press of Harvard University Press.
Bergad, Laird, and Stuart Schwartz. 2007. *The Comparative Histories of Slavery in Brazil, Cuba, and the United States*. Cambridge: Cambridge University Press.
Berlin, Ira. 1992. *Slaves without Masters: The Free Negro in the Antebellum South*. New York: New Press.
Bhadwal, Suruchi, Ghanashyam Sharma, Ganesh Gorti, and Sudeshna Maya Sen. 2019. "Livelihoods, Gender and Climate Change in the Eastern Himalayas." *Environmental Development* 31: 68–77.
Bhandar, Brenna. 2018. *Colonial Lives of Property: Law, Land, and Racial Regimes of Ownership*. Durham, NC: Duke University Press.

Bialuschewski, Arne, and Linford D. Fisher, eds. 2017. "Native American Slavery in the Seventeenth Century." Special issue of *Ethnohistory* 64(1).
Biello, David. 2015. "Mass Deaths in Americas Start New CO_2 Epoch." *Scientific American*, March 11. https://www.scientificamerican.com/article/mass-deaths-in-americas-start-new-co2-epoch/.
Bilge, Sirma. 2013. "Intersectionality Undone: Saving Intersectionality from Feminist Intersectionality Studies." *Du Bois Review* 10(2): 405–424.
Bird-David, Nurit. 2017. *Us, Relatives: Scaling and Plural Life in a Forager World*. Berkeley: University of California Press.
Blackbird, Leila K. 2018. "Entwined Threads of Red and Black: The Hidden History of Indigenous Enslavement in Louisiana, 1699–1824." PhD diss., University of New Orleans. https://scholarworks.uno.edu/td/2559.
Blackmon, Douglas A. 2008. *Slavery by Another Name: The Re-Enslavement of Black Americans from the Civil War to World War II*. New York: Doubleday Books.
Boetto, Heather, and Jennifer McKinnon. 2013. "Gender and Climate Change in Rural Australia." *Critical Social Work* 14(1): 15–31.
Borgen Project. 2018. "10 Facts about Poverty in Brazil." March 2. https://borgenproject.org/10-facts-about-poverty-in-brazil/.
Box, Jason E., William T. Colgan, Torben Røjle Christensen, Niels Martin Schmidt, Magnus Lund, Frans-Jan W. Parmentier, Ross Brown, Uma S. Bhatt, Eugénie S. Euskirchen, Vladimir E. Romanovsky, John E. Walsh, James E. Overland, Muyin Wang, Robert W. Corell, Walter N. Meier, Bert Wouters, Sebastian Mernild, Johanna Mård, Janet Pawlak, and Morten Skovgård Olsen. 2019. "Key Indicators of Arctic Climate Change: 1971–2017." *Environmental Research Letters* 14(045010): 1–18.
Boyd, Emily. 2002. "The Noel Kempff Project in Bolivia: Gender, Power, and Decision-Making in Climate Mitigation." *Gender and Development* 10(2): 70–77.
Brainard, Lael, Derek Chollet, and Vinca LaFleur. 2007. "The Tangled Web: The Poverty-Insecurity Nexus." In *Too Poor for Peace? Global Poverty, Conflict, and Security in the 21st Century*, ed. Lael Brainard and Derek Chollet, 1–30. Washington, DC: Brookings Institution Press.
The Brazilian Report. 2020. "Coronavirus Aid Sees Brazil's Poverty Rates Drop to Lowest Level since 2004." *Wilson Center, Brazil Institute*, August 14. https://www.wilsoncenter.org/blog-post/coronavirus-aid-sees-brazils-poverty-rates-drop-lowest-level-2004.
Brody, Alyson, Justina Demetriades, and Emily Esplen. 2008. *Gender and Climate Change: Mapping the Linkages. A Scoping Study on Knowledge and Gaps*. Vol. 44. Brighton, UK: Institute of Development Studies.
Broome, John. 2012. *Climate Matters: Ethics in a Warming World*. New York: W. W. Norton.
Brown, Donald A. 2012. *Climate Change Ethics: Navigating the Perfect Moral Storm*. New York: Routledge.
Buck, Holly Jean, Andrea R. Gammon, and Christopher J. Preston. 2014. "Gender and Geoengineering." *Hypatia* 29(3): 651–669.
Buckingham, Susan, and Virginie Le Masson, eds. 2019. *Understanding Climate Change through Gender Relations*. New York: Routledge.
Buffon, Georges Louis Leclerc, comte de. 2018. *The Epochs of Nature*. Trans. and ed. Jan Zalasiewicz, Anne-Sophie Milon, and Mateusz Zalasiewicz. Chicago: University of Chicago Press.

Bullard, Robert D. 1994. *Dumping in Dixie: Race, Class, and Environmental Quality*. 2nd edition. Boulder, CO: Westview Press.
Bullard, Robert D., Paul Mohai, Robin Saha, and Beverly Wright. 2007. *Toxic Wastes and Race at Twenty 1987–2007: A Report Prepared for the United Church of Christ Justice & Witness Ministries*. Cleveland, OH: United Church of Christ.
Burkhart, Brian. 2019. *Indigenizing Philosophy through the Land: A Trickster Methodology for Decolonizing Environmental Ethics and Indigenous Futures*. East Lansing: Michigan State University Press.
Butler, Rhett A. 2020. "Brazil Revises Deforestation Data: Amazon Rainforest Loss Topped 10,000 sq km in 2019." *Mongabay*, June 10. https://news.mongabay.com/2020/06/brazil-revises-deforestation-data-amazon-rainforest-loss-topped-10000-sq-km-in-2019/.
Butler, Tom, ed. 2015. *Overdevelopment, Overpopulation, Overshoot*. San Francisco: Goff Books.
Cadena, Marisol de la. 2015. *Earth Beings: Ecologies of Practice across Andean Worlds*. Durham, NC: Duke University Press.
Cadena, Marisol de la. 2019. "Uncommoning Nature: Stories from the Anthropo-Not-Seen." In *Anthropos and the Material*, ed. Penny Harvey, Christian Krohn-Hansen, and Knut G. Nustad, 35–58. Durham, NC: Duke University Press.
Californians for Population Stabilization. 2020a. "Earth Day at 50: A Message from Its Founder on Environmentalism, Population Growth, and Immigration." https://capsweb.org/ad-campaigns/earth-day-at-50-a-message-from-its-founder-on-environmentalism-population-growth-and-immigration.
Californians for Population Stabilization. 2020b. "Who We Are." https://capsweb.org/about.
Callicott, J. Baird. 1989. *In Defense of the Land Ethic: Essays in Environmental Philosophy*. Albany: State University of New York Press.
Calmore, John O. 1993. "Spatial Equality and the Kerner Commission Report: A Back-to-the-Future Essay." *North Carolina Law Review* 71(5): 1487–1518.
Campanella, Richard. 2008. *Bienville's Dilemma: A Historical Geography of New Orleans*. Baton Rouge: Louisiana State University Press.
Campbell, Kurt M., ed. 2008. *Climatic Cataclysm: The Foreign Policy and National Security Implications of Climate Change*. Washington, DC: Brookings Institute.
Campt, Tina M. 2017. *Listening to Images*. Durham, NC: Duke University Press.
Caney, Simon. 2006. "Environmental Degradation, Reparations, and the Moral Significance of History." *Journal of Social Philosophy* 37: 464–482.
Cannon, Terry. 2002. "Gender and Climate Hazards in Bangladesh." *Gender and Development* 10(2): 45–50.
Capizzi, Dario, Sandro Bertolino, and Alessio Mortellit. 2014. "Rating the Rat: Global Patterns and Research Priorities in Impacts and Management of Rodent Pests." *Mammal Review* 44:148–162.
Carastathis, Anna. 2016. *Intersectionality: Origins, Contestations, Horizons*. Lincoln: University of Nebraska Press.
Carbado, Devon W. 2013. "Colorblind Intersectionality." *Signs: Journal of Women in Culture and Society* 38(4): 811–845.
Carbado, Devon W., Kimberlé Williams Crenshaw, Vickie M. Mays, and Barbara Tomlinson. 2013. "Intersectionality: Mapping the Movements of a Theory." *Du Bois Review: Social Science Research on Race* 10(2): 303–312.

Carmichael, Stokely, and Charles V. Hamilton. 1967. *Black Power: The Politics of Liberation.* New York: Vintage Books.

Carrying Capacity Network. n.d. https://www.carryingcapacity.org/.

Carter, Jacob. 2020. "Superfund Sites in Path of Hurricane Laura Could Leach Toxic Contaminants." *The Equation,* August 26. https://blog.ucsusa.org/jacob-carter/superfund-sites-in-path-of-hurricane-laura-could-leach-toxic-contaminants.

Castañeda Camey, Itzá, Laura Sabater, Cate Owren, and A. Emmett Boyer. 2020. *Gender-Based Violence and Environment Linkages: The Violence of Inequality.* Ed. Jamie Wen. Gland, Switzerland: IUCN.

Centers for Disease Control. 2022. "Health Disparities." Accessed January 17, 2022. https://www.cdc.gov/nchs/nvss/vsrr/covid19/health_disparities.htm#RaceHispanicOrigin.

Chakrabarty, Dipesh. 2000. *Provincializing Europe: Postcolonial Thought and Historical Difference.* Princeton, NJ: Princeton University Press.

Chakrabarty, Dipesh. 2021. *The Climate of History in a Planetary Age.* Chicago: University of Chicago Press.

Chamberlain, Gethin. 2012. "'They Are Killing Us': World's Most Endangered Tribe Cries for Help." *The Observer,* April 21. https://www.theguardian.com/world/2012/apr/22/brazil-rainforest-awa-endangered-tribe.

Chen, Mel. 2012. *Animacies: Biopolitics, Racial Mattering and Queer Affect.* Durham, NC: Duke University Press.

Chartoff, Michael, Marc Morial, Mike Tidwell, Mark Fischetti, David Wessel, Haley Barbour and Aaron Brossard. 2005. "Transcript for September 4." CNN News, September 4. https://www.nbcnews.com/id/wbna9179790.

Christian Aid. 2007. "Human Tide: The Real Migration Crisis." https://reliefweb.int/sites/reliefweb.int/files/resources/47F1DFB5696BEE43C12572DB0035D16A-Full_Report.pdf.

Cho, Sumi, Kimberlé Williams Crenshaw, and Leslie McCall. 2013. "Toward a Field of Intersectionality Studies: Theory, Applications, and Praxis." *Signs* 38(4): 785–810.

Clare, Stephanie D. 2019. *Earthly Encounters: Sensation, Feminist Theory, and the Anthropocene.* Albany: State University of New York Press.

CNA Military Advisory Board. 2014. *National Security and the Accelerating Risks of Climate Change.* Alexandria, VA: CNA Corporation.

Cohen, Leonard. 1972. *The Energy of Slaves: Poems.* London: Johnathan Cape.

Cole, Luke W., and Sheila R. Foster. 2001. *From the Ground Up: Environmental Racism and the Rise of the Environmental Justice Movement.* New York: New York University Press.

Collins, Patricia Hill. 1990. *Black Feminist Thought: Knowledge, Consciousness, and the Politics of Empowerment.* Boston: Unwin Hyman.

Collins, Patricia Hill. 2019. *Intersectionality as Critical Social Theory.* Durham, NC: Duke University Press.

Collins, Patricia Hill, and Sirma Bilge. 2016. *Intersectionality.* Cambridge and Malden: Polity Press.

Colten, Craig. 2007. "Environmental Justice in a Landscape of Tragedy." *Technology in Society* 29(2): 173–179.

Combahee River Collective. 1979. "The Combahee River Collective Statement." In *Capitalist Patriarchy and the Case for Socialist Feminism,* ed. Zillah Eisenstein, 362–372. New York: Monthly Review Press.

Connors, Libby. 1997. "Environmental Racism: Australia, Shell and Nigeria." *Social Alternatives* 16(2): 50–52.
Cooper, Anna Julia. 1892. *A Voice from the South*. Xenia, OH: Aldine.
Costa, Federico, Caio Graco Zeppelini, Guilherme S. Riberio, Norlan Santos, Renato Barbosa Reis, Ridalva D. Martins, Deborah Bittencourt, Carlos Santos, Jonas Brant, Mitermayer G. Reis, and Albert I. Ko. 2021. "Household Rat Infestation in Urban Slum Populations: Development and Validation of a Predictive Score for Leptospirosis." *PLoS Neglected Tropical Diseases* 15(3): 1–13. e0009154.
Cotton, William R., and Roger A. Pielke. 2007. *Human Impacts on Weather and Climate*. Cambridge: Cambridge University Press.
Coulthard, Glen Sean. 2014. *Red Skin, White Masks: Rejecting the Colonial Politics of Recognition*. Minneapolis: University of Minnesota Press.
Couvillion, Brady R., John A. Barras, Gregory D. Steyer, William Sleavin, Michelle Fischer, Holly Beck, Nadine Holly, Brad Griffin, and David Heckman. 2011. *Land Area Change in Coastal Louisiana from 1932 to 2010*. U.S. Geological Survey Scientific Investigations Map 3164. Pamphlet. Reston, VA: U.S. Geological Survey.
Crenshaw, Kimberlé. 1989. "Demarginalizing the Intersection of Race and Sex: A Black Feminist Critique of Antidiscrimination Doctrine, Feminist Theory and Antiracist Politics." *University of Chicago Legal Forum*, 1, article 8: 139–168.
Crenshaw, Kimberlé. 1991. "Mapping the Margins: Intersectionality, Identity Politics, and Violence against Women of Color." *Stanford Law Review* 43(6):1244–1299.
Crenshaw, Kimberlé. 1993. "Beyond Racism and Misogyny: Black Feminism and 2 Live Crew." In *Words That Wound: Critical Race Theory, Assaultive Speech and the First Amendment*. ed. Mari J. Matsuda, Charles R. Lawrence III, Richard Delgado, and Kimberlé Williams Crenshaw, 111–132. Boulder, CO: Westview Press.
Crenshaw, Kimberlé. 2020. "Interview by Katy Steinmetz." *Time*, February 20. https://time.com/5786710/kimberle-crenshaw-intersectionality/.
Crepelle, Adam. 2018. "Standing Rock in the Swamp: Oil, the Environment, and the United Houma Nation's Struggle for Federal Recognition." *Loyola Law Review* 64: 141–186.
Crutzen, Paul J. 2006. "The 'Anthropocene.'" In *Earth System Science in the Anthropocene: Emerging Issues and Problems*, ed. Eckart Ehlers and Thomas Krafft, 13–18. Berlin: Springer.
Cuomo, Chris J. 2011. "Climate Change, Vulnerability, and Responsibility." *Hypatia* 26(4): 690–714.
Cuomo, Chris, and Nancy Tuana, eds. 2014. "Climate Change." Special issue of *Hypatia: A Journal of Feminist Philosophy* 29(3).
Cusicanqui, Silvia Rivera. 2019. *Ch'ixinakax Utxiwa: On Decolonising Practices and Discourses*. Trans. Molly Geidel. Cambridge, UK: Polity Press.
Dados, Nour, and Raewyn Connell. 2012. "The Global South." *Contexts* 11(1): 12–13.
Dankelman, Irene. 2010. *Gender and Climate Change: An Introduction*. London: Earthscan.
Daniel, Roxanne. 2020. "Since You Asked: What Data Exists about Native American People in the Criminal Justice System?" *Prison Polity Initiative*, April 22. https://www.prisonpolicy.org/blog/2020/04/22/native/.
Dardar, T. Mayheart. 2000. *Women-Chiefs and Crawfish Warriors: A Brief History of the Houma People*. Trans. Clint Bruce. New Orleans, LA: United Houma Nation.
Data USA. 2019. "St. John the Baptist Parish, LA." https://datausa.io/profile/geo/st-john-the-baptist-parish-la#about.

Delegates to the First National People of Color Environmental Leadership Summit. 1991. "The Principles of Environmental Justice." https://www.nrdc.org/sites/default/files/ej-principles.pdf.

Denton, Fatma. 2002. "Climate Change Vulnerability, Impacts, and Adaptation: Why Does Gender Matter?" *Gender and Development* 10(2): 9–20.

Deyle, Steven. 2005. *Carry Me Back: The Domestic Slave Trade in American Life.* New York: Oxford University Press.

Djoudi, Houria, Bruno Locatelli, Chloe Vaast, Kira Asher, Maria Brockhaus, and Bimbika Basnett Sijapati. 2016. "Beyond Dichotomies: Gender and Intersecting Inequalities in Climate Change Studies." *Ambio* 45(Suppl 3): 248–262.

Dodge, Richard Irving. 1877. *The Plains of the Great West and Their Inhabitants.* New York: G. P. Putnam's Sons.

Donoghue, Katy. 2021. "Allison Janae Hamilton Interrogates Myths around Landscape and Stories of Paradise." *Whitewall Art*, August 13. https://whitewall.art/art/allison-janae-hamilton-interrogates-myths-around-landscape-and-stories-of-paradise.

Dougherty, Sarah, John Taylor, Rizqa Hidaynai, and Dati Fatimah. 2016. *Lessons from Improving a Gender-based Climate Change Vulnerability Assessment.* London: International Institute for Environment and Development.

"Dow in Louisiana." n.d. Dow Corporate. https://corporate.dow.com/en-us/locations/louisiana.html.

Drèze, Jean, and Amartya Sen. 1989. *Hunger and Public Action.* Oxford: Clarendon Press.

Dubow, Saul. 1989. *Racial Segregation and the Origins of Apartheid in South Africa, 1919–36.* New York: Palgrave Macmillan.

Dubow, Saul. 2014. *Apartheid, 1948–1994.* Oxford: Oxford University Press.

Dunn, Christopher. E. 2007. "The Intergenerational Transmission of Lifetime Earnings: Evidence from Brazil." *The B.E. Journal of Economic Analysis & Policy* 7(2): 2–40.

Duru, O. Kenrick, Nina T. Harawa, Dulcie Kermah, and Keith C. Norris. 2012. "Allostatic Load Burden and Racial Disparities in Mortality." *Journal of the National Medical Association* 104(1): 89–95.

Dyer, Gwynne. 2008. *Climate Wars: The Fight for Survival as the World Overheats.* London: Random House.

The Economist. 2016. "Slavery's Legacies; Race Relations." 420(9006, September 8): 51.

Eichen, Joshua R. 2020. "Cheapness and (Labor-)Power: The Role of Early Modern Brazilian Sugar Plantations in the Racializing Capitalocene." *Environment and Planning D: Society and Space* 38(1): 35–52.

Eko Atlantic. N.d. "Real Estate Solutions to Meet Your Needs." Accessed August 1, 2022. https://www.ekoatlantic.com/invest/residential/.

Ellis, Aunjanue. 2021. "'The Landscape Is a Witness': Aunjanue Ellis Talks with Allison Janae Hamilton." *Bitter Southerner*, July 27. https://bittersoutherner.com/summer-voices/aunjanue-ellis/allison-janae-hamilton.

den Elzen, Michel G. J., Jos G. J. Olivier, Niklas Höhne, and Greet Janssens-Maenhout. 2013. "Countries' Contributions to Climate Change: Effect of Accounting for All Greenhouse Gases, Recent Trends, Basic Needs and Technological Progress." *Climatic Change* 121(2): 397–412.

Energy Information Administration. 2005. *Household Vehicles Energy Use: Latest Data and Trends.* Washington, DC: U.S. Department of Energy.

Engineering and Mining Journal. 1908. "Metal, Mineral, Coal and Stock Markets: Current Prices, Market Conditions and Commercial Statistics of the Metals, Minerals and Mining Stocks: Quotations from Important Sources." December 26: 1279–1284.

Engineering and Mining Journal. 1909. "Texas May Stop Convict Mining." November 27: 1068.

Environmental Protection Agency. 2021a. "Environmental Justice." Accessed May 2021. https://www.epa.gov/environmentaljustice.

Environmental Protection Agency. 2021b. "Particulate Matter (PM) Pollution." Accessed May 2021. https://www.epa.gov/pm-pollution.

Evans, Simon. 2020. "Analysis: Coronavirus Set to Cause Largest Ever Annual Fall in CO_2 Emissions." Carbon Brief, April 9. https://www.carbonbrief.org/analysis-coronavirus-set-to-cause-largest-ever-annual-fall-in-co2-emissions.

Evers, D. 2018. "The Effects of Methylmercury on Wildlife: A Comprehensive Review and Approach for Interpretation." In *The Encyclopedia of the Anthropocene*, ed. Dominick A. DellaSala, and Michael I. Goldstein, 5: 181–194. Oxford: Elsevier.

Farmer, Blake. 2020. "The Coronavirus Doesn't Discriminate, but U.S. Health Care Showing Familiar Biases." National Public Radio, April 2. https://www.npr.org/sections/health-shots/2020/04/02/825730141/the-coronavirus-doesnt-discriminate-but-u-s-health-care-showing-familiar-biases.

Fashae, Olutoyin Adeola, and Olumide David Onafeso. 2011. "Impact of Climate Change on Sea Level Rise in Lagos, Nigeria." *International Journal of Remote Sensing* 32(24): 9811–9819.

Federal Bureau of Investigation. 2017. "Hate Crime Statistics." https://ucr.fbi.gov/hate-crime/2017.

Felzemburgh, Ridalva D. M., Guilherme S. Ribeiro, Federico Costa, Renato B. Reis, José E. Hagan, Astrid X. T. O. Melendez, Deborah Fraga, Francisco S. Santana, Sharif Mohr, Balbino L. dos Santos, Adriano Q. Silva, Andréia C. Santos, Romy R. Ravines, Wagner S. Tassinari, Marília S. Carvalho, Mitermayer G. Reis, and Albert I. Ko. 2014. "Prospective Study of Leptospirosis Transmission in an Urban Slum Community: Role of Poor Environment in Repeated Exposures to the Leptospira Agent." *PLoS Neglected Tropical Diseases* 8(5): e2927.

Ferrer, Ada. 2014. *Freedom's Mirror: Cuba and Haiti in the Age of Revolution*. Cambridge: Cambridge University Press.

de Figueiredo Correia, Jader. 1967. "Relatório Figueiredo/The Figueiredo Report." http://www.mpf.mp.br/atuacao-tematica/ccr6/dados-da-atuacao/grupos-de-trabalho/violacao-dos-direitos-dos-povos-indigenas-e-registro-militar/relatorio-figueiredo.

Foucault, Michel. 1966. *The Order of Things: An Archaeology of the Human Sciences*. New York: Vintage Books.

Foucault, Michel. 1977. "Nietzsche, Genealogy, History." In *Language, Counter-Memory, Practice*, ed. Donald F. Bouchard, trans. Donald F. Bouchard and Sherry Simon, 139–164. Ithaca, NY: Cornell University Press.

Foucault, Michel. 1991. "Question of Method." In *The Foucault Effect: Studies in Governmentality with Two Lectures by and an Interview with Michel Foucault*, ed. Graham Burchell, Colin Gordon, and Peter Miller, 73–86. Chicago: University of Chicago Press.

Fox-Genovese, Elizabeth, and Eugene D. Genovese. 2008. *Slavery in White and Black: Class and Race in the Southern Slaveholders' New World Order*. Cambridge: Cambridge University Press.

Frazier, Chelsea M. 2016. "Troubling Ecology: Wangechi Mutu, Octavia Butler, and Black Feminist Interventions in Environmentalism." *Critical Ethnic Studies* 2(1): 40–72.
Freese, Curtis H., Keith E. Aune, Delaney P. Boyd, James N. Derr, Steve C. Forrest, C. Cormack Gates, Peter J. P. Gogan, Shaun M. Grassel, Natalie D. Halbert, Kyran Kunkel, and Kent H. Redford. 2007. "Second Chance for the Plains Bison." *Biological Conservation* 136(2): 175–184.
Fuhlendorf, Samuel D., and David M. Engle. 2001. "Restoring Heterogeneity on Rangelands: Ecosystem Management Based on Evolutionary Grazing Patterns." *BioScience* 51(8): 625–632.
Fujikane, Candace. 2021. *Mapping Abundance for a Planetary Future: Kanaka Maoli and Critical Settler Cartographies in Hawai'i*. Durham, NC: Duke University Press.
Gallay, Alan. 2009. *The Indian Slave Trade: The Rise of the English Empire in the American South, 1670–1717*. New Haven, CT: Yale University Press.
Gandy, Matthew. 2006. "Planning, Anti-Planning and the Infrastructure Crisis Facing Metropolitan Lagos." *Urban Studies* 43(2): 371–396.
Gardiner, Stephen M. 2006. "A Perfect Moral Storm: Climate Change, Intergenerational Ethics and the Problem of Moral Corruption." *Environmental Values* 15(3): 397–413.
Gardiner, Stephen M. 2011. *A Perfect Moral Storm: The Ethical Challenge of Climate Change*. Oxford: Oxford University Press.
Gardiner, Stephen M., Simon Caney, Dale Jamieson, and Henry Shue, eds. 2010. *Climate Ethics: Essential Readings*. Oxford: Oxford University Press.
Gardiner, Stephen M., and David A. Weisbach. 2016. *Debating Climate Ethics*. New York: Oxford University Press.
Garner, Robert. 2013. *A Theory of Justice for Animals: Animal Rights in a Nonideal World*. Oxford: Oxford University Press.
Garutsa, Tendayi C. 2021. "Considering an Intersectional Lens in Agriculture and Climate Change: A Systematic Literature Review." *African Journal of Gender, Society and Development* 10(4): 163–186.
Garvey, James. 2008. *The Ethics of Climate Change: Right and Wrong in a Warming World*. London: Continuum International.
Genovese, Eugene D. 1998. *A Consuming Fire: The Fall of the Confederacy in the Mind of the White Christian South*. Vol. 41. Athens: University of Georgia Press.
Genovese, Eugene D., and Elizabeth Fox-Genovese. 2011. *Fatal Self-Deception: Slaveholding Paternalism in the Old South*. Cambridge: Cambridge University Press.
Geronimus, Arline T., John Bound, Timothy A. Waidmann, Cynthia G. Colen, and Dianne Steffick. 2001. "Inequality in Life Expectancy, Functional Status, and Active Life Expectancy across Selected Black and White Populations in the United States." *Demography* 38(2): 227–251.
Geronimus, Arline T., Margaret Hicken, Danya Keene, and John Bound. 2006. "'Weathering' and Age Patterns of Allostatic Load Scores among Blacks and Whites in the United States." *American Journal of Public Health* 96(5): 826–833.
Gilmore, Ruth Wilson. 2006. *Golden Gulag: Prisons, Surplus, Crisis, and Opposition in Globalizing California*. Berkeley: University of California Press.
Glacken, Clarence J. 1960. "Count Buffon on Cultural Changes of the Physical Environment." *Annals of the Association of American Geographers* 50(1): 1–22.
Glazebrook, Patricia. 2011. "Women and Climate Change: A Case-Study from Northeast Ghana." *Hypatia* 26(4): 762–782.

Godfrey, Phoebe C., ed. 2012. "Race, Gender and Class and Climate Change." Special issue of *Race, Gender & Class* 19(1–2).
Godfrey, Phoebe, and Denise Torres. 2016a. *Emergent Possibilities for Global Sustainability: Intersections of Race, Class and Gender*. Abingdon: Routledge.
Godfrey, Phoebe, and Denise Torres, eds. 2016b. *Systemic Crises of Global Climate Change: Intersections of Race, Class and Gender*. Abingdon: Routledge.
Goel, Sharad, Justin M. Rao, and Ravi Shroff. 2016. "Precinct or Prejudice? Understanding Racial Disparities in New York City's Stop-and-Frisk Policy." *Annals of Applied Statistics* 10(1): 365–394.
Goldsworthy, Heather. 2010. "Women, Global Environmental Change, and Human Security." In *Global Environmental Change and Human Security*, ed. Richard A. Matthew, Jon Barnett, Bryan McDonald, and Karen O'Brien, 215–236. Cambridge, MA: MIT Press.
Global Slavery Index. 2018. "Brazil." https://www.globalslaveryindex.org/2018/findings/country-studies/brazil/.
Gómez-Barris, Macarena. 2017. *The Extractive Zone: Social Ecologies and Decolonial Perspectives*. Durham, NC: Duke University Press.
Goodall, Jane. 2019. "Inside the Amazon: The Dying Forest." *Time*, September 12. https://time.com/longform/inside-amazon-rain-forest-vr-app/.
Goodalle, Stephanie E. 2019. "At the River's Edge: Allison Jane Hamilton Interviewed by Stephanie E. Goodalle." *Bomb*, August 27. https://bombmagazine.org/articles/at-the-rivers-edge-allison-janae-hamilton-interviewed/.
Grandin, Greg. 2014. *The Empire of Necessity: Slavery, Freedom, and Deception in the New World*. New York: Metropolitan Books/Henry Holt.
Green, Lesley. 2020. *Rock | Water | Life: Ecology and Humanities for a Decolonial South Africa*. Durham, NC: Duke University Press.
Guthman, Julie, and Sandy Brown. 2016. "Whose Life Counts: Biopolitics and the 'Bright Line' of Chloropicrin Mitigation in California's Strawberry Industry." *Science, Technology, & Human Values* 41(3): 461–482.
Gyasi, Yaa. 2016. *Homegoing: A Novel*. New York: Alfred A. Knopf.
Hage, Ghassan. 2017. *Is Racism an Environmental Threat? Debating Race*. Cambridge, UK: Polity.
Hage, Ghassan. 2018. "Up to Our Neck." *Journal of Sociology* 54(2): 272–275.
Hall, G. Stanley. 1916. *Adolescence: Its Psychology and Its Relations to Physiology, Anthropology, Sociology, Sex, Crime, Religion and Education*. London: D. Appleton.
Hallum-Montes, Rachel. 2012. "'Para el Bien Común': Indigenous Women's Environmental Activism and Community Care Work in Guatemala." *Race, Gender & Class* 19(1–2): 104–130.
Halme, Pia. 2007. "Carbon Debt and the (In)significance of History." *TRAMES* 11: 346–365.
Haraway, Donna J. 1991. "A Cyborg Manifesto: Science, Technology, and Socialist-Feminism in the Late Twentieth Century." In *Simians, Cyborgs and Women: The Reinvention of Nature*, 149–181. New York; Routledge, 1991.
Haraway, Donna J. 1997. *Modest_Witness@Second_Millennium: FemaleMan_Meets_OncoMouse: Feminism and Technoscience*. New York: Routledge.
Haraway, Donna J. 2015. "Anthropocene, Capitalocene, Plantationocene, Chthulucene: Making Kin." *Environmental Humanities* 6(1): 159–165.

Haraway, Donna J. 2016. *Staying with the Trouble: Making Kin in the Chthulucene.* Durham, NC: Duke University Press.

Haraway, Donna, Noboru Ishikawa, Scott F. Gilbert, Kenneth Olwig, Anna L. Tsing, and Nils Bubandt. 2016. "Anthropologists Are Talking—About the Anthropocene." *Ethnos* 81(3): 535–564.

Haraway, Donna, and Anna L. Tsing. 2019. "Reflections on the Plantationocene: A Conversation with Donna Haraway and Anna Tsing." *Edge Effects.* http://edgeeffects.net/wp-content/uploads/2019/06/PlantationoceneReflections_Haraway_Tsing.pdf.

Hardin, Garrett. 1974. "Living on a Lifeboat." *Bioscience* 24(10): 561–568.

Harding, Sandra. 2008. *Sciences from Below: Feminisms, Postcolonialities, and Modernities.* Durham, NC: Duke University Press.

Harris, Melanie L. 2017. *Ecowomanism: African American Women and Earth-Honoring Faiths.* Maryknoll, NY: Orbis Books.

Harris, Paul G. 2010. *World Ethics and Climate Change: From International to Global Justice.* Edinburgh: Edinburgh University Press.

Hartman, Saidiya V. 1997. *Scenes of Subjection: Terror, Slavery, and Self-Making in Nineteenth-Century America.* New York: Oxford University Press.

Hartman, Saidiya V. 2008. *Lose Your Mother: A Journey along the Atlantic Slave Route.* New York: Farrar, Straus and Giroux.

Hartman, Saidiya V., and Frank B. Wilderson. 2003. "The Position of the Unthought." *Qui parle* 13(2): 183–201.

Hartmann, Betsy. 1998. "Population, Environment, and Security: A New Trinity." *Environment and Urbanization* 10(2): 113–128.

Hartmann, Betsy. 2016. *Reproductive Rights and Wrongs: The Global Politics of Population Control.* Chicago: Haymarket Books.

Harvey, Penny, Christian Krohn-Hansen, and Kunt G. Nustad, eds. 2019. *Anthropos and the Material.* Durham, NC: Duke University Press.

Hathaway, Julia Robertson. 2020. "Climate Change, the Intersectional Imperative, and the Opportunity of the Green New Deal." *Environmental Communication* 14(1): 13–22.

Hecht, Gabrielle. 2018a. "The African Anthropocene." *Aeon,* February 6. https://aeon.co/essays/if-we-talk-about-hurting-our-planet-who-exactly-is-the-we.

Hecht, Gabrielle. 2018b. "Interscalar Vehicles for an African Anthropocene: On Waste, Temporality, and Violence." *Cultural Anthropology* 33(1): 109–141.

Hemmati, Minu, and Ulrike Rohr. 2009. "Engendering the Climate-Change Negotiations: Experiences, Challenges, and Steps Forward." *Gender and Development* 17(1): 19–32.

Henderson, Taja-Nia Y., and Jamila Jefferson-Jones. 2020. "#LivingWhileBlack: Blackness as Nuisance." *American University Law Review* 69(3): 863–914.

Heyward, Clare, and Dominic Roser, eds. 2016. *Climate Justice in a Non-Ideal World.* Oxford: Oxford University Press.

Hird, Myra J. 2009. "Feminist Engagements with Matter." *Feminist Studies* 35(2): 329–346.

Hoffman, Jeremy S., Vivek Shandas, and Nicholas Pendleton. 2020. "The Effects of Historical Housing Policies on Resident Exposure to Intra-Urban Heat: A Study of 108 US Urban Areas." *Climate* 8(1): 1–15.

Hogan, Linda. 1995. *Dwellings: A Spiritual History of the Living World.* New York: Touchstone.

Holmes, Meghan. 2018. "Justice Continues to Be Elusive for Gordon Plaza Residents." *Louisiana Weekly,* August 27.

Hopkins, Hop. 2020. "Racism Is Killing the Planet." *Sierra*, June 8. https://www.sierraclub.org/sierra/racism-killing-planet.

Hornaday, William Temple. 1889. *The Extermination of the American Bison*. Smithsonian Institution. Washington, DC: Government Printing Office.

Horowitz, Andy. 2020. *Katrina: A History, 1915–2015*. Cambridge, MA: Harvard University Press.

Howard, Jeffrey T., and P. Johnelle Sparks. 2016. "The Effects of Allostatic Load on Racial/Ethnic Mortality Differences in the United States." *Population Research and Policy Review* 35(4): 421–443.

Hubbard, Tasha. 2014. "Buffalo Genocide in Nineteenth-Century North America: 'Kill, Skin, and Sell.'" In *Colonial Genocide in Indigenous North America*, ed. Andrew John Woolford, Jeff Benvenuto, and Alexander Laban Hinto, 292–305. Durham, NC: Duke University Press.

Hughes, Margaret, and Stuart Barlo. 2021. "Yarning with Country: An Indigenist Research Methodology." *Qualitative Inquiry* 27(3–4):353–363.

Hultgren, John. 2015. *Border Walls Gone Green: Nature and Anti-immigrant Politics in America*. Minneapolis: University of Minnesota Press.

Human Rights Watch. 2020. "Covid-19 Fueling Anti-Asian Racism and Xenophobia Worldwide." May 12. https://www.hrw.org/news/2020/05/12/covid-19-fueling-anti-asian-racism-and-xenophobia-worldwide.

Hunter, Lori, and Emmanuel David. 2009. "Climate Change and Migration: Considering Gender Dimensions." https://www.researchgate.net/publication/229051887_Climate_Change_and_Migration_Considering_the_Gender_Dimensions.

Hurtado, Sylvia, Jeffrey F. Milem, Alma R. Clayton-Pedersen, and Walter R. Allen. 1998. "Enhancing Campus Climates for Racial/Ethnic Diversity through Educational Policy and Practice." *Review of Higher Education* 21(3): 279–302.

Huyer, Sophia, ed. 2016. "Gender, Climate Change and Agriculture." Special issue of *Gender, Technology and Development* 20(2).

Huyer, Sophia, and Samuel T. Partey. 2020. "Gender Equality in Climate Smart Agriculture: Framework, Approaches and Technologies." *Climatic Change* 158(1): 1–106.

Instituto Brasileiro de Geografia e Estatística. 2018. "Síntese de Indicadores Sociais." https://www.ibge.gov.br/estatisticas/sociais/saude/9221-sintese-de-indicadores-sociais.html?=&t=o-que-e.

Intergovernmental Panel on Climate Change. n.d. "About the IPCC." https://www.ipcc.ch/about/.

Intergovernmental Panel on Climate Change. 2013a. "Annex III: Glossary." In *Climate Change 2013: The Physical Science Basis. Contribution of Working Group I to the Fifth Assessment Report of the Intergovernmental Panel on Climate Change*, ed. T. F.Stocker, D. Qin, G.-K. Plattner, M. Tignor, S. K. Allen, J. Boschung, A. Nauels, Y. Xia, V. Bex, and P. M. Midgley, 1447–1465. Cambridge: Cambridge University Press.

Intergovernmental Panel on Climate Change. 2013b. *Climate Change 2013: The Physical Science Basis. Contribution of Working Group I to the Fifth Assessment Report of the Intergovernmental Panel on Climate Change*. Ed. T. F. Stocker, D. Qin, G.-K. Plattner, M. Tignor, S. K. Allen, J. Boschung, A. Nauels, Y. Xia, V. Bex, and P. M. Midgley. Cambridge: Cambridge University Press.

Intergovernmental Panel on Climate Change. 2018. *Global Warming of 1.5 °C: An IPCC Special Report on the Impacts of Global Warming of 1.5 °C above Pre-industrial Levels and Related Global Greenhouse Gas Emission Pathways, in the Context of Strengthening the Global Response to the Threat of Climate Change, Sustainable Development, and Efforts to Eradicate Poverty.* Ed. V. Masson-Delmotte, P. Zhai, H.-O. Pörtner, D. Roberts, J. Skea, P. R. Shukla, A. Pirani, W. Moufouma-Okia, C. Péan, R. Pidcock, S. Connors, J. B. R. Matthews, Y. Chen, X. Zhou, M. I. Gomis, E. Lonnoy, T. Maycock, M. Tignor, and T. Waterfield. Geneva: World Meteorological Organization.

International Energy Agency. 2017. *Key World Energy Statistics.* Paris: IEA Publications.

Irons, Charles F. 2008. *The Origins of Proslavery Christianity: White and Black Evangelicals in Colonial and Antebellum Virginia.* Chapel Hill: University of North Carolina Press.

Isenberg, Andrew C. 2000. *The Destruction of the Bison: An Environmental History, 1750–1920.* New York: Cambridge University Press.

Issa, Daniela. 2017. "Reification and the Human Commodity: Theorizing Modern Slavery in Brazil." *Latin American Perspectives* 44(6): 90–106.

Jackson, Mark S. 2018. "Introduction: A Critical Bridging Exercise." In *Coloniality, Ontology, and the Question of the Posthuman,* ed. Mark Jackson, 1–18. Abingdon: Routledge.

Jackson, Zakiyyah Iman. 2020. *Becoming Human: Matter and Meaning in an Antiblack World.* New York: New York University Press.

Jafry, Tahseen, Karin Helwig, and Michael Mikulewicz, eds. 2018. *Routledge Handbook of Climate Justice.* London: Routledge.

James, Guillermo. 2013. *Community Engaged Research in Salvador, Brazil.* Berkeley: Center for Latin American Studies, University of California. https://clas.berkeley.edu/research/community-engaged-research-salvador-brazil.

James, Wesley, Chunrong Jia, and Satish Kedia. 2012. "Uneven Magnitude of Disparities in Cancer Risks from Air Toxics." *International Journal of Environmental Research and Public Health* 9(12): 4365–4385.

Johnson, Walter. 2017. *River of Dark Dreams: Slavery and Empire in the Cotton Kingdom.* Cambridge, MA: Harvard University Press.

Kaijser, Anna, and Annica Kronsell. 2014. "Climate Change through the Lens of Intersectionality." *Environmental Politics* 23(3): 417–433.

Kajdacsi, Brittney, Federico Costa, Chaz Hyseni, Fleur Porter, Julia Brown, Gorete Rodrigues, Helena Farias, Mitermayer G. Reis, James E. Childs, Albert I. Ko, and Adalgisa Caccone. 2013. "Urban Population Genetics of Slum-Dwelling Rats (*Rattus norvegicus*) in Salvador, Brazil." *Molecular Ecology* 22(20): 5056–5070.

Kanbur, Ravi, and Henry Shue, eds. 2018. *Climate Justice: Integrating Economics and Philosophy* Oxford: Oxford University Press.

Kaplan, Robert D. 1994. "The Coming Anarchy: How Scarcity, Crime, Overpopulation, Tribalism, and Disease Are Rapidly Destroying the Social Fabric of Our Planet." *The Atlantic* 273(2): 44–77.

Kaplan, Robert D. 1996. *The Ends of the Earth: A Journey at the Dawn of the 21st Century.* New York: Random House.

Kasperson, Jeanne X., and Roger E. Kasperson. 2001. *Global Environmental Risk.* Tokyo: United Nations University Press.

Keith, David. 2013. *A Case for Climate Engineering.* Cambridge, MA: MIT Press.

Kelbaugh, Doug. 2019. *The Urban Fix: Resilient Cities in the War against Climate Change, Heat Islands and Overpopulation.* New York: Routledge.

Kidd, Ian James, José Medina, and Gaile Pohlhaus Jr. 2017. *The Routledge Handbook of Epistemic Injustice.* New York: Routledge.

Kidder, Tristram R. 2000. "Making the City Inevitable: Native Americans and the Geography of New Orleans." In *Transforming New Orleans and Its Environs: Centuries of Change*, ed. Craig E. Colton, 9–21. Pittsburgh: University of Pittsburgh Press.

Kim, Claire Jean. 2015. *Dangerous Crossings: Race, Species, and Nature in a Multicultural Age*. New York: Cambridge University Press.

Kimmerer, Robin Wall. 2013. *Braiding Sweetgrass: Indigenous Wisdom, Scientific Knowledge and the Teachings of Plants*. Minneapolis, MN: Milkweed Editions.

King, Tiffany Lethabo. 2016. "The Labor of (Re)reading Plantation Landscapes Fungible(ly)." *Antipode* 48(4): 1022–1039.

Klein, Herbert S. 1999. *The Atlantic Slave Trade*. Cambridge: Cambridge University Press.

Klein, Herbert S., and Francisco Vidal Luna. 2010. *Slavery in Brazil*. Cambridge: Cambridge University Press.

Kline, Davie, and Thomas Cole. 2017. "Toward a New Humanism in the Age of Anthropogenic Climate Change: On Sylvia Wynter." In *Encyclopedia of the Anthropocene*, Vol. 4: *Ethics*, ed. Bruce Jennings, 175–180. Amsterdam: Elsevier.

Klinenberg, Eric. 2015. *Heat Wave: A Social Autopsy of Disaster in Chicago*. Chicago; University of Chicago Press.

Klinsky, Sonja, and Jasmina Brankovic. 2018. *The Global Climate Regime and Transitional Justice*. Abingdon: Routledge.

Klopotek, Brian, Brenda Lintinger, and John Barbry. 2008. "Ordinary and Extraordinary Trauma: Race, Indigeneity, and Hurricane Katrina in Tunica-Biloxi History." *American Indian Culture and Research Journal* 32(2): 55–77.

Knapp, Alan K., John M. Blair, John M. Briggs, Scott L. Collins, David C. Hartnett, Loretta C. Johnson, and E. Gene Towne. 1999. "The Keystone Role of Bison in North American Tallgrass Prairie." *Bioscience* 49(1): 39–50.

Kronlid, David O. 2014. *Climate Change Adaptation and Human Capabilities: Justice and Ethics in Research and Policy*. London: Palgrave Macmillian.

Lambrou, Yianna, and Grazia Piana. 2006. *Gender: The Missing Component in the Response to Climate Change*. Rome: Food and Agriculture Organization of the United Nations.

Larson, Anne M., David Solis, Amy E. Duchelle, Stibniati Atmadja, Ida Aju Pradnja Resosudarmo, Therese Dokken, and Mella Komalasari. 2018. "Gender Lessons for Climate Initiatives: A Comparative Study of REDD+ Impacts on Subjective Wellbeing." *World Development* 108: 86–102.

Lartey, Jamiles, and Oliver Laughland. 2019. "This Is Cancer Town: A Year-Long Series from Reserve, Louisiana." *The Guardian*, May 6. https://www.theguardian.com/us-news/ng-interactive/2019/may/06/cancertown-louisana-reserve-special-report.

Lau, Colleen L., Lee D. Smythe, Scott B. Craig, and Philip Weinstein. 2010. "Climate Change, Flooding, Urbanisation and Leptospirosis: Fuelling the Fire?" *Transactions of the Royal Society of Tropical Medicine and Hygiene* 104(10): 631–638.

Laughland, Oliver, and Jamiles Larty. 2019. "'It's Been Killing Us for 50 Years'" Residents on Living in Cancer Town." *The Guardian*, May 7. https://www.theguardian.com/us-news/2019/may/07/cancertown-reserve-louisiana-residents-stories.

Lawson, Elaine T., Rahinatu Sidiki Alare, Abdul Rauf Zanya Salifu, and Mary Thompson-Hall. 2020. "Dealing with Climate Change in Semi-Arid Ghana: Understanding Intersectional Perceptions and Adaptation Strategies of Women Farmers." *GeoJournal* 85(2): 439–452.

Lee, So-Young, and Eric Zusman. 2018. "Participatory Climate Governance in Southeast Asia: Lessons Learned from Gender-Responsive Climate Mitigation." In *Routledge Handbook of Climate Justice*, ed. Tahseen Jafry, Michael Mikulewicz, and Karin Helwig, 393–404. London: Routledge.

Leopold, Aldo. 1949. *A Sand County Almanac: And Sketches Here and There*. Oxford: Oxford University Press.

Lerner, Sharon. 2020. "The Coronavirus Pandemic and Police Violence Have Reignited the Fight against Toxic Racism." *The Intercept*, June 17. https://theintercept.com/2020/06/17/coronavirus-environmental-justice-racism-robert-bullard/.

Lerner, Steve. 2010. *Sacrifice Zone: The Front Lines of Toxic Chemical Exposure in the United States*. Cambridge, MA: MIT Press.

Levitus, Sydney, John I. Antonov, Timothy P. Boyer, and Cathy Stephens. 2000. Warming of the World Ocean *Science* 287, 5461: 2225–2229.

Lewis, Shireen K., ed. 2016. "Climate Justice: Blacks and Climate Change." Special issue of *Black Scholar: Journal of Black Studies and Research* 46(3).

Lewis, Simon L., and Mark A. Maslin. 2015. "Defining the Anthropocene." *Nature* (London) 519: 171–180.

López, Alfred J. 2001. *Posts and Pasts: A Theory of Postcolonialism*. Albany: State University of New York Press.

López, Alfred J. 2018. "Contesting the Material Turn; Or, the Persistence of Agency." *Cambridge Journal of Postcolonial Literary Inquiry* 5(3): 371–386.

Lopez, Mark Hugo, Ana Gonzalez-Barrera, and Jens Manuel Krogstad. 2018. "Latinos and Discrimination." Pew Research Center. https://www.pewresearch.org/hispanic/2018/10/25/latinos-and-discrimination/.

Louisiana Department of Natural Resources. n.d. Office of Conservation: Pipeline Operations Program. http://www.dnr.louisiana.gov/index.cfm/page/150.

Lovejoy, Thomas E., and Carlos Nobre. 2018. "Amazon Tipping Point." *Science Advances* 4(2): 2340.

Lowe, Ian, and Jouni Paavola, eds. 2005. *Environmental Values in a Globalizing World: Nature, Justice and Governance*. Abingdon: Routledge.

Lugones, María. 2007. "Heterosexualism and the Colonial/Modern Gender System." *Hypatia: A Journal of Feminist Philosophy* 22(1): 186–209.

Lugones, María. 2010. "Toward a Decolonial Feminism." *Hypatia: A Journal of Feminist Philosophy* 25(4): 742–759.

Lykke, Nina. 2009. "Non-Innocent Intersections of Feminism and Environmentalism." *Kvinder, Køn & Forskning*, 3–4: 37–44.

Lykke, Nina. 2019. "Making Live and Letting Die: Cancerous Bodies between Anthropocene Necropolitics and Chthulucene Kinship." *Environmental Humanities* 11(1): 108–136.

MacGregor, Sherilyn. 2009. "A Stranger Silence Still: The Need for Feminist Social Research on Climate Change." *Sociological Review* 57(2 suppl): 124–140.

MacGregor, Sherilyn. 2010. "'Gender and Climate Change': From Impacts to Discourses." *Journal of the Indian Ocean Region* 6(2): 223–238.

Mainlay, Jony, and Su Fei Tan. 2012. *Mainstreaming Gender and Climate Change in Nepal*. London: International Institute for Environment and Development.

Malm, Andreas, and Rikard Warlenius. 2019. "The Grand Theft of the Atmosphere: Sketches for a Theory of Climate Injustice in the Anthropocene." In *Climate*

Futures: Re-Imagining Global Climate Justice, ed. Kum-Kum Bhavnai, John Foran, Priya A. Kurian, and Debashish Munshi, 32–39. London: Zed Books.
Mann, Kristin. 2007. *Slavery and the Birth of an African City: Lagos, 1760–1900*. Bloomington: Indiana University Press.
Manzo, Kate. 2010. "Imaging Vulnerability: The Iconography of Climate Change." *Area* 42(1): 96–107.
Maranhão Costa, Patricía Trindade. 2009. *Fighting Forced Labour: The Example of Brazil*. Geneva: International Labour Office.
Masi, Eduardo de, Pedro José Vilaça, and Maria Tereza Pepe Razzolini. 2009. "Evaluation on the Effectiveness of Actions for Controlling Infestation by Rodents in Campo Limpo Region, Sao Paulo Municipality, Brazil." *International Journal of Environmental Health Research* 19(4): 291–304.
Masika, Rachel. 2002. *Gender, Development, and Climate Change*. Oxford: Oxfam Publishing.
Massey, Douglas S., and Nancy A. Denton. 1993. *American Apartheid: Segregation and the Making of the Underclass*. Cambridge, MA: Harvard University Press.
McNamara, Karen E., and Rachel Clissold. 2019. "Vulnerable Groups and Preliminary Insights into Intersecting Categories of Identity in Laamu Atoll, Maldives." *Singapore Journal of Tropical Geography* 40(3): 410–428.
McWhorter, Ladelle. 1994. "Foucault's Genealogy of Homosexuality." *Journal of French and Francophone Philosophy* 6(1–2):44–58.
Medina, José. 2012. *The Epistemology of Resistance: Gender and Racial Oppression, Epistemic Injustice, and Resistant Imaginations*. Oxford: Oxford University Press.
Mele, Christopher. 2016. "'Using' Race in the Politics of Siting Environmentally Hazardous Facilities." *Environmental Sociology* 2(2): 166–179.
Melo, Luís Antônio Camargo. 2007. "Atuação do Ministério Público do Trabalho no Combate ao Trabalho Escravo." In *Possibilidades Jurídicas de Combate à Escravidão Contemporânea*, ed. Ruth Beatriz V. Vilela, 60–99. Brasilia: International Labour Organization.
Mensah, Michael, Paul L. G. Vlek, and Benedicta Y. Fosu-Mensah. 2020. "Gender and Climate Change Linkages in the Semi-Arid Region of Ghana." *GeoJournal* 87: 363–376. https://doi.org/10.1007/s10708-020-10261-w.
Merchant, Carolyn. 2003. "Shades of Darkness: Race and Environmental History." *Environmental History* 8(3): 380–394.
Meyer, Lukas H. 2004. "Compensating Wrongless Historical Emissions of Greenhouse Gases." *Ethical Perspectives* 11(1):20–35.
Mikati, Ihab, Adam F. Benson, Thomas J. Luben, Jason D. Sacks, and Jennifer Richmond-Bryant. 2018. "Disparities in Distribution of Particulate Matter Emission Sources by Race and Poverty Status." *American Journal of Public Health* 108(4): 480–485.
Mills, Charles. 1997. *The Racial Contract*. Ithaca, NY: Cornell University Press.
Mills, Charles. 2001. "Black Trash." In *Faces of Environmental Racism: Confronting Issues of Global Justice*, ed. Laura Westra and Bill E. Lawson, 2nd edition, 73–92. Lanham, MD: Rowman and Littlefield.
Miranda, Raul F. C., Carolina Grottera, and Mario Giampietro. 2016. "Understanding Slums: Analysis of the Metabolic Pattern of the Vidigal Favela in Rio De Janeiro, Brazil." *Environment, Development and Sustainability* 18(5): 1297–1322.

Mirzoeff, Nicholas. 2018. "It's Not the Anthropocene, It's the White Supremacy Scene; Or, The Geological Color Line." In *After Extinction*, ed. Richard Grusin, 122–149. Minneapolis: University of Minnesota Press.

Mishra, Ashok K., and Valerian O Pede. 2017. "Perception of Climate Change and Adaptation Strategies in Vietnam: Are There Intra-Household Gender Differences?" *International Journal of Climate Change Strategies and Management* 9(4): 501–516.

Mitchell, Bruce, and Juan Franco. 2018. "HOLC 'Redlining' Maps: The Persistent Structure of Segregation and Economic Inequality." https://ncrc.org/wp-content/uploads/dlm_uploads/2018/02/NCRC-Research-HOLC-10.pdf.

Mix, Jacqueline, Lisa Elon, Valerie Vi Thien Mac, Joan Flocks, Eugenia Economos, Antonio J. Tovar-Aguilar, Vicki Stover Hertzberg, and Linda A. McCauley. 2018. "Hydration Status, Kidney Function, and Kidney Injury in Florida Agricultural Workers." *Journal of Occupational and Environmental Medicine* 60(5): e253–e260.

Moellendorf, Darrel. 2014. *The Moral Challenge of Dangerous Climate Change: Values, Poverty, and Policy*. Cambridge: Cambridge University Press.

Mohai, Paul, and Robin Saha. 2007. "Racial Inequality in the Distribution of Hazardous Waste: A National-Level Reassessment." *Social Problems* 54(3): 343–370.

Mohai, Paul, and Robin Saha. 2015. "Which Came First, People or Pollution? Assessing the Disparate Siting and Post-Siting Demographic Change Hypotheses of Environmental Injustice." *Environmental Research Letters* 10(11): 1–17.

Moore, Jason W. 2015. *Capitalism in the Web of Life: Ecology and the Accumulation of Capital*. New York: Verso.

Moore, Jason W. 2016. "The Rise of Cheap Nature." In *Anthropocene or Capitalocene? Nature, History, and the Crisis of Capitalism*, ed. Jason W. Moore, 78–115. Oakland, CA: PM Press.

Moore, Jason W. 2017. "The Capitalocene, Part I: On the Nature and Origins of Our Ecological Crisis." *Journal of Peasant Studies* 44(3): 594–630.

Moore, Jason W. 2018. "The Capitalocene Part II: Accumulation by Appropriation and the Centrality of Unpaid Work/Energy." *Journal of Peasant Studies* 45(2): 237–279.

Moss, Jeremy, ed. 2018. *Climate Change and Justice*. Cambridge: Cambridge University Press.

Moura, Maria Cecilia P., Steven J. Smith, and David B. Belzer. 2015. "120 Years of U.S. Residential Housing Stock and Floor Space." *PLoS ONE* 10(8): e0134135.

Müller, B. 2001. "Varieties of Distributive Justice in Climate Change: An Editorial Comment." *Climatic Change* 48: 273–288.

Mullin, Rick. 2020. "The Rise of Environmental Justice." *Chemical and Engineering News*, August 24, 28–41.

Muñoz Martinez, Monica. 2014. "Recuperating Histories of Violence in the Americas: Vernacular History-Making on the US-Mexico Border." *American Quarterly* 66(3): 661–689.

NAACP. 2012. "Coal Blooded: Putting Profits before People." https://naacp.org/resources/coal-blooded-putting-profits-people.

Nadel, Ira B. 1996. *Various Positions: A Life of Leonard Cohen*. New York: Pantheon Books.

Nagel, Joane. 2016. *Gender and Climate Change: Impacts, Science, Policy*. New York: Routledge, Taylor & Francis.

NASA. n.d.a. "Global Climate Change: Vital Signs of the Climate." https://climate.nasa.gov/.

NASA. n.d.b. "Global Climate Change: Vital Signs of the Planet: How Do We Know Climate Change Is Real?" https://climate.nasa.gov/evidence/.

Nash, Michael P. 2010. *Climate Refugees*. Los Angeles: LA Think Tank and Beverly Hills Productions.

National Academies of Sciences, Engineering, and Medicine 2016. *Attribution of Extreme Weather Events in the Context of Climate Change*. Washington, DC: National Academies Press.

National Association of Real Estate Boards. 1924. "Code of Ethics." https://www.nar.realtor/about-nar/history/1924-code-of-ethics.

Ndugga, Nambi, Olivia Pham, Samantha Artiga, Raisa Alam, and Noah Parker. 2021. "Latest Data on COVID-19 Vaccinations Race/Ethnicity." KFF, March 17. https://www.kff.org/coronavirus-covid-19/issue-brief/latest-data-on-covid-19-vaccinations-race-ethnicity/.

Nelson, Julie A. 2007. "Economists, Value Judgments, and Climate Change: A View from Feminist Economics." *Ecological Economics* 65(3): 441–447.

Nesmith, Ande A., Cathryne L. Schmitz, Yolanda Machado-Escudero, Shanondora Billiot, Rachel A. Forbes, Meredith C. F. Powers, Nikita Buckhoy, Lucy A. Lawrence, and Lacey M. Sloan. 2021. *The Intersection of Environmental Justice, Climate Change, Community, and the Ecology of Life*. Cham: Springer Nature Switzerland.

Ngai, Mae M. 2004. *Impossible Subjects: Illegal Aliens and the Making of Modern America*. Princeton, NJ: Princeton University Press.

Nicoson, Christie. 2021. "Towards Climate Resilient Peace: An Intersectional and Degrowth Approach." *Sustainability Science* 16(4): 1147–1158.

Nightingale, Andrea J. 2011. "Bounding Difference: Intersectionality and the Material Production of Gender, Caste, Class and Environment in Nepal." *Geoforum* 42(2): 153–162.

Nixon, Rob. 2011. *Slow Violence and the Environmentalism of the Poor*. Cambridge, MA: Harvard University Press.

Nussbaum, Martha. C. 2006. *Frontiers of Justice: Disability, Nationality, Species Membership*. Cambridge, MA: Belknap Press.

O'Brien, Karen, Asunción Lera St. Clair, and Berit Kristoffersen, eds. 2010. *Climate Change, Ethics and Human Security*. Cambridge: Cambridge University Press.

O'Brien, Kevin J. 2020. "Climate Change and Intersectionality: Christian Ethics, White Supremacy, and Atmospheric Defilement." *Journal of the Society of Christian Ethics* 40(2): 311–328.

The Observer. 2005. "Shock Snaps US Media Out of Its Long Trance." September 10. https://www.theguardian.com/media/2005/sep/11/business.hurricanekatrina.

O'Dwyer, Kathryn. 2020a. "Local Residents Demand Closure of Agriculture Street Landfill in 1950s." New Orleans Historical, accessed November 7, 2020. https://neworleanshistorical.org/items/show/1464.

O'Dwyer, Kathryn. 2020b. "Toxic Chemicals Deposited at Agriculture Street Landfill." New Orleans Historical, accessed November 7, 2020. https://neworleanshistorical.org/items/show/1503.

O'Dwyer, Kathryn, Shelby Loyacano, and Ella McIntire. 2020. "Gordon Plaza Deemed EPA Superfund Site." New Orleans Historical, accessed November 7, 2020. https://neworleanshistorical.org/items/show/1466.

Ogra, M. V., and R. Badola. 2015. "Gender and Climate Change in the Indian Himalayas: Global Threats, Local Vulnerabilities, and Livelihood Diversification at the Nanda Devi Biosphere Reserve." *Earth System Dynamics* 6(2): 505–523.

Okude, A. S., and I. A. Ademiluyi. 2006. "Coastal Erosion Phenomenon in Nigeria: Causes, Control and Implications." *World Applied Science Journal* 1(1): 44–51.

Olsson, L., M. Opondo, P. Tschakert, A. Agrawal, S. H. Eriksen, S. Ma, L. N. Perch, and S. A. Zakieldeen. 2014. "Livelihoods and Poverty." In *Climate Change 2014: Impacts, Adaptation, and Vulnerability. Part A: Global and Sectoral Aspects*. Contribution of Working Group II to the Fifth Assessment Report of the Intergovernmental Panel on Climate Change. Ed. C. B.Field, , V. R. Barros, D. J. Dokken, K. J. Mach, M. D. Mastrandrea, T. E. Bilir, M. Chatterjee, K. L. Ebi, Y. O. Estrada, R. C. Genova, B. Girma, E. S. Kissel, A. N. Levy, S. MacCracken, P. R. Mastrandrea, and L. L. White, 793–832. Cambridge: Cambridge University Press.

Olukoju, Ayodeji. 1993. "Population Pressure, Housing and Sanitation in West Africa's Premier Port-City: Lagos, 1900–1939." *Great Circle* 15(2): 91–106.

Omolo, Nancy A. 2011. "Gender and Climate Change-Induced Conflict in Pastoral Communities: Case Study of Turkana in Northwestern Kenya." *African Journal on Conflict Resolution* 10(2): 81–102.

Online Etymology Dictionary. 2018. "incorporate." Accessed March 7, 2021. https://www.etymonline.com/word/incorporate.

Opperman, Romy. 2019. "A Permanent Struggle against an Omnipresent Death: Revisiting Environmental Racism with Frantz Fanon." *Critical Philosophy of Race* 7(1): 57–80.

Organization of the Petroleum Exporting Countries. 2022. "Nigeria Facts and Figures." https://www.opec.org/opec_web/en/about_us/167.htm.

Oro, Daniel, Meritzell Genovart, Giacomo Tavecchia, Mike S. Fowler, and Alejandro Martínez-Abraín. 2013. "Ecological and Evolutionary Implications of Food Subsidies from Humans." *Ecology Letters* 16: 1501–1514.

Osava, Mario. 2020. "Slavery Modernises, Adapts to Stay Alive in Brazil." *Inter Press Service*, March 5. http://www.ipsnews.net/2020/03/slavery-modernises-adapts-stay-alive-brazil/.

Osborne, Natalie. 2015. "Intersectionality and Kyriarchy: A Framework for Approaching Power and Social Justice in Planning and Climate Change Adaptation." *Planning Theory* 14(2): 130–151.

Owusu, Mensah, Melissa Nursey-Bray, and Diane Rudd. 2019. "Gendered Perception and Vulnerability to Climate Change in Urban Slum Communities in Accra, Ghana." *Regional Environmental Change* 19(1): 13–25.

Page, Edward. A. 2005. *Climate Change, Justice, and Future Generations*. Northampton, MA: Edward Elgar.

Paine, Robert T. 1969. "A Note on Trophic Complexity and Community Stability." *American Naturalist* 103(929): 91–93.

Park, Lisa Sun-Hee, and David N. Pellow. 2011. *The Slums of Aspen: Immigrants vs. the Environment in America's Eden*. New York: New York University Press.

Parker, Emily Anne. 2021. *Elemental Difference and the Climate of the Body*. New York: Oxford University Press.

Partey, Samuel T., Angela D. Dakorah, Robert B. Zougmore, Mathieu Ouedraogo, Mary Nyasimi, Gordon K. Nikoi, and Sophia Huyer. 2020. "Gender and Climate Risk Management: Evidence of Climate Information Use in Ghana." *Climatic Change* 158: 61–75.

Pearse, Rebecca. 2017. "Gender and Climate Change." *Wiley Interdisciplinary Reviews: Climate Change* 8(2): 8:e451. doi:10.1002/wcc.451.
Pellow, David Naguib. 2007. *Resisting Global Toxins: Transnational Movements for Environmental Justice*. Cambridge, MA: MIT Press.
Pellow, David Naguib. 2016. "Toward a Critical Environmental Justice Studies: Black Lives Matter as an Environmental Justice Challenge." *Du Bois Review* 13(2): 221–236.
Pellow, David Naguib. 2018. *What Is Critical Environmental Justice?* Cambridge, UK: Polity Press.
Pellow, David Naguib, and Robert J. Brulle, eds. 2005. *Power, Justice, and the Environment: A Critical Appraisal of the Environmental Justice Movement*. Cambridge, MA: MIT Press.
Pereira, Claudiney. 2018. "Brazil: Fiscal Policy and Ethno-Racial Poverty and Inequality." In *Commitment to Equity Handbook: Estimating the Impact of Fiscal Policy on Inequality and Poverty*, ed. Nora Lustig, 554–567. New Orleans, LA: CEQ Institute at Tulane University and Brookings Institution Press.
Perry, Andre M., and David Harshbarger. 2019. "America's Formerly Redlined Neighborhoods Have Changed, and So Must Solutions to Rectify Them." Brookings Institute. Report, October 14. https://www.brookings.edu/research/americas-formerly-redlines-areas-changed-so-must-solutions/.
Pew Research Center. 2015. "A Global Middle Class Is More Promise Than Reality." July 8. http://www.pewglobal.org/2015/07/08/a-global-middle-class-is-more-promise-than-reality.
Phillips, Dom. 2020. "'We Are Facing Extermination': Brazil Losing a Generation of Indigenous Leaders to Covid-19." *The Guardian*, June 21. https://www.theguardian.com/global-development/2020/jun/21/brazil-losing-generation-indigenous-leaders-covid-19.
Pickering, Andrew. 1995. *The Mangle of Practice: Time, Agency, and Science*. Chicago: University of Chicago Press.
Pickering, Andrew. 2005. "Asian Eels and Global Warming: A Posthumanist Perspective on Society and the Environment." *Ethics and the Environment* 10(2): 29–43.
Piedalue, Amy, and Susmita Rishi. 2017. "Unsettling the South through Postcolonial Feminist Theory." *Feminist Studies* 43(3): 548–570.
Plumwood, Val. 1993. *Feminism and the Mastery of Nature*. London: Routledge.
Plumwood, Val. 2009. "Nature in the Active Voice." *Australian Humanities Review* 46: 1–14.
Population Matters. 2022. "About Us." https://populationmatters.org/about-us.
Posner, Eric, and David Weisbach. 2010. *Climate Change Justice*. Princeton, NJ: Princeton University Press.
Preston, Christopher J., ed. 2016 *Climate Justice and Geoengineering: Ethics and Policy in the Atmospheric Anthropocene*. London: Rowman and Littlefield International.
Prison Polity Initiative. 2021. "Louisiana Profile." https://www.prisonpolicy.org/profiles/LA.html.
Pulido, Laura. 2015. "Geographies of Race and Ethnicity I: White Supremacy vs White Privilege in Environmental Racism Research." *Progress in Human Geography* 39(6): 809–817.
Pulido, Laura. 2016. "Flint, Environmental Racism, and Racial Capitalism." *Capitalism Nature Socialism* 27(3): 1–16.

Pulido, Laura. 2017a. "Geographies of Race and Ethnicity II: Environmental Racism, Racial Capitalism and State-Sanctioned Violence." *Progress in Human Geography* 41(4): 524–533.

Pulido, Laura. 2017b. "Geographies of Race and Ethnicity III: Settler Colonialism and Nonnative People of Color." *Progress in Human Geography* 42(2): 309–318.

Pulido, Laura. 2018. "Racism and the Anthropocene." In *The Remains of the Anthropocene*. ed. G. Mitman, R. Emmett. and M. Armiero, 116–128. Chicago: University of Chicago Press.

Quandt, Amy. 2018. "Variability in Perceptions of Household Livelihood Resilience and Drought at the Intersection of Gender and Ethnicity." *Climatic Change* 152(1): 1–15.

Radley, Jack. 2020. "Privileging Utterances as Forms: An Interview with Allison Janae Hamilton." Berlin Art Link, June 12. https://www.berlinartlink.com/2020/06/12/privileging-utterances-as-forms-an-interview-with-allison-janae-hamilton/.

Ravera, Federica, Irene Iniesta-Arandia, Berta Martín-López, Unai Pascual, and Purabi Bose, eds. 2016. "Gender Perspectives in Resilience, Vulnerability and Adaptation to Global Environmental Change." Special issue of *Ambio* 45(3 Suppl).

Ravera, Federica, Berta Martín-López, Unai Pascual, and Adam Drucker. 2016. "The Diversity of Gendered Adaptation Strategies to Climate Change of Indian Farmers: A Feminist Intersectional Approach." *Ambio* 45(S3): 335–351.

Reis, Renato B., Guilherme S. Ribeiro, Ridalva D. M. Felzemburgh, Francisco S. Santana, Sharif Mohr, Astrid X. T. O. Melendez, Adriano Queiroz, Andréia C. Santos, Romy R. Ravines, Wagner S. Tassinari, Marília S. Carvalho, Mitermayer G. Reis, and Albert I. Ko. 2008. "Impact of Environment and Social Gradient on Leptospira Infection in Urban Slums." *PLoS Neglected Tropical Diseases* 2(4): e228.

Reséndez, Andrés. 2016. *The Other Slavery: The Uncovered Story of Indian Enslavement in America*. Boston: Houghton Mifflin Harcourt.

Reyes, G. Mitchell, and Kundai Chirindo. 2020. "Theorizing Race and Gender in the Anthropocene." *Women's Studies in Communication* 43(4): 429–442.

Rice, Susan E. 2007. "Poverty Breeds Insecurity." In *Too Poor for Peace? Global Poverty, Conflict, and Security in the 21st Century*, ed. Lael Brainard and Derek Chollet, 31–49. Washington, DC: Brookings Institution Press.

Rifkin, Mark. 2011. *When Did Indians Become Straight? Kinship, the History of Sexuality, and Native Sovereignty*. New York: Oxford University Press.

Robinson, Cedric J. 2019. *On Racial Capitalism, Black Internationalism, and Cultures of Resistance*. London: Pluto Press.

Robinson, Fiona. 2011. *The Ethics of Care: A Feminist Approach to Human Security*. Philadelphia, PA: Temple University Press.

Robinson, Michael D. 2017. *A Union Indivisible: Secession and the Politics of Slavery in the Border South*. Chapel Hill: University of North Carolina Press.

Rose, Deborah Bird. 2009. "Introduction: Writing in the Anthropocene." *Australian Humanities Review* 47: 87.

Rosen, Julia 2021. "How Heat Waves Warp Ecosystems." *High Country News,* November 22. https://www.hcn.org/issues/53.12/north-climate-change-how-heat-waves-warp-ecosystems.

Roser, Dominic, and Christian Seidel. 2016. *Climate Justice: An Introduction*. London: Routledge.

Rothman, Adam. 2007. *Slave Country: American Expansion and the Origins of the Deep South*. Cambridge, MA: Harvard University Press.

Rothstein, Richard. 2017. *The Color of Law: A Forgotten History of How Our Government Segregated America*. New York: Liveright.
Rousset, Patrick, Armando Caldeira-Pires, Alexander Sablowski, and Thiago Rodrigues. 2011. "LCA of Eucalyptus Wood Charcoal Briquettes." *Journal of Cleaner Production* 19(14): 1647–1653.
Rowan, Rory. 2014. "Notes on Politics after the Anthropocene." *Progress in Human Geography* 38(3): 439–456.
Roy, Sajal. 2019. *Climate Change Impacts on Gender Relations in Bangladesh: Socio-environmental Struggle of the Shora Forest Community in the Sundarbans Mangrove Forest*. Singapore: Springer International.
Russell, Gordon. 2019. "In 'Cancer Alley,' Toxic Polluters Face Little Oversight from Environmental Regulators." *ProPublica*, December 19, https://www.propublica.org/article/in-cancer-alley-toxic-polluters-face-little-oversight-from-environmental-regulators.
Ryder, Stacia S. 2018. "Developing an Intersectionally-Informed, Multi-Sited, Critical Policy Ethnography to Examine Power and Procedural Justice in Multiscalar Energy and Climate Change Decisionmaking Processes." *Energy Research & Social Science* 45: 266–275.
Said, Edward W. 1978. *Orientialism*. New York: Pantheon Books.
Salamanca, Carlos. 2019. "Indigenous Peoples' Experiences: Some Observations about the New Political Era in Latin America." *Peace Research Institute Frankfort Blog*, August 7. https://blog.prif.org/2019/08/07/indigenous-peoples-experiences-some-observations-about-the-new-political-era-in-latin-america/.
Salleh, Ariel, ed. 2009. *Eco-Sufficiency and Global Justice: Women Write Political Ecology*. London: Pluto Press.
Sánchez Barba, Mayra G. 2020. "Keeping Them Down: Neurotoxic Pesticides, Race, and Disabling Biopolitics." *Catalyst* 6(1): 1–31.
Sandy, Matt. 2019. "The Amazon Rainforest Is Nearly Gone." *Time*. https://time.com/amazon-rainforest-disappearing/.
Saxton, Dvera I. 2015. "Strawberry Fields as Extreme Environments: The Ecobiopolitics of Farmworker Health." *Medical Anthropology* 34(2): 166–183.
Schermerhorn, Calvin. 2015. *The Business of Slavery and the Rise of American Capitalism, 1815–1860*. New Haven, CT: Yale University Press.
Schlosberg, David. 2014. "Ecological Justice for the Anthropocene." In *Political Animals and Animal Politics*, ed. Marcel Wissenburg and David Schlosber, 75–92. London: Palgrave Macmillan.
Schneider, Stephen H., and Janica Lane. 2006. "Dangers and Thresholds in Climate Change and the Implications for Justice." In *Fairness in Adaptation to Climate Change*, ed. W. Neil Adger, Jouni Paavola, Saleemul Huq, and M. J. Mace, 23–52. Cambridge, MA: MIT Press.
Seager, Joni. 2009. "Death by Degrees: Taking a Feminist Hard Look at the 2^0 Climate Policy." *Kvinder, Køn & Forskning*, 3–4: 11–21.
Sealey-Huggins, Leon. 2018. "'The Climate Crisis Is a Racist Crisis': Structural Racism, Inequality and Climate Change." In *The Fire Now: Anti-Racist Scholarship in Times of Explicit Racial Violence*. ed. Azeezat Johnson, Remi Joseph-Salisbury, and Beth Kamunge, 99–113. London: Zed Books.
Sen Roy, Shouraseni. 2018. *Linking Gender to Climate Change Impacts in the Global South*. Cham, Switzerland: Springer International.

Shah, Purvi, Colette Pichon Battle, Vincent Warren, Alicia Garza, and Elle Hearns. 2015. "RadTalks: What Could Be Possible If the Law Really Stood for Black Lives?" *City University of New York Law Review* 19(1): 91–130.

Shapiro, Ari. 2018. "Why White Americans Call the Police on Black People in Public Spaces." National Public Radio, May 15. https://www.npr.org/2018/05/15/611389765/why-white-americans-call-the-police-on-black-people-in-public-spaces.

Sharp, Tyler M., Brenda Rivera García, Janice Pérez-Padilla, Renee L. Galloway, Marta Guerra, Kyle R. Ryff, Dana Haberling, Sharada Ramakrishnan, Sean Shadomy, Dianna Blau, Kay M. Tomashek, and William A. Bower. 2016. "Early Indicators of Fatal Leptospirosis during the 2010 Epidemic in Puerto Rico." *PLoS Neglected Tropical Diseases* 10(2): e0004482.

Sharpe, Christina. 2016. *In the Wake: On Blackness and Being*. Durham, NC: Duke University Press.

Shefveland, Kristalyn Marie. 2016. *Anglo-Native Virginia Trade, Conversion, and Indian Slavery in the Old Dominion, 1646–1722*. Athens: University of Georgia Press.

Sheridan, Philip Henry. 1868. Letter of Philip Henry Sheridan to William T Sherman, October 15. William T. Sherman Papers, Library of Congress. https://www.loc.gov/resource/mss39800.013_0316_0641/?sp=120&r=0.039,0.983,1.072,0.68,0.

Sherman, William T. 1868. Letter of William T Sherman to Philip Henry Sheridan, May 10. Philip Henry Sheridan Papers, Library of Congress. https://www.loc.gov/resource/mss39768.017_0007_0246/?sp=6&r=-0.047,0.31,0.463,0.293,0.

Showalter, Kevin, David López-Carr, and Daniel Ervin. 2019. "Climate Change and Perceived Vulnerability: Gender, Heritage, and Religion Predict Risk Perception and Knowledge of Climate Change in Hawaii." *Geographical Bulletin* 60(1): 49–71.

Shue, Henry. 2014. *Climate Justice: Vulnerability and Protection*. Oxford: Oxford University Press.

Sikka, Tina. 2018. "Technology, Gender, and Climate Change: A Feminist Examination of Climate Technologies." *Societies* 8(4): 109–145.

Silliman, Jael Miriam, and Ynestra King, eds. 1999. *Dangerous Intersections: Feminist Perspectives on Population, Environment, and Development*. Cambridge, MA: South End Press.

Silva Junior, Celso H. L., Ana C. M. Pessôa, Nathália S. Carvalho, João B. C. Reis, Liana O. Anderson, and Luiz E. O. C. Aragão. 2021. "The Brazilian Amazon Deforestation Rate in 2020 Is the Greatest in the Decade." *Nature, Ecology and Evolution* 5: 144–145.

Simpson, Leanne Betasamosake. 2017. *As We Have Always Done: Indigenous Freedom through Radical Resistance*. Minneapolis: University of Minnesota Press.

Simpson, Michael. 2020. "The Anthropocene as Colonial Discourse." *Environment and Planning D: Society and Space* 38(1): 53–71.

Smits, David, D. 1994. "The Frontier Army and the Destruction of the Buffalo: 1865–1883." *Western Historical Quarterly* 25(3): 312–338.

Soares, José Maria, José M. Gomes, Marcelo R. Anjos, Josianne N. Silveira, Flavia B. Custódio, and M. Beatriz A Gloria. 2018. "Mercury in Fish from the Madeira River and Health Risk to Amazonian and Riverine Populations. *Food Research International* 109: 537–543.

South Energyx Nigeria Limited. N.d. *Eko Atlantic Milestones*, 1. www.ekoatlantic.com.

Spring, Jake. 2021. "Deforestation in Brazil's Amazon Rainforest Rises for Fourth Straight Month." Reuters, July 6. https://www.reuters.com/business/environment/deforestation-brazils-amazon-rainforest-rises-fourth-straight-month-2021-07-09/.

Stern, Nicholas. 2007. *The Economics of Climate Change: The Stern Review*. Cambridge: Cambridge University Press.

Stern, Walter. 2018. *Race and Education in New Orleans: Creating the Segregated City, 1764–1960*. Baton Rouge: Louisiana State University Press.

Stewart, Nikita. 2020. "The White Dog Walker and #LivingWhileBlack in New York City." *New York Times*, May 30. https://www.nytimes.com/2020/05/30/nyregion/central-park-video.html.

Stillman, Jonathon H. 2019. "Heat Waves, the New Normal: Summertime Temperature Extremes Will Impact Animals, Ecosystems, and Human Communities." *Physiology* 34(2): 86–100.

Sublette, Ned, and Constance Sublette. 2015. *The American Slave Coast: A History of the Slave-Breeding Industry*. Chicago: Chicago Review Press.

Subramaniam, A. 2008. "Amazon River Enhances Diazotrophy and Carbon Sequestration in the Tropical North Atlantic Ocean." *PNAS* 105: 10460–10465.

Sullivan, Shannon, and Nancy Tuana, eds. 2007. *Race and Epistemologies of Ignorance*. Albany: State University of New York Press.

Sultana, Farhana. 2013. "Gendering Climate Change: Geographical Insights." *Professional Geographer* 66(3): 372–381.

Sundberg, Juanita. 2014. "Decolonizing Posthumanist Geographies." *Cultural Geographies* 21(1): 33–47.

Survival International. 2019. "The Yanomami." September 25. https://www.survivalinternational.org/tribes/yanomami.

Swim, Janet K., Theresa K. Vescio, Julia L. Dahl, and Stephanie J. Zawadzki. 2018. "Gendered Discourse about Climate Change Policies." *Global Environmental Change* 48: 216–225.

TallBear, Kim. 2011. "Why Interspecies Thinking Needs Indigenous Standpoints." *Fieldsights*, November 18. https://culanth.org/fieldsights/why-interspecies-thinking-needs-indigenous-standpoints.

Tan, Shirlee W., Jesse C. Meiller, and Kathryn R. Mahaffey. 2009. "The Endocrine Effects of Mercury in Humans and Wildlife." *Critical Reviews in Toxicology* 39(3): 228–269.

Tangwa, Godfrey B. 2000. "The Traditional African Perception of a Person: Some Implications for Bioethics." *Hastings Center Report* 30(5): 39–43.

Tattersall, Nick. 2008. "Sea Surges Could Uproot Millions in Nigeria Megacity." *Reuters, Environment*. November 19. https://www.reuters.com/article/us-climate-nigeria-sea-surges-could-uproot-millions-in-nigeria-megacity-idUSTRE4AI74G20081119.

Taylor, Chloe. 2021. "Deforestation in Brazil's Amazon Rainforest Hits a 15-Year High, Data Shows." *CNBC Sustainable Future*, November 19. https://www.cnbc.com/2021/11/19/deforestation-in-brazils-amazon-rainforest-hits-15-year-high.html.

Taylor, Dorceta E. 2014. *Toxic Communities: Environmental Racism, Industrial Pollution, and Residential Mobility*. New York: New York University Press.

Taylor, Keeanga-Yamahtta. 2019. *Race for Profit: How Banks and the Real Estate Industry Undermined Black Homeownership*. Chapel Hill: University of North Carolina Press.

Taylor, Kennith I. 1988. "Deforestation and Indians in Brazilian Amazonia." In *Biodiversity*, ed. E. O. Wilson and Frances M. Peter, 128–144. Washington, DC: National Academy Press.

Taylor, M. Scott. 2011. "Buffalo Hunt: International Trade and the Virtual Extinction of the North American Bison." *American Economic Review* 101(7): 3162–3195.

Taylor, Paul. 1986. *Respect for Nature: A Theory of Environmental Ethics*. Princeton, NJ: Princeton University Press.

Teaching American History. 2022. Mississippi Black Code. November 1865. Accessed June 14, 2022. http://teachingamericanhistory.org/library/document/mississippi-black-code/.

Terry, Geraldine. 2009. "No Climate Justice without Gender Justice: An Overview of the Issues." *Gender and Development* 17(1): 5–18.

Teixeira, Fabio. 2021. "Lost 'Libraries': Brazil's Indigenous People Lament COVID Deaths of Elders." Reuters, February 28. https://www.reuters.com/article/us-brazil-coronavirus-indigenous-elders-idUSKCN2AT10U.

Thomas, Mike. 2015. "Chicago's Deadly 1995 Heat Wave: An Oral History." *Chicago Magazine*, June 29. https://www.chicagomag.com/Chicago-Magazine/July-2015/1995-Chicago-heat-wave/.

Thompson, Allen, and Jeremy Bendik-Keymer. 2012. *Ethical Adaptation to Climate Change: Human Virtues of the Future*. Cambridge, MA: MIT Press.

Thompson, Kara. 2017. "Traffic Stops, Stopping Traffic: Race and Climate Change in the Age of Automobility." *ISLE: Interdisciplinary Studies in Literature and Environment* 24(1): 92–112. https://doi.org/10.1093/isle/isw091.

Thompson-Hall, Mary, Edward R. Carr, and Unai Pascual. 2016. "Enhancing and Expanding Intersectional Research for Climate Change Adaptation in Agrarian Settings." *Ambio* 45(S3): 373–382.

Todd, Zoe. 2015a. "Fish Pluralities: Human-Animal Relations and Sites of Engagement in Paulatuuq, Arctic Canada." *Etudes Inuit* 38(1–2): 217–238.

Todd, Zoe. 2015b. "Indigenizing the Anthropocene." In *Art in the Anthropocene: Encounters among Aesthetics, Politics, Environments and Epistemologies*, ed. Heather Davis and Etienne Turpin, 241–254. London: Open Humanities Press.

Todd, Zoe. 2016. "An Indigenous Feminist's Take on the Ontological Turn: 'Ontology' Is Just Another Word for Colonialism." *Journal of Historical Sociology* 29(1): 4–22.

Tomfohr, Lianne M., Meredith A. Pung, and Joel E. Dimsdale. 2016. "Mediators of the Relationship between Race and Allostatic Load in African and White Americans." *Health Psychology* 35(4): 322–332.

Tosam, Mbih Jerome. 2019. "African Environmental Ethics and Sustainable Development." *Open Journal of Philosophy* 9(2): 172–192.

Tremmel, Joerg, and Katherine Robinson. 2014. *Climate Ethics: Environmental Justice and Climate Change*. London: I. B. Tauris.

Tschakert, Petra, Raymond A. Tutu, and Anna Alcaro. 2013. "Embodied Experiences of Environmental and Climatic Changes in Landscapes of Everyday Life in Ghana." *Emotion, Space and Society* 7: 13–25.

Tsing, Anna Lowenhaupt. 2015. *The Mushroom at the End of the World: On the Possibility of Life in Capitalist Ruins*. Princeton, NJ: Princeton University Press.

Tuana, Nancy. 2001. "Material Locations: An Interactionist Alternative to Realism/Social Constructivism." In *Engendering Rationalities*, ed. Nancy Tuana and Sandra Morgen, 221–244. Albany, NY: SUNY Press.

Tuana, Nancy. 2007. "Viscous Porosity: Witnessing Katrina." In *Material Feminisms*, ed. Susan Hekman and Stacy Alaimo, 188–213. Durham, NC: Duke University Press.

Tuana, Nancy. 2017. "Climate Change and Place: Delimiting Cosmopolitanism." In *Cosmopolitanism and Place*, ed. Jessica Wahman, José Medina, and John Stuhr, 181–196. Bloomington: Indiana University Press.

Tuana, Nancy. 2019. "Climate Apartheid: The Forgetting of Race in the Anthropocene." *Critical Philosophy of Race* 7(1): 1–31.
Tuana, Nancy. 2020. "From a Lifeboat Ethic to Anthropocenean Sensibilities." *Environmental Philosophy* 17(1): 101–123.
Tuana, Nancy, and Robert Bernasconi, eds. 2019. "Race and the Anthropocene." Special issue of *Critical Philosophy of Race* 7(1).
Tuana, Nancy, and Chris Cuomo, eds. 2014. "Climate Change." Special issue of *Hypatia* 29.
Tuana, Nancy, and Charles Scott. 2020. *Beyond Philosophy: Nietzsche, Foucault, Anzaldúa*. Bloomington: Indiana University Press.
Tutu, Desmond. 2007. "We Do Not Need Climate Change Apartheid in Adaptation." In *Human Development Report 2007/2008, Fighting Climate Change: Human Solidarity in a Divided World*, ed. United Nations Development Programme, 166. New York: Palgrave Macmillan.
Unger, Alon, Albert Ko, and Guillermo Douglass-Jaime. 2016. "Favela Health in Pau Da Lima, Salvador, Brazil." In *Slum Health: From the Cell to the Street*, ed. Jason Corburn and Lee Riley, 101–117. Oakland: University of California Press.
Union of Concerned Scientists. 2017. "How Coal Works." December 18. http://www.ucsusa.org/clean_energy/our-energy-choices/coal-and-other-fossil-fuels/how-coal-works.html#.WczUnsZrx5Q.
United Church of Christ. 1987. "Toxic Wastes and Race in the United States." United Church of Christ Commission for Racial Justice. https://www.nrc.gov/docs/ML1310/ML13109A339.pdf.
United Nations. 2016. "Framework Convention on Climate Change." https://unfccc.int/process-and-meetings/the-paris-agreement/the-paris-agreement.
United Nations. 2019. "Climate Justice." Sustainable Development Goals. Goal 13: Climate Action, Goal of the Month, May 31. https://www.un.org/sustainabledevelopment/blog/2019/05/climate-justice/.
United Nations Department of Economic and Social Affairs. 2020. "COVID-19 and Indigenous People." https://www.un.org/development/desa/indigenouspeoples/covid-19.html.
United Nations Development Programme. 2004. "Forging a Global South: United Nations Day for South-South Cooperation." December 19.https://www.undp.org/content/dam/china/docs/Publications/UNDP-CH-PR-Publications-UNDay-for-South-South-Cooperation.pdf.
United Nations Development Programme, ed. 2007. *Human Development Report 2007/8: Fighting Climate Change: Human Solidarity in a Divided World*. New York: Palgrave Macmillan.
United Nations Development Programme. 2009. "Resource Guide on Gender and Climate Change." http://www.un.org/womenwatch/downloads/Resource_Guide_English_FINAL.pdf.
United Nations Women Watch. 2022. "Women, Gender Equality and Climate Change." http://www.un.org/womenwatch/feature/climate_change/.
U.S. Census. 2021. "QuickFacts: Louisiana." The United States Census Bureau. https://www.census.gov/quickfacts/fact/table/US/PST045221.
United States Environmental Protection Agency. n.d. "Agriculture Street Landfill New Orleans, LA." https://cumulis.epa.gov/supercpad/CurSites/csitinfo.cfm?id=0600646&msspp=med.

U.S. Congress. *The Statutes at Large and Treaties of the United States of America. From December 1, 1845, to March 3, 1851, Arranged in Chronological Order; with References to the Matter of Each Act and to the Subsequent Acts on the Same Subject. Vol. IX.* United States, Periodical. https://www.loc.gov/item/llsl-v9/.

Van Aelst, Katrien, and Nathalie Holvoet. 2016. "Intersections of Gender and Marital Status in Accessing Climate Change Adaptation: Evidence from Rural Tanzania." *World Development* 79: 40–50.

Van der Geest, Kees, and Koko Warner. 2015. "What the IPCC 5th Assessment Report Has to Say about Loss and Damage. UNU-EHS Working Paper, *No. 21.* Bonn: United Nations University Institute of Environment and Human Security.

Vanderheiden, Stephen. 2008. *Atmospheric Justice: A Political Theory of Climate Change.* Oxford: Oxford University Press.

Vega, Claudia, Jesem D. Y. Orellana, Marcos W. Oliveira, Sandra S. Hacon, and Paulo C. Basta. 2018. "Human Mercury Exposure in Yanomami Indigenous Villages from the Brazilian Amazon." *International Journal of Environmental Research and Public Health* 15(6): 1051–1064.

Venkatasubramanian, Kalpana, and Smita Ramnarain. 2018. "Gender and Adaptation to Climate Change: Perspectives from a Pastoral Community in Gujarat, India." *Development and Change* 49(6): 1580–1604.

Vergès, Françoise. 2017. "Racial Capitalocene." In *The Futures of Black Radicalism*, ed. Gaye Theresa Johnson and Alex Lubin, 72–82. London: Verso.

Vinyeta, Kirsten, Powys Whyte, Kyle, and Lynn, Kathy. 2015. Climate Change through an Intersectional Lens: Gendered Vulnerability and Resilience in Indigenous Communities in the United States. Gen. Tech. Rep. PNW-GTR-923. Portland, OR: U.S. Department of Agriculture, Forest Service, Pacific Northwest Research Station.

Viveiros de Castro, Eduardo. 2007. "The Crystal Forest: Notes on the Ontology of Amazonian Spirits." *Inner Asia* 9(2): 153–172.

Viveiros de Castro, Eduardo. 2015. *The Relative Native: Essays on Indigenous Conceptual Worlds.* Chicago: HUA Books.

Voyles, Traci Brynne. 2015. *Wastelanding: Legacies of Uranium Mining in Navajo Country.* Minneapolis: University of Minnesota Press.

Walker, Heidi M., Angela Culham, Amber J. Fletcher, and Maureen G. Reed. 2019. "Social Dimensions of Climate Hazards in Rural Communities of the Global North: An Intersectionality Framework." *Journal of Rural Studies* 72: 1–10.

Wark, McKenzie. 2016. *Molecular Red: Theory for the Anthropocene.* New York: Verso.

Washick, Bonnie, and Elizabeth Wingrove. 2015. "Politics That Matter: Thinking about Power and Justice with the New Materialists." *Contemporary Political Theory* 14: 63–79.

Wazana Tompkins, Kyla. 2016. "On the Limits and Promise of New Materialist Philosophy." *Lateral: Journal of the Cultural Studies Association* 5(1). https://www.jstor.org/stable/48671431.

Weinstein, Rachel, and Allison Plyer. 2020. "Detailed Data Sheds New Light on Racial Disparities in COVID-19 Deaths." Data Center, June 25. https://www.datacenterresearch.org/reports_analysis/lack-of-data-obscures-true-levels-of-racial-inequity-in-covid-deaths/.

Weizman, Eyal, and Fazal Sheikh. 2015. *The Conflict Shoreline: Colonization as Climate Change in the Negev Desert.* Göttingen: Steidl.

Weston, Burns H. 2008. "Climate Change and Intergenerational Justice: Foundational Reflections." *Vermont Journal of Environmental Law* 9: 375–430.

White, Andrew. 2017. "BioLab's Robert Gelinas Leading Lake Charles Site through Modernization." *BIC Magazine,* October 30. https://www.bicmagazine.com/departments/maintenance-reliability/nov-2017-biolabs-robert-gelinas/.
Whittenbury, Kerri. 2013. "Climate Change, Women's Health, Wellbeing and Experiences of Gender Based Violence in Australia." In *Research, Action and Policy: Addressing the Gendered Impacts of Climate Change,* ed. Margaret Alston and Kerri Whittenbury, 207–222. Dordrecht: Springer.
Whyte, Kyle. 2016. "Is It Colonial Déjà Vu? Indigenous Peoples and Climate Justice." In *Humanities for the Environment: Integrating Knowledge, Forging New Constellations of Practice,* ed. Joni Adamson, Michael Davis, and Hsinya Huang, 88–104. Abingdon: Routledge.
Whyte, Kyle. 2017. "Indigenous Climate Change Studies: Indigenizing Futures, Decolonizing the Anthropocene." *English Language Notes* 55(1–2): 153–162.
Whyte, Kyle. 2018. "Settler Colonialism, Ecology, and Environmental Injustice." *Environment and Society* 9(1): 125–144.
Williams, David R., and Selina A. Mohammed. 2009. "Discrimination and Racial Disparities in Health: Evidence and Needed Research." *Journal of Behavioral Medicine* 32: 20–47.
Williams, Patricia J. 1991. *The Alchemy of Race and Rights.* Cambridge, MA: Harvard University Press.
Williams, Walter L., ed. 2009. *Southeastern Indians since the Removal Era.* Athens: University of Georgia Press.
Williston, Bryon. 2019. *The Ethics of Climate Change: An Introduction.* London: Routledge.
Winter, Susanne. 2020. "Mehr Wald geht durch Corona verloren." World Wildlife Fund, May 21. https://blog.wwf.de/wald-corona/.
Women's Environment and Development Organization, with ABANTU, Action Aid, and ENDA. 2008. "Gender, Climate Change and Human Security: Lessons from Bangladesh, Ghana and Senegal." http://www.gdnonline.org/resources/WEDO_Gender_CC_Human_Security.pdf.
Wong, Kaufui V., Andrew Paddon, and Alfredo Jimenez. 2013. "Review of World Urban Heat Islands: Many Linked to Increased Mortality." *Journal of Energy Resources and Technology* 135(2): 022101.
Wood, Alexa L., Prince Ansah, Louie Rivers, and Arika Ligmann-Zielinska. 2021. "Examining Climate Change and Food Security in Ghana through an Intersectional Framework." *Journal of Peasant Studies* 48(2): 329–348.
World Bank. 2017. *Atlas of Sustainable Development Goals 2017: World Development Indicators.* Washington, DC: World Bank. doi:10.1596/978-1-4648-1080-0.
World Health Organization. N.d. "Air Pollution." https://www.who.int/health-topics/air-pollution#tab=tab_1.
Wu, Xiao, Rachel C. Nethery, Benjamin M. Sabath, Danielle Braun, and Francesca Dominici. 2020. "Exposure to Air Pollution and COVID-19 Mortality in the United States." *Science Advances* 6(45): eabd4049.
Wynter, Sylvia. 1971. "Novel and History, Plot and Plantation." *Savacou* 5: 95–102.
Wynter, Sylvia. 2001. "Towards the Sociogenic Principle: Fanon, Identity, the Puzzle of Conscious Experience, and What It Is Like to Be 'Black.'" In *National Identities and Sociopolitical Changes in Latin America,* ed. Mercedes F. Durán-Cogan and Antonio Gómez-Moriana, 3066. New York: Routledge.

Wynter, Sylvia. 2003. "Unsettling the Coloniality of Being/Power/Truth/Freedom: Towards the Human, after Man, Its Overrepresentation—An Argument." *New Centennial Review* 3(3): 257–337.

Wynter, Sylvia, and Katherine McKittrick. 2015. "Unparalleled Catastrophe for Our Species? Or, to Give Humanness a Different Future: Conversations." In *Sylvia Wynter: On Being Human as Praxis*, ed. Katherine McKittrick, 9–89. Durham, NC: Duke University Press.

Yale Environment 360. 2013. "Coal Pollution and the Fight for Environmental Justice." http://e360.yale.edu/features/naacp_jacqueline_patterson_coal_pollution_and_fight_for_environmental_justice.

Yancy, George. 2008. *Black Bodies, White Gazes: The Continuing Significance of Race*. Lanham, MD: Rowman and Littlefield.

Young, Iris Marion. 1990. *Justice and the Politics of Difference*. Princeton, NJ: Princeton University Press.

Yusoff, Kathryn. 2015. "Queer Coal: Genealogies in/of the Blood." *philoSOPHIA* 5(2): 203–229.

Yusoff, Kathryn. 2018. *A Billion Black Anthropocenes or None*. Vol. 53. Minneapolis: University of Minnesota Press.

Zimring, Carl A. 2015. *Clean and White: A History of Environmental Racism in the United States*. New York: New York University Press.

Index

For the benefit of digital users, indexed terms that span two pages (e.g., 52–53) may, on occasion, appear on only one of those pages.
Figures are indicated by *f* following the page number

Abbey, Edward, 136
Abram, David, 19, 20n.19
Adams-Onis Treaty, x
adaptation and mitigation policies
   climate change apartheid, 39–40, 61–63
   heatwaves and, 41–46
   in Lagos, Nigeria, 63–69
   mitigation targets, 40–41
   in multidimensional framework, 37, 39–40
afterlives of slavery, 49, 70, 79–80, 86, 110
agency, dance of, 90, 90n.7, 91
agential realism, 23
Agriculture Street Landfill, New Orleans, 105–8
air pollution, 1–2, 11–12, 100
Akrãtikatêjê, Katia Silene, 3–4
Alchemy of Race and Rights, The (Williams), 113–14
Allen, Barbara, 100
allostatic load, 114–15n.6
Al-Saji, Alia, 110n.31
Alter, Jonathan, 109
Amazon deforestation, 48–55
American Apartheid: Segregation and the Making of the Underclass (Massey and Denton), 42–43
American bison, extermination of, 27–30, 30n.35
American Lung Association, 2
Anthropocene
   beginning of, 4n.5
   conceptual antecedents of concept, 125, 125n.14
   humanocentrism in, 141–43
   meaning of *anthropos*, 34
   meaning of *cene*, 55
   new forms of writing in, 150–51
   promise of, 147–48
   as singular versus plural, 149–50
anthropocenean sensibilities, 141–51
   anthropo-not-seen, 145–49
   meaning of *anthropos*, 143–44
   paradox of, 141, 142–43, 145–46
   place-based analyses, 149–50
   promise of, 150
anthropogenic climate change, overview of, 112
anthropo-not-seen, 145–49
anti-Blackness in United States, 112–13, 114–16
anti-immigration discourse, 134–39
Apalachee people, ix–x
Appiah, Kwame Anthony, 2n.3
Articulation of the Indigenous People of Brazil (APIB), 3–4
Asafu-Adjaye, John, 142–43
Asians, racism towards in U.S., 115–16, 116n.7
Asunción Valdivia Heat Illness and Fatality Prevention Act, 45n.13
Awajún Wampis, 145–46

backgrounding of nature, 19n.18
Bales, Kevin, 50–52
Barad, Karen, 23–24
Barbry, John, 97–98, 109
Baré, Nara, 3–4
Battle, Colette Pichon, 97
Beck, Roy, 139
Bederman, Gail, 123–24
Bennett, Jane, 23

186 INDEX

Bennett, Joshua, 147n.7
Bhandar, Brenna, 125
Bilge, Sirma, 9–10, 14
Billion Black Anthropocenes or None, A (Yusoff), 34, 149
biocentrism, 23n.25
Biolab plant (Louisiana), fire at, 99
biosequestration, 48
Black Lives Matter, 1, 1n.2, 2
black lung disease, 76
Blackmon, Douglas, 73n.24, 76,
Black Power: The Politics of Liberation (Carmichael & Hamilton), 15–16
Blacks
　black trash, 104–8
　differential impacts of coal-fired plants, 71–72
　impact of COVID-19 pandemic on, 1–2, 11–12, 108
　racial climate in U.S., 112–13, 115–16
　racial segregation in U.S. cities and heat island effect, 42–46
　toxic chemical exposure in Louisiana, 101–4
black trash, 104–8
Bolsonaro, Jair, 4–5, 53–55
Brainard, Lael, 132–33
Brazil
　charcoal industry in, 47–49
　impact of pandemic on Indigenous population in, 2–5
　poverty and urban ecosystems in, 77–82
　unfree labor and environmental destruction in, 49–55
breathing room, 110, 110n.31
buffalo, extermination of, 27–30, 30n.35
Buffon, le Comte de (Georges Louis Leclerc), 124–25
Bullard, Robert D., 110
Burkhart, Brian, 21n.22
Bush, George W., 89

Cadena, Marisol de la, 145–49
Californians for Population Stabilization, 137
Campt, Tina M., 130–31
Cancer Alley, Louisiana, 100–4

Carastathis, Anna, 58–59
Carbado, Devon, 10–11, 38–39, 55–56
Carmichael, Stokely, 15–16
carrying capacity, 134–35, 136–37
Carrying Capacity Network, 136–37
Castro-Sotomayor, José, 19
cene, alternate meaning of, 55
Chakrabarty, Dipesh, 125–26, 141–42
charcoal industry, in Brazil, 47–49
chattel slavery, 70, 73n.24
Chavis, Benjamin, 60n.5
chemical industry, in Louisiana, 99–104
Chen, Mel, 21n.22
Chertoff, Michael, 89, 89–90n.5
Chinese, racism towards, 115–16, 116n.7
chlorine gas exposure, in Louisiana, 99
Chollet, Derek, 132–33
Christian Aid, 138
Clare, Stephanie, 20n.21
civilization, 123–26
climate, defined, 111–12
climate adaptation in Lagos, Nigeria, 63–69
climate change
　anthropogenic, 112
　climate refugees, 138–39
　impact on Indigenous population in Brazil, 5
　inequal effects of, xii
　moral responsibility for, 118, 131, 131n.16
climate change apartheid
　climate adaptation practices in Lagos, Nigeria, 63–69
　and ecological indifference, 61–62, 67–68
　general discussion, 39–40, 61–63
climate engineering, 142n.2
climate injustice
　ecological indifference as key component of, 20–22, 86, 116–17
　genealogical sensibilities, 7–9, 85
　indifference to, 6–7
　intersectional analyses and, 12–15
climate justice
　climate adaptation in Lagos, Nigeria, 63–69
　climate change apartheid, 61–69

coal mining in post–Civil War U.S. South, 69–77
differential distribution of harms and benefits, 26–27
"not without us" slogan, 57–60
poverty and urban ecosystems in Brazil, 77–82
race and gender justice perspectives in, 118–21, 120n.10
UN definition of, 34–35
Climate Justice: Vulnerability and Protection (Shue), 129–30, 129f
Climate of History in a Planetary Age, The (Chakrabarty), 141–42
climate refugees, 138–39
Climate Refugees (film), 138–39
Coal Blooded: Putting Profits Before People study, 71–72
coal mining in post–Civil War U.S. South, 69–77
Coulthard, Glenn, 21n.22
Cohen, Leonard, 69–70
Collins, Patricia Hill, 9–11
colonialism, 4n.5, 79–80, 122–23, 125–26, 128
Connell, Raewyn, 122–23
contemporary slave labor, 50–53, 51n.19
convict lease programs, 75–76, 94n.10
"COVID-19 And Indigenous Peoples" report (United Nations Department of Economic and Social Affairs), 2–3
COVID-19 pandemic, 1, 1n.1
  impact on Black population, 2, 11–12, 108
  impact on Indigenous population, 2–5
Cramer, Stefan, 63
Crenshaw, Kimberlé, 9–11, 14, 57–58
critical environmental justice, 57–58n.2
Crutzen, Paul, 143–44
culture/nature divide, 22, 23n.26, 141–42, 147–49

Dados, Nour, 122–23
dance of agency, 90, 90n.7, 91
deficit model of "Global South," 121–31, 132
deforestation in Brazil
  charcoal industry in, 47–49

unfree labor practices and, 49–55
denial, 89–90
Denton, Fatma, 127–28
Denton, Nancy, 42–43
Desire Housing Project in New Orleans, 105–8
differential distribution of ecological harms and benefits, 25–27
differential impacts, 37–38, 37n.5, 59–60, 71–72
Dodge, Richard Irving, 27–28
domains of systemic racisms/environmental degradation intersections
  differential distribution of harms and benefits, 25–27
  interrelations of, 32–33
  overview, 24–25, 35–36
  racist institutions and practices, 27–30
  social structures, 30–32
domestication, generalized, 21n.23, 30–31
Dow Chemical, purchase of plantations in Louisiana by, 100n.16
Drèze, Jean, 6–7

ecocentrism, 21n.23
ecointersectional analyses
  genealogical sensibilities in, 47, 49, 56, 59–60, 85–86, 99, 109–10, 140–41
  overview, 14–15, 18n.15, 19n.16, 56
  of racial climates, 38–39, 45, 118, 140
  systemic racisms/environmental degradation interconnections, 14–18
ecological harms and benefits, differential distribution of, 25–27
ecological indifference, 38–39
  differential distribution of harms and benefits, 25–27
  general discussion, 19–22
  and Hurricane Katrina, 86, 100, 102–4, 109–10
  of Jair Bolsonaro, 53–55
  and racial climates, 27, 31–32, 54–55, 116–17, 140–41, 149–50
  racist institutions and practices and, 27–30, 52–53, 101n.17, 102–4, 108
  social structures and, 30–32

toxin exposure, 102–4
ecological justice, 21–22
ecowomanism, 146–47
Ecowomanism: African American Women and Earth-Honoring Faiths (Harris), 146–47
education, racial climates in, 36
Edwards, John Bel, 99
Eko Atlantic, Nigeria, 63–68, 63n.10, 64n.12
enchanted materialism, 23
Energy of Slaves, The (Cohen), 69–70
environment, 22n.24
  ecological indifference, 19–22
  ecological justice approaches, 19–22
  environmental destruction
    in Brazil, 49–55
    coal mining in post–Civil War South, 71–77
    differential distribution of harms and benefits, 25–27
    domains interlocking systemic racisms and, 24–25, 35–36
    intermeshing of systemic racisms and, 46–47
    poverty and urban ecosystems in Brazil, 77–82
    racist institutions and practices causing, 27–30, 45–46
    sacrifice zones, 32–33
    social structures generating, 30–32
    systemic racisms connected to, 17–18
  environmental injustice
    complexities of, 5–7
    examples of, 1–5
    genealogical sensibilities, 7–9, 85, 140
  environmental justice, 18, 19n.17
    differential distribution of ecological harms and benefits, 25–27
    ecological indifference as key component of, 19–22
    EPA definition of, 25–26
  Environmental Protection Agency (EPA), 25–26
  environmental racism, 18, 25–27, 60, 60n.5
  epistemology of ignorance, 61n.6, 69, 118–20

Fair Housing Act of 1968, 44, 44n.10
farmworkers, impact of climate change on, 45n.13
favelas, in Brazil, 77–82
Federal Housing Administration (FHA), 43
feminist "new" materialisms, 22–23
Fifth Assessment Report (Intergovernmental Panel on Climate Change), 12–14, 13*f*
First National People of Color Environmental Leadership Summit, The, 19–20
five-dimensional conception of racial climates, 36
Florida, human history of, ix–xiii
forced labor, in Brazil, 49–55
Formosa Plastic Group, 103–4, 103–4n.20
Foucault, Michel, 5–6, 7–8, 59–60
framing of climate-related policies, 37, 39–41, 44–45
Frazier, Chelsea M., 23–24

garimperios (illegal gold miners), in Brazil, 3–5, 4n.6
gas industry, in Louisiana, 95–99, 96*f*
gender
  climate impacts in "Global South," 127–31, 130*f*
  gender justice in climate justice accounts, 118–21, 120n.10
  "not without us" slogan, 57–58
genealogical sensibilities
  cultivation of, 47, 110, 116–17
  in ecointersectional analyses, 49, 59–60, 85, 99, 140–41
  general discussion, 7–9, 109–10, 140–41
  ordinary trauma, 97–98
  racial climates and, 38–39, 115–18, 139
  unfree labor and environmental destruction in Brazil, 49–55
genealogies, 7–8
generalized domestication, 21n.23, 30–31
Geronimus, Arline, 114
ghettoization of Blacks, 42–46
Global North/South labels
  association of vulnerability with "Global South," 127–31

in climate policy and
  discussions, 126–31
 debates about population
  control, 131–38
 as racist conceptualizations, 121–31
Global Warming of 1.5°C report
 (Intergovernmental Panel on Climate
 Change), 41
Gómez-Barris, Macarena, 147
Gordon Plaza housing development, New
 Orleans, 107–8
Gyasi, Yaa, 75

Hage, Ghassan, 17, 21n.23, 30–32
Hall, G. Stanley, 124
Hallum-Montes, Rachel, 18n.15
Hamilton, Allison Janae, ix–xiii
Hamilton, Charles V., 15–16
Haraway, Donna, 22–23, 150–51
Hardin, Garrett, 134–35
Harding, Sandra, 122–23, 126–27
Harris, Melanie L., 21n.22, 146–47
Hartman, Saidiya, 20n.19, 38, 39, 127–28
Hartmann, Betsy, 132, 137–38
hazardous substance exposure, in
 Louisiana, 99–104
health, impact of racial climates
 on, 114–15
heat island effect, 41–43, 44–45, 44n.11
heatwaves, 41–46
Hecht, Gabrielle, 141–43, 149–50
Hird, Myra, 23n.27
 in Brazil, 79–80
 coal mining in post–Civil War U.S.
  South, 71–77
 general discussion, 37, 46–47
 in Nigeria, 64–67
 unfree labor and environmental
  destruction in Brazil, 49–55
historical responsibility for climate
 change, 118, 131, 131n.16
historicism, 125–26
Hogan, Linda, 34
Homegoing: A Novel (Gyasi), 75
Home Owners' Loan Corporation
 (HOLC), 43
Homer-Dixon, Thomas, 136, 136n.18
Hopkins, Hop, 32–33

Hornaday, William, 27–28
Houma people, 97–99
housing projects in New Orleans, 105–8
Hultgren, John, 137–38
human agency, 89–92, 90n.7
human/nonhuman separation
 and ecological indifference, 19–22,
  32, 109–10
 ecological justice approaches, 19–22,
  22n.24, 92
 nature/culture divide, 22, 23n.26, 141–
  42, 147–49
 new materialisms, 22–23
 and racial climates, 140, 141–43
humanocentrism, 141–43
hunger, indifference to, 6–7
Hurricane Beta, 84
Hurricane Betsy, 106–7, 107n.29
Hurricane Ida, 84n.1
Hurricane Katrina, 84–85, 86, 109
 black trash, 104–8
 chemical industry in Louisiana, 99–104
 flooding of Mississippi River and
  swamps, 93–95
 and genealogical sensibilities, 85–86,
  92, 93–94, 97–98, 99
 geography of New Orleans, 89–93
 oil and gas industries in
  Louisiana, 95–99
 viscous porosity, 86–89, 95–97, 99
Hurricane Laura, 99–100
Hurtado, Sylvia, 36
hygienist discourse, 66
hyperseparation, 23n.26, 141–43, 145–49

ignorance, epistemology of, 118–20
illegal mining in Yanomami land in Brazil,
 3–5, 4n.7
ILO (International Labour
 Organization), 52–53
Ilubirin, Nigeria, 66–67
immigration, 134–39
Immigration and Liberal Taboos
 (Abbey), 136
incarceration rate, in Louisiana, 104–5
incorporated racism, 72–77
Indigenous peoples
 anthropo-not-seen, 145–46

Indigenous peoples (*cont.*)
　impact of Amazon deforestation on, 48–55
　impact of COVID-19 pandemic on, 2–5
　in Louisiana, 97–99
　in Nigeria, impact of adaptation policies on, 66–68, 68n.17
　racism behind extermination of buffalo in U.S., 28–30
　racism in U.S. towards, 115–16
　uranium mining in Navajo Nation, 104n.23
individual versus systemic racisms, 15–17
institutional versus individual racism, 15–17
Intergovernmental Panel on Climate Change, 12–14, 13*f*, 41, 111
International Labour Organization (ILO), 52–53
intersectional analyses, 9–15, 58–59
　goals of, 10–11
　multidimensional vulnerability, 12–14, 13*f*
　racial disparities in COVID-19 rates, 11–12
　relevance to climate injustice, 12–15
　whitening of intersectionality, 14
In the Wake: On Blackness and Being (Sharpe), 112–13
Islamophobia, 30–31
Is Racism an Environmental Threat? (Hage), 17, 30–31
"I Threw Open the Shutters" (Cohen), 69–70

Jackson, Mark, 145
James, Guillermo, 78
James, Wesley, 101–2
Jia, Chunrong, 101–2

kairos, 55
Kaplan, Robert, 135–36
Kedia, Satish, 101–2
Kelbaugh, Douglas, 133
keystone species, 10n.9, 30
Klopotek, Brian, 97–98, 109
Knapp, Alan K., 30

LaFleur, Vinca, 132–33
Lagos (Nigeria), climate adaptation practices in, 63–69
land distribution in Brazil, 80
Lane, Janica, 126–27
Latinos
　differential impacts of coal-fired plants, 71–72
　racial climate in U.S., 113–14, 115–16
　term, 113n.4
Leclerc, Georges Louis (le Comte de Buffon), 124–25
leptospirosis, 78–81
Lerner, Steve, 32
levee system of New Orleans, 91, 93–95
Lewis, Simon, 4n.5
lifeboat ethic, 134–35, 139
Lintinger, Brenda, 97–98, 109
logging industry, in Wacissa watershed, xi
López, Alfred, 25n.29, 125–26
Louisiana, United States
　black trash, 104–8
　Desire Housing Project in New Orleans, 105–8
　flooding of Mississippi River and swamps, 93–95
　geography of New Orleans, 89–93
　Hurricane Katrina, 84–85, 109
　incarceration rate in, 104–5
　oil and gas industries, 95–99
　toxic chemical exposure risk in, 99–104
　viscous porosity, 86–89, 93–94

Ma'a, Pire'i, 53–55
Makoko, Nigeria, 66–67
mankind, meaning of term, 143–44
Manliness and Civilization (Bederman), 123–24
Maranhão Costa, Patrícia Trindade, 51n.17, 51n.20, 52–53
Marxist-inspired materialisms, 22–23
Maslin, Mark, 4n.5
Massey, Douglas, 42–43
McDonogh 35 high school, New Orleans, 105, 105n.26
McWhorter, Ladelle, 7–8
mercury exposure, 4, 102–3
migration due to climate change, 138–39

INDEX

Mills, Charles, 61n.7, 104, 118–19
Milon, Anne-Sophie, 125n.14
Milstein, Tema, 19
mining in Yanomami land in Brazil, 3–5, 4n.7
Mississippi River flooding, 93–95
mitigation policies
   climate change apartheid, 62–63
   heatwaves and, 41–46
   mitigation targets, 40–41, 44–45
moral responsibility for climate change, 118, 131, 131n.16
more-than-human, 19–20, 20n.21, 22–23, 38–39, 38n.7, 55–56, 71
   and Hurricane Katrina, 71, 88–89, 90, 91–92, 97, 116–17
Moton Elementary School, New Orleans, 107–8
Movement for Survival of the Ogoni People (MOSOP), 68, 68n.17
multidimensional framework for racial climates, 37–38
multidimensional vulnerability, 12–14, 13f
Mushroom at the End of the World: On the Possibility of Life in Capitalist Ruins, The (Tsing), 82, 140–41

Nash, Michael, 138–39
nature
   backgrounding of, 19n.18
   biocentrism and ecocentrism, 23n.25
   ecological indifference, 19–22
   ecological justice approaches, 21–22
   new materialisms, 22–24
nature/culture divide, 22, 23n.26, 141–42, 147–49
Navajo Nation, uranium mining in, 104n.23
Nelson, Gaylord, 137
new materialisms, 22–24, 25n.29
New Orleans, Louisiana
   chemical industry, 99–104
   Desire Housing Project in, 105–8
   flooding of Mississippi River and swamps, 93–95
   geography of, 89–93
   Hurricane Katrina, 84–85, 86, 109
   oil and gas industries, 95–99, 96f

Nigeria, climate adaptation practices in Lagos, 63–69
Noranda Alumina plant, Louisiana, 102
Norway rat (*Rattus norvegicus*) infestations in Brazil, 79, 80–81
"Notes toward a 'Native' Theory of History" (Robinson), 125–26
"not without us" slogan, 57–60

Ogoni people, 68, 68n.17
Ogu people, 66–67
oil industry, in Louisiana, 95–99, 96f
Olsson, L., 12–14, 13f
Opperman, Romy, 34, 60n.5, 72
ordinary trauma, 97–99, 100, 109
Otodo Gbame, Nigeria, 66–67
overpopulation, 131–38

Park, Lisa Sun-Hee, 137–38
Patterson, Jacqueline, 71–72
Pau da Lima (Salvador), Brazil, 77–82
Pellow, David Naguib, 57–58n.2, 137–38
Peru, Indigenous beliefs in, 145–46
petrochemical plants, in Louisiana, 100–4
Pickering, Andrew, 90, 90n.7, 91
Piedalue, Amy, 122–23
pipelines, in Louisiana, 95–99
Plumwood, Val, 19n.18, 23n.26, 141
pneumoconiosis, 76
polyhedron of intelligibility, 5–6, 10–11
population control
   anti-immigration discourse, 134–39
   carrying capacity, 134–35, 136–37
   climate refugees, 138–39
   overpopulation, 131–38
Population Matters, 133–34
posthumanism, 147–48, 147n.8
poverty
   in Nigeria, 64
   and population control, 132–33
   and urban ecosystems in Brazil, 77–82
Press Park Townhouses, New Orleans, 107
psychological dimensions, 37
public housing projects, in New Orleans, 105–8

race riots, 42–43

racial climates, 113–14, 116–18, 139
   debates about population
      control, 131–38
   ecointersectional analyses of, 38–
      39, 116–17
   and ecological indifference, 27, 31–32,
      54–55, 116–17, 140–41, 150
   in education, 36
   Global North/South labels, 121–31
   and Hurricane Katrina, 86, 97–98
   interfusing of dimensions, 39–40
   mitigation policies and
      heatwaves, 40–46
   multidimensional framework for, 37–38
   overview, 34–36
   systemic racisms and environmental
      destruction, 46–47
   understanding and addressing, 117–18
   weathering, 112–18
Racial Contract (Mills), 61n.7
racial segregation in U.S. cities, 42–
   46, 106–7
racism. *See also* systemic racisms
   environmental, 18, 25–27, 60, 60n.5
   incorporated, 72–77
   systemic versus individual, 15–17
racist institutions and practices
   general discussion, 27–30
   overview, 25, 35
   poverty and urban ecosystems in
      Brazil, 77–82
   racial segregation in U.S. cities, 45–46
rat-born disease in Brazilian favelas, 78–81
redlining, 43–46, 44n.11, 105
Red Summer, 42–43
refugees, climate, 138–39
relationality of things, 21n.22
*Reproductive Rights and Wrongs: The
   Global Politics of Population Control*
   (Hartmann), 132
Rice, Susan E., 133
Rishi, Susmita, 122–23
River Road, Louisiana, 100–4
Roberts, Michelle, 110
Robinson, Cedric, 125–26
Rose, Debra Bird, 150–51
Rowan, Rory, 147–48
Russell, Gordon, 102

sacrifice zones, 32–33
*Sacrifice Zone: The Front Lines of Toxic
   Chemical Exposure in the United
   States* (Lerner), 32
Said, Edward, 122–23
Salvador, Brazil, 77–82
Saro-Wiwa, Ken, 68, 68n.17
Schneider, Stephen H., 126–27
school siting in New Orleans, 105
Sciences from Below (Harding), 122–23
Seager, Joni, 41
Sealey-Huggins, Leon, 45
sea wall in Lagos, Nigeria, 63–69
Sen, Amartya, 6–7
sensibilities, 1–33, 35, 37, 39, 58–59,
   59n.4, 73n.23, 126–27, 140,
   141, 146–49
Sharpe, Christina, 112–13
shell middens, New Orleans, 91–93
Sheridan, Philip H., 28–29
Sherman, William Tecumseh, 28–29
Shue, Henry, 129–30, 129f
Simpson, Leanne Betasamosake, 21n.22
Simpson, Michael, 4n.5, 125, 144
slavery
   afterlives of, 49, 70, 79–80, 86, 110, 112–
      13, 114–16
   in Brazil, 49–52, 50n.15, 52n.21, 55, 80
   in Nigeria, 64–66
   in United States, ix–x, 70–71, 73–
      74, 73n.24, 75, 93–94, 93n.9,
      94n.10, 100–1
socialist feminism, 22–23
social structures
   coal mining in post–Civil War U.S.
      South, 71–77
   general discussion, 30–32
   overview, 25, 36
South Africa, apartheid in, 61–62
Spanish settlement of Florida, ix–x
"State of the Air" report (American Lung
   Association), 2
Stern, Walter, 105
St. James Parish, Louisiana, 100–1,
   102, 103–4
"stop and frisk" efforts by police, 113–14
stress response to racial climates, 112–18
structural dimensions of diversity, 37

structural racism, heatwaves and, 41–46
Sundberg, Juanita, 147–48, 147n.8
superfund sites in Louisiana, 100, 108
swamp lands in Louisiana, 94–95
systemic racisms
   differential distribution of harms and benefits, 25–27
   domains interlocking environmental degradation and, 24–25, 35–36, 38–39
   environmental degradation connected to, 17–18, 46–47, 121–22
   general discussion, 15–17
   racist institutions and practices, 27–30
   social structures, 30–32
   weathering racial climates, 112–18

"Tangled Web: The Poverty-Insecurity Nexus, The" (Brainard, Chollet, & LaFleur), 132–33
Thompkins, Wazana, 23–24
Thompson, Kara, 24
Todd, Zoe, 149
toxic chemical exposure risk in Louisiana, 99–104
trabalho escravo contemporâneo (contemporary slave labor), 50–53, 51n.19
transatlantic slave trade in Brazil, legacies of, 49–55
trauma, ordinary and extraordinary, 97–98, 98n.14, 100, 109
Tsing, Anna, 82, 140–41
Tutu, Desmond, 39–40, 61–63

unavoidable impacts of climate change, 37, 37n.5
unavoided impacts of climate change, 37, 37n.5, 62n.8
unfree labor practices
   in Brazil, 49–55
   in post–Civil War U.S. South, 73–77
United Houma Nation, 97–99

United Nations Department of Economic and Social Affairs, 2–3
United Nations Development Programme, 121–22
uranium mining in Navajo Nation, 104n.23
Urban Fix: Resilient Cities in the War against Climate Change, Heat Islands and Overpopulation, The (Kelbaugh), 133
urban heat island effect and systemic racisms, 41–43, 44–45, 44n.11

vagrancy laws, 74–75
Vergès, Françoise, 49
viscous porosity, 69n.18, 87–89, 110
   Hurricane Katrina, 86–89, 95–97, 99
   New Orleans, 91–94
Voyles, Traci Brynne, 104n.23

Wacissa River, Florida, ix–xiii
Washick, Bonnie, 23–24
Wazana Tompkins, Kyla, 24
wastelanding, 104n.23
weather, 111
weathering racial climates, 112–18
Western modernity, 123
wetland loss in Louisiana, 94–97
whitening of intersectionality, 14
Whyte, Kyle, 147
Wilderson, Frank B., 38
Williams, Patricia, 113–14
Wingrove, Elizabeth, 23–24
Wiwa, Owens, 68
world-making, 1–33, 140–41, 145–47
Wynter, Sylvia, 23n.26, 70

Yanomami people, Brazil, 3–5, 4n.6, 7n.8
Young, Iris Marion, 35
Yusoff, Kathryn, 34, 69n.18, 149

Zalasiewicz, Jan, 125n.14
Zalasiewicz, Mateusz, 125n.14